ANNE NEVILLE

ANNE NEVILLE

QUEEN AND WIFE OF RICHARD III

REBECCA BATLEY

AN IMPRINT OF PEN & SWORD BOOKS LTD.
YORKSHIRE – PHILADELPHIA

First published in Great Britain in 2024 by
PEN AND SWORD HISTORY
An imprint of
Pen & Sword Books Ltd
Yorkshire – Philadelphia

Copyright © Rebecca Batley, 2024

ISBN 978 1 39905 878 0

The right of Rebecca Batley to be identified as Author of this work has been asserted by her in accordance with the Copyright, Designs and Patents Act 1988.

A CIP catalogue record for this book is available from the British Library.

All rights reserved. No part of this book may be reproduced or transmitted in any form or by any means, electronic or mechanical, including photocopying, recording or by any information storage and retrieval system, without permission from the Publisher in writing.

Typeset in Times New Roman 11/15 by
SJmagic DESIGN SERVICES, India.
Printed and bound in the UK by CPI Group (UK) Ltd.

Pen & Sword Books Limited incorporates the imprints of After the Battle, Atlas, Archaeology, Aviation, Discovery, Family History, Fiction, History, Maritime, Military, Military Classics, Politics, Select, Transport, True Crime, Air World, Frontline Publishing, Leo Cooper, Remember When, Seaforth Publishing, The Praetorian Press, Wharncliffe Local History, Wharncliffe Transport, Wharncliffe True Crime and White Owl.

For a complete list of Pen & Sword titles please contact
PEN & SWORD BOOKS LIMITED
George House, Units 12 & 13, Beevor Street, off Pontefract Road, Barnsley, South Yorkshire, S71 1HN, England
E-mail: enquiries@pen-and-sword.co.uk
Website: www.pen-and-sword.co.uk

or
PEN AND SWORD BOOKS
1950 Lawrence Road, Havertown, PA 19083, USA
E-mail: uspen-and-sword@casematepublishers.com
Website: www.penandswordbooks.com

For my Nan and Grandad
Doris and William Turner – I love you.

'What you leave behind is not what is engraved in stone monuments but what is woven into the lives of others.'

Pericles

Contents

Acknowledgements	ix
List of Images	xi
Key Characters	xiv
Family Tree	xxii
Timeline	xxiii
The End	1
Chapter 1 Childhood	4
Chapter 2 Daughter of Calais	16
Chapter 3 Daughter of a Traitor	25
Chapter 4 The Kingmaker's Daughter	36
Chapter 5 Uncertain Times	47
Chapter 6 Isobel's Sister	57
Chapter 7 Princess of Wales	67
Chapter 8 Wife of Lancaster	80
Chapter 9 The Prince's Widow	88
Chapter 10 Wife and Mother	100
Chapter 11 The Death of the King	113
Chapter 12 Queen of England	123
Chapter 13 Queen of the North	138
Chapter 14 Tragedy	153

Chapter 15	Christmastide	160
Chapter 16	Eclipse of the Sun	169
Chapter 17	After Anne	177

Endnotes	186
Select Bibliography	208
Index	215

Acknowledgements

There are several people I need to thank for their help and support in writing this book. Firstly, I'd like to thank author Alex Marchant for her early encouragement; it was much appreciated. My thanks must also go to Kim Harding of the Richard IIII Society, whose help and comments were absolutely invaluable. I must also thank Lucy and Sarah-Beth at Pen and Sword for their support and patience in answering my numerous questions. I also wish to thank my editor, Linne, for her patience and help.

I would like to acknowledge the help of several individuals in securing images for the book. Christine Reynolds at Westminster Abbey was particularly helpful, as was Sally Jennings at Eton College. The image of Warwick on the Beauchamp tomb is reproduced by kind permission of St Mary's Church and their encouragement was much appreciated.

I need to thank everyone at BTR for being so supportive, in particular Carole, for talking history with me; Elaine, for being awesome; Jo H and Jo E, simply for being totally amazing human beings; Lisa, Emily and Dee for making me smile, and Craig, for being our incredible emotional support colleague and helping to keep me sane(ish).

The staff at The National Archives are unfailingly helpful and their support has proved invaluable.

I would also like to acknowledge the contribution of the late, great, Dr Anne Sutton to Ricardian studies. Her scholarship and passion have been, and continue to be, an inspiration.

Without fellow author Amy, this book would literally never have been written, and it certainly wouldn't have had any images or the family tree! Thank you for everything – for your constant support, for making me laugh and for reading everything through and editing my persistent misspelling of Warwick and Somerset.

Special thanks must go to Louise, as always and for everything. *Tak for alt*, my dearest friend. And to Toyah, for listening to me ramble on with patience – thank you, lovely, you're amazing. Hi Adam, I said I'd give you a mention. I hope Donna and Cerys smile at seeing their names here.

Lastly, I must thank my wonderful family. Thanks Mum, as always, for your love and support. My brother, sister-in-law, and wonderful nephews and niece: Dylan, Lily and Deacon, I love you.

Finally, thanks must go to Jem, my hard-working secretary, loyal member of the Richard III Society and associate of Flooble, Flooblet and Poofle. I love you more than anything in the entire universe – except for Molly and Joan, naturally.

List of Images

1. Anne Neville. Digitised image from Knight, Charles, *The Popular History of England* (1856), p. 223. Courtesy of The British Library, via Flickr DS 09504.k.4.
2. Warwick Castle. Digitised image from *England Delineated*, Volume II (1804, Lackington: Allen & Co.). Courtesy of The British Library, via Flickr DS 10348.f.10.
3. Warwick Castle. Image from the author's own collection.
4. Richard Neville, depicted on the tomb of Richard Beauchamp, 13th Earl of Warwick, in St Mary's church, Warwick. By kind permission of St Mary's, Warwick.
5. John of Gaunt. CC Wikipedia image from Armitage-Smith, S., *John of Gaunt: King of Castile and Leon, Duke of Aquitaine and Lancaster, Earl of Derby, Lincoln, and Leicester, Seneschal of England* (1905, Archibald Constable), p. 100. Wikimedia Commons.
6. Richard III Society plaque, Clare Priory. Image from the author's own collection.
7. Richard Plantagenet, Duke of York. Courtesy of the LUNA: Folger Digital Image Collection.
8. Cecily Neville, Duchess of York, depicted in a *Book of Hours* belonging to the Neville family, c.1430. Wikimedia Commons.
9. Henry VI. Digitised image from Hume, D., *The History of England to the Revolution in 1688*, Volume III (1802). Courtesy of the British Library via Flickr DS 9505.ee.2.
10. The coronation of Henry VI and Margaret of Anjou. Courtesy of the Wellcome Collection.
11. Cardiff Castle window depicting Isobel Neville, in the entrance hall to the castle apartments. Courtesy of Wolfgang Sauber, via Wikimedia Commons.

12. Elizabeth Woodville. Digitised image from Knight, Charles, *The Popular History of England* (1856). Courtesy of the British Library via Flickr DS 09504.k.4.
13. George, Duke of Clarence. Courtesy of the LUNA: Folger Image Collection.
14. Rose Noble coin of Edward IV dating to 1464. Courtesy of Daderot, via Wikimedia Commons.
15. Amboise Castle. Courtesy of 7777777kz via Wikimedia Commons.
16. Men re-enacting the Battle of Barnet in 2023. From the author's own collection and with kind permission of Barnet Medieval Festival.
17. Bisham Abbey manor house. Courtesy of WyrdLight.com, via Wikimedia Commons.
18. Gobes Hall/Gupshill Manor. Courtesy of www.gupshillmanor.com.
19. The Bloody Meadow at Tewkesbury, where the Lancastrian army was finally routed. From the author's own collection.
20. Tewkesbury Abbey interior. From the author's own collection and used with the kind permission of Tewkesbury Abbey.
21. The plaque marking the burial place of Edward of Westminster. From the author's own collection and used with the kind permission of Tewkesbury Abbey.
22. The grill over the steps in Tewkesbury Abbey, which lead down to the Clarence vault. From the author's own collection and used with the kind permission of Tewkesbury Abbey.
23. Anne Neville after the Rous Roll. Wikimedia Commons.
24. The great keep of Middleham Castle. Courtesy of leestuartsherriff, via Wikimedia Commons.
25. King Edward IV. Wikimedia Commons.
26. White Boar watercolour, symbol of Richard III. Courtesy of artist Marion Moffatt at MadeMarionArt.
27. Richard, Duke of Gloucester, and the Lady Anne, by Edwin Austin Abbey. Courtesy of Yale University Art Gallery.
28. Third-party image from *Writhe's Garter Book*. From the author's own collection.
29. The Middleham Jewel. Courtesy of York Museum Trust CC BT-SA 4.0.
30. Portrait of Anne Neville, by Jo Romero, @sketcherjoey.

List of Images

31. Statue of Richard III at Middleham. From the author's own collection and used with the kind permission of English Heritage.
32. Eton wall paintings. Image reference FDA-A 427-2014. Reproduced by permission of the Provost and Fellows of Eton College.
33. Plaque commemorating the investiture of Prince Edward. From the author's own collection.
34. Elizabeth of York. Digitised image from Knight, Charles, *The Popular History of England* (1856), p. 50. Courtesy of The British Library, via Flickr DS 09504.k.4.
35. The plaque marking Anne Neville's final resting place. Copyright Dean and Chapter of Westminster.

Key Characters

Anne's immediate family

Richard Neville, 16th Earl of Warwick, known to history as the Kingmaker. Anne's father. Born 22 November 1428. Died 14 April 1471. He married Anne Beauchamp in 1436 and made it his business to make and unmake kings.

Anne Beauchamp, 16th Countess of Warwick. Anne's mother. Born 13 July 1426. Died September 1492 in obscurity, having outlived both her daughters. She married Richard Neville in 1436.

Richard Neville, 5th Earl of Salisbury. Anne's paternal grandfather. Born 1400. Died 31 December 1460. He was the third son of Ralph Neville, Earl of Westmorland, and his second wife, Joan Beaufort, daughter of John of Gaunt. Married Alice Monatgu in 1420. He was heavily involved in, and an instigator of, the Neville–Percy feud in the north. Originally loyal to Henry VI, he threw in his lot with the Yorkists.

Alice Monatgu, 5th Countess of Salisbury. Anne's paternal grandmother. Born 1407. Died before 9 December 1462. In 1420, she married Richard Neville and he became Earl of Salisbury in right of his wife. Reputedly formidable, she has the somewhat dubious honour of being the only noblewoman who was attainted for treason during the Wars of the Roses.

Richard Beauchamp, 13th Earl of Warwick, Anne's maternal grandfather. Born January 1382. Died 30 April 1439. Married 1. Elizabeth de Berkeley

2. Isabel le Despenser. A soldier of his king, he acquired quite the reputation for chivalry.

Isabel le Despenser, Countess of Worcester and Warwick, Anne's maternal grandmother. Born 26 July 1400. Died 27 December 1439. Married 1. Richard Beauchamp, 1st Earl of Worcester 2. Richard Beauchamp, 13th Earl of Warwick. Both her husbands, as well as sharing a name, were cousins, and grandsons of the 11th Earl of Warwick.

Isobel Neville, Duchess of Clarence. Anne's older sister. Born 5 September 1451. Died 22 December 1476. Married George, Duke of Clarence, in 1469, and by him had four children. After the various and repeated defections of their male relations, Isobel and Anne often found themselves on opposite sides of the Wars of the Roses.

Margaret Huddleston, Anne's older half-sister, illegitimate daughter of the Kingmaker. Born *c.*1450. Died *c.*1499. She married Sir Richard Huddleston of Millom in a strategic match by which her father sought to secure Huddleston's support. He gave Margaret land in Coverdale and the manors of Blennerhasset and Upmanby as her dowry. As she was one of Anne's ladies at her coronation and preceded other ladies of higher birth, we can perhaps infer that Anne was close to her half-sister. Margaret and her husband had three children: Richard, Margaret and Joan.

Edward of Middleham, Prince of Wales. Born *c.*1476. Died *c.*9 April 1484. Anne and Richard's only son and heir. His premature death devastated her, and destroyed her hopes for the future.

Extended family

John Neville, Marquess of Montagu. Anne's paternal uncle, her father's younger brother. Born *c.*1431. Died 14 April 1471. He was a leading figure in the northern Percy–Neville feud. He emerged as Edward IV's powerful representative in the north. Ultimately, though, he threw in his lot with his brother.

Thomas Neville, Anne's paternal uncle and another of her father's younger brothers. Born c.1429. Died 1460. His wedding to Maud Stanhope is said to have sparked the Percy–Neville feud in the north. He fought alongside the Duke of York and went down with him at Wakefield.

George Neville, Archbishop of York and Chancellor of England. Anne's paternal uncle and the youngest of Salisbury's sons. Born c.1432. Died 8 June 1476. Highly educated and a respected scholar, his enthronement at Cawood Castle looms large in history. Loyal to his family at heart, he somehow managed to act as chancellor to both Edward IV and Henry VI, and keep his head. Finally arrested in 1472 for treason, he was imprisoned near Calais for a time before returning to England to die.

Joan Neville, Countess of Arundel. Anne's paternal aunt. Born c.1424. Died September 1462. She married William FitzAlan, the Earl of Arundel, in 1438; her marriage was reputedly a love match. William fought with his brother-in-law Warwick at the Second Battle of St Albans and at Towton, but after his wife's death he took little further interest in national politics.

Cecily Neville, Duchess of Warwick and Countess of Worcester, Anne's paternal aunt. Born c.1425. Died 26 July 1450. She married her first husband, Henry de Beauchamp, Duke of Warwick, in 1434. Her second marriage was to John Tiptoft, 1st Earl of Worcester, in 1449. Cecily was the sister closest to the Kingmaker in age and her premature death caused the family great distress.

Eleanor Neville. Born c.1430. Died c.1472. Anne's paternal aunt. Her marriage in 1451 to Thomas Stanley, 1st Earl of Derby, brought Stanley firmly into the Yorkist fold. Two of her surviving letters suggest that she was trusted by her husband and wielded considerable influence. After her death, Thomas Stanley's second marriage, to Lady Margaret Beaufort, would help rewrite history.

Alice Neville, Baroness FitzHugh. Born c.1430. Died after 1503. Anne's paternal aunt. She married Henry FitzHugh, 5th Baron FitzHugh, and was close to her niece Anne, whom she served as lady-in-waiting. She was both powerful and formidable, being credited by some as the instigator of the

Key Characters

1470 rebellion, which lured Edward IV north and allowed her brother, the Kingmaker, to land. She would become the great-grandmother of Henry VIII's sixth wife, Katherine Parr.

Katherine Neville, Baroness Hastings. Born 1442. Died 1503–4. Anne's paternal aunt. She married twice; by her first husband, William Bonville, she had a daughter, Cecily, who became a wealthy heiress after her father's death at the Battle of Wakefield. She then married William Hastings, who was beheaded in 1483 on the orders of Richard III, following a now infamous council meeting. Richard placed her under his protection and she lived on in relative obscurity, dying before March 1504.

Margaret Neville, Countess of Oxford. Born 1442. Died 1506. Anne's paternal aunt. The youngest of the Kingmaker's sisters, she married the loyal Lancastrian commander John de Vere, 13th Earl of Oxford. For fourteen years, she suffered relative poverty and numerous trials when her husband was attainted a traitor, and she found herself stranded on the wrong side of the Wars of the Roses. When de Vere helped Henry Tudor to victory, they were well rewarded for their loyalty.

Key Lancastrians

King Henry VI. Son of Henry V and Katherine of Valois. Anne's first father-in-law. Born 6 December 1421. Died 21 May 1471. The Lancastrian king whose ill health ultimately cost him the throne.

Margaret of Anjou, Queen consort of England. Anne's first mother-in-law. Born 1430. Died 1482. Nicknamed the 'She-wolf of France' by her enemies, her tenacious desire to preserve her son's inheritance added fuel to the Wars of the Roses. From 1453 onwards, she effectively spearheaded the Lancastrian cause.

Edward of Westminster, Prince of Wales. Anne's first husband. Born 1453. Died 1471. He was the only son of Henry VI and Margaret of Anjou, the 'last hope of his race'.

John Beaufort, 1st Duke of Somerset. Born 1404. Died 1444. His disastrous campaign in France in 1443 cost him his career and reputation.

Edmund Beaufort, 2nd Duke of Somerset. Born *c.*1406. Died 1455. An important figure in the Hundred Years War, his rivalry with the Duke of York, his cousin, was a leading cause of the Wars of the Roses. He was killed at the First Battle of St Albans in a final desperate charge; his son Henry would never forgive either Warwick or York for his father's death.

Henry Beaufort, 3rd Duke of Somerset. Born 1436. Died 1464. Henry was badly injured at St Albans, where his father was slain. Furious and seeking revenge, he never forgave the Yorkists. He ultimately met his end at Yorkist hands following the Battle of Hexham.

Edmund Beaufort, 4th Duke of Somerset. Born *c.*1438. Died 1471. Henry's Beaufort's younger brother and, like him, a diehard Lancastrian. His death at Tewkesbury ended the male Beaufort line.

Lady Margaret Beaufort. Born 31 May 1443. Died 29 June 1509. Edmund Beaufort's death left Margaret as the sole legitimate Beaufort heir. Formidable, powerful and brilliant, Margaret bore her only child, Henry Tudor, at just 13 years of age and plotted continually to put him on the throne. Her influence, and marriage to Lord Stanley, were instrumental in bringing about Richard III's defeat.

King Henry VII (Tudor), Born 28 January 1457. Died 21 April 1509. The only son of Margaret Beaufort and Edmund Tudor, he spent most of his early life in exile as the only surviving male Lancastrian heir. He returned to claim the throne of England in 1485.

Henry Holland, 2nd Duke of Exeter. Born 1430. Died 1475. A cousin of Henry VI, with royal blood in his veins, he married Richard, Duke of York's daughter Anne in 1445. He fought for Henry VI and was captured following the Battle of Barnet in 1471. Anne promptly divorced him and he drowned in suspicious circumstances in 1475.

Key Characters

Cardinal John Kempe, Archbishop of York, Cardinal and Archbishop of Canterbury. Born *c.*1380. Died 1454. Henry VI's chancellor, who helped to hold together his rule after his ill health. His death in 1454 was disastrous and precipitated the Duke of York's protectorate.

Key Yorkists

Richard Duke of York. Anne's second father-in-law. Born 1411. Died 1460. Proud and ambitious, York's royal descent made him powerful. In 1447, he became King Henry VI's heir and increasingly came into conflict with Margaret of Anjou and the Lancastrian faction. His death at the Battle of Wakefield further fuelled his son's desire for power and revenge.

Cecily Neville, Duchess of York. 'The Rose of Raby'. Anne's second mother-in-law and her great-aunt. Wife of Richard, Duke of York. Born 3 May 1415. Died 31 May 1495. Youngest daughter of Ralph Neville, 1st Earl of Westmorland, and his second wife, Joan Beaufort. Cecily was the aunt of Anne's father, the Kingmaker. She was the mother of two kings and grandmother of Elizabeth of York. Pious but with a proud, formidable temper, she latterly continually tried to broker peace between her warring children. She lived to see the birth in 1491 of her great-grandson, who became King Henry VIII.

Anne of York, Duchess of Exeter. Born 10 August 1439. Died 14 January 1476. She was the eldest child of Richard, Duke of York, and Cecily Neville. She was married to Henry Holland, 3rd Duke of Exeter, who remained staunchly Lancastrian and commanded the Lancastrian force at Wakefield, where Anne's father was killed. After her brother, Edward IV, acceded to the throne, she and her husband separated and finally divorced in 1472. She married again, to Thomas St Leger, who was a loyal Yorkist until Richard III assumed the throne, when he joined the October rebellion, and was executed in 1483.

King Edward IV. Born 28 April 1442. Died April 1483. Anne's brother-in-law and the eldest son of Richard, Duke of York, and Cecily Neville.

A skilled warrior, brave man and astute politician, he held his throne peacefully following Tewkesbury for many years but his unexpected death provoked a succession crisis.

Edmund of Rutland. Born 17 May 1443. Died 30 December 1460. Richard of York's second son, he died alongside his father at Wakefield. Tradition says he was executed by Lord Clifford when his youth should have spared him. Clifford would be killed in retaliation at the Battle of Ferrybridge.

Elizabeth of York, Duchess of Suffolk. Born 22 April 1444. Died *c.*1503. A daughter of Richard, Duke of York, and sister to two kings, she married John de la Pole. Her son John was considered by some for a time to be Richard III's heir. Her other sons would all meet violent ends on account of their Plantagenet blood.

Margaret of York, Duchess of Burgundy. Born 3 May 1446. Died 23 November 1503. She was the learned and impressive third wife of Charles the Bold, Duke of Burgundy. After his death, she acted as Protector of Burgundy and is credited with preventing French dominance.

George, Duke of Clarence. Anne's brother-in-law twice over. Born 21 October 1449. Died 18 February 1478. Brother to King Edward IV, his position as the second son and 'spare' led to him repeatedly switching sides. He was married to Anne's sister, Isobel. He finally went too far and was executed on his brother's orders in 1478.

Richard III, Duke of Gloucester. Anne's second husband. Born 2 October 1452. Died 22 August 1485. He was the youngest son of Richard, Duke of York, and Cecily Neville, and brother to Edward IV. He claimed the throne after the death of his brother in June 1483 and would be killed in a final cavalry charge at the Battle of Bosworth.

Elizabeth Woodville, Queen of England. Anne's sister-in-law and wife of Edward IV. Born *c.*1437. Died 8 June 1492. Her second marriage, to the Yorkist claimant Edward IV, led to a schism between him and Anne's

Key Characters

father. After the disappearance of her sons, she eventually left sanctuary and permitted her daughters to join Richard III's court. Ultimately, she was involved in the plot to marry her daughter Elizabeth to Henry Tudor and overthrow Richard.

Key figures during Richard III's rule

Sir William Catesby. Born *c.*1446. Died August 1485. Richard III's 'Catte', he was one of Richard's most loyal supporters and received lands after Buckingham's rebellion. He spoke out against Richard marrying his niece, Elizabeth of York, but fought alongside his king at Bosworth, after which he was executed.

John Howard, Duke of Norfolk. Born *c.*1420. Died 2 August 1485. A loyal supporter of Richard III, he was rewarded for his loyalty with the dukedom of Norfolk. He died at Bosworth trying to repel the attack of the Earl of Oxford.

Francis, Viscount Lovell. Richard III's 'dogge' and most loyal supporter, the two men had spent time alongside each other at Middleham as teenagers, and became close friends. After Richard's death, he was involved in Lambert Simnel's rebellion and fought at the Battle of Stoke Field, after which he disappeared from history.

Sir Richard Ratcliffe. Died 22 August 1485. Richards III's 'ratte', he was a royal councillor and trusted supporter. He had northern connections and supported Richard following his marriage to Anne Neville; he spoke out against Richard marrying Elizabeth of York but he died alongside his king at Bosworth.

Sir James Tyrell. Born *c.*1455. Died 1502. A key supporter of Richard II and royal councillor. After Bosworth, he transferred his loyalties to Henry VII, but was executed in 1502 for conspiring with one of the last Plantagenet male heirs, Edmund de la Pole.

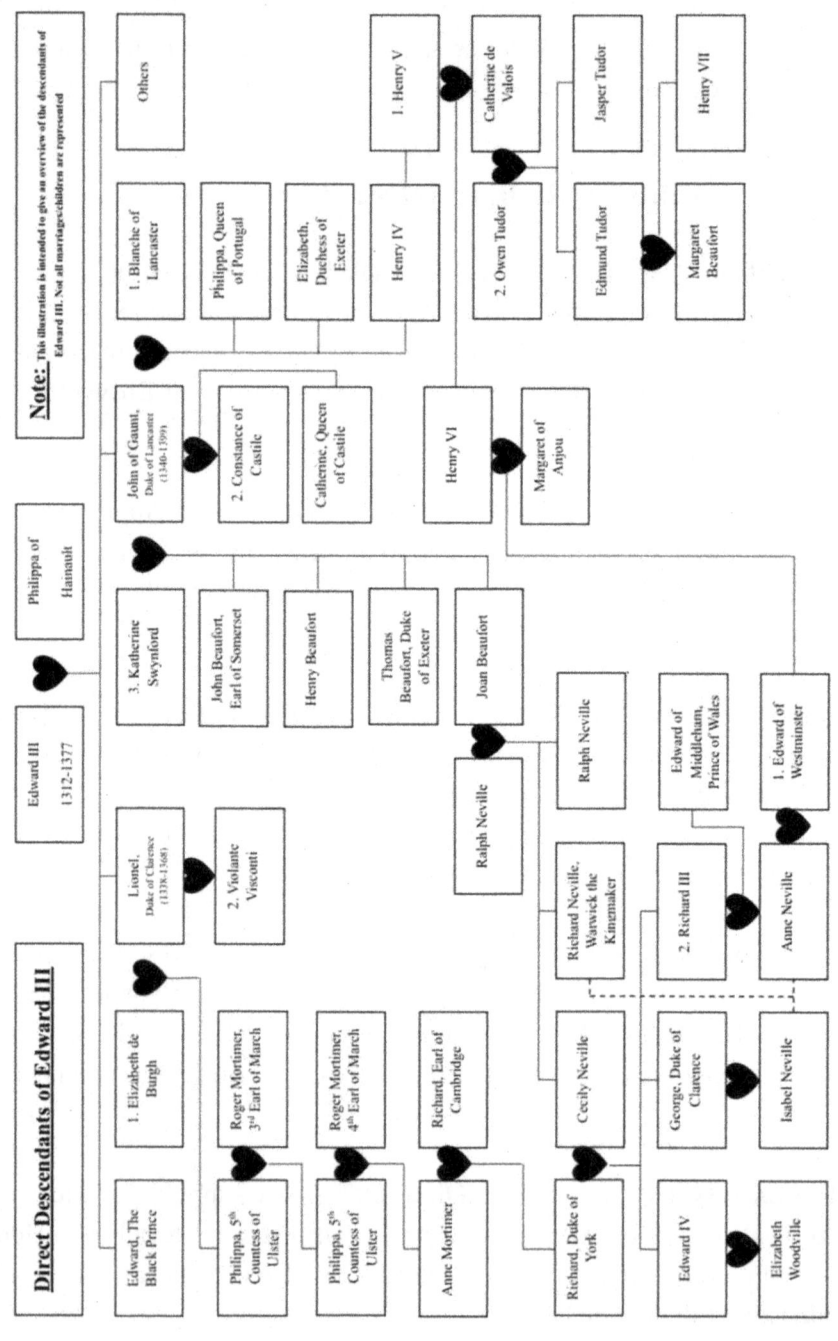

Timeline

Naturally, Anne Neville did not fight in any battles during the Wars of the Roses, but the outcomes of the battles fought defined her life and times.

22 May 1455
The First Battle of St Albans
Yorkist victory for Richard, Duke of York, and Anne's father, Warwick.

23 September 1459
The Battle of Blore Heath
Yorkist victory.

12–13 October 1459
The Battle of Ludford Bridge
Lancastrian victory, the Duke of York fled to Ireland, Anne's father to Calais.

10 July 1460
The Battle of Northampton
Yorkist victory. Henry VI was captured.

30 December 1460
The Battle of Wakefield
Lancastrian victory, the Duke of York and his second son, Edmund, were killed.

2 February 1461
The Battle of Mortimer's Cross
Yorkist victory.

Anne Neville: Queen and Wife of Richard III

17 February 1461
The Second Battle of St Albans
Lancastrian victory. Henry VI was liberated from Yorkist captivity.

29 March 1461
The Battle of Towton
Decisive victory for the Yorkists under King Edward IV, son of Richard, Duke of York.

25 April 1464
The Battle of Hedgeley Moor
Yorkist victory.

15 May 1464
The Battle of Hexham
Yorkist victory. This was followed by five years of relative peace until Anne's father, Warwick, switched sides and rebelled.

24 July 1469
The Battle of Edgecote
Lancastrian victory.

12 March 1470
The Battle of Losecoat Field
Yorkist victory.

14 April 1471
The Battle of Barnet
Yorkist victory. Anne's father was killed.

4 May 1471
The Battle of Tewkesbury
Yorkist victory. Anne's first husband was killed, alongside nearly the entire Lancastrian nobility, including the last male of the direct Beaufort line.

Timeline

22 August 1485
The Battle of Bosworth
After many years of peace, Anne's second husband, King Richard III, died at Bosworth Field, defeated by the forces of Henry Tudor.

16 June 1487
The Battle of Stoke Field
The last battle. Henry Tudor, now King Henry VII, defeated the last vestiges of serious resistance to his rule.

The End

> Anointed let me be with deadly venom
> And die ere men can say 'God save the queen'.
> *Richard III*, William Shakespeare

On 16 March 1485, deep inside the medieval palace of Westminster, inside a hot and foetid room, a queen of England lay dying. As she struggled for breath, with her flaxen hair plastered to her skull, she was attended by a small group of her ladies. The air was infused with spices – cinnamon and cloves – but they could not conceal the earthy smells of vomit and blood. The queen had been ailing ever since Christmas and her husband was conspicuously absent from the sickroom on the advice of his physician, who had told him to 'shun her bed'.[1] Royal physicians were in daily attendance but even given her youth, the 28-year-old queen was long past saving in this pre-antibiotic age.

Outside the sick room door, the court was alive with intrigue and rumour. The previous year had seen the birth of the idea that, following the death of their only son and heir, the king was plotting to replace his infertile wife with his 18-year-old niece. In consequence, Christmas had, according to the *Crowland Chronicle*, been held with 'far too much attention [being] given to dancing and gaiety'.[2] The queen and her niece had been dressed the same, causing many to comment on the insult to rank in a society where the type of clothing you could wear was closely governed by sumptuary laws. The right to wear such fabrics as purple silk and cloth of gold was limited to the legitimate royal family by a law passed in 1482, so when Anne's bastardised niece was arrayed as a queen, people began to whisper.[3] The fact that Crowland was not in favour of court living generally and that it is now considered that the two women exchanged gowns because they were of similar size and colouring was not enough to quell the gossips. These were no idle rumours; they were championed by such sources as the later Clerkenwell Declaration and perhaps most tellingly by the queen's niece herself, who wrote a letter expressing her hopes and fears to John Howard, the Duke of Norfolk.[4]

Whatever the truth behind them, these rumours had taken root and it was soon said that the king in truth meant to be rid of his queen either by death or 'by means of a divorce for which he believed he had sufficient grounds'.[5] It is impossible that such rumours failed to reach the sanctity of the dying queen's chamber. There were suggestions that the queen had previously railed at her husband in fury upon hearing them or even that she was already dead.[6] Her ladies tried to conceal the worst from her, but even the walls of the sickroom could not be sealed entirely; few secrets stayed secret for long in the hotbed of gossip that was England's medieval court. These tales would later grow to include the idea that many now believed the king had determined to use poison if the queen were to show signs of recovery.[7] The air inside the queen's room was therefore poisonous with both words and germs, and everyone was uneasy as the queen's breath rattled in her chest.

It is not known if the queen was conscious enough to view the solar eclipse that occurred that same day, when London was plunged into darkness, filling the superstitious citizens with panic. When the queen breathed her last, at some time in the early evening, it was said, even as the bells began to toll to announce her death, that the eclipse foretold not just her end but also her husband's doom.

The queen in question was Anne Neville, wife to the last Plantagenet king, Richard III, and what she felt as she lay dying can only be guessed at. Whether or not she gave credence to the court rumours is unknown but her husband's absence would certainly have given her the time and space to doubt. That is not to say that there was necessarily anything malevolent behind his absence; today, most historians believe that Anne was dying of tuberculosis. The king's doctor's advice in that case was eminently sensible given the disease's highly contagious nature. It does seem likely, however, that Richard III was considering marriage to his niece, Elizabeth, the daughter of his brother, Edward IV, and Elizabeth Woodville. Key contemporary figures at court such as Sir Richard Ratcliffe and William Catesby attest to

The End

the fact and give the rumours credence. People were shocked and appalled as, even in the medieval period, morality required a decent interval between the death of one wife and a man's remarriage.

Anne's feelings are beyond our reach; perhaps she was deeply hurt, or tentatively approved the plan knowing that her husband would require a new wife to produce a new heir if his dynasty was to survive. Whichever way her feelings swung, and simple humanity suggests it was a mixture of both, there is no evidence that she bore her niece any ill will. Indeed, Anne is steadfastly silent during these months. She appears not to have made a will, which is extremely unusual for the time, especially given that by the beginning of March at the latest, she would surely have known that she was dying. We cannot discount the possibility that her will has been lost but sadly, for historians today, this silence is something that characterised her entire life. We know less about Anne Neville than about almost any other queen consort of England since the Norman Conquest. That does not mean that she is totally lost to us, however; we can glean glimpses of her life, her actions and even perhaps her feelings from the plethora of surviving documentation from the period.

Anne lived through one of the most turbulent times in English history: during the Wars of the Roses. She was born into the House of York, and was married to the Lancastrian heir before finally becoming the wife of England's last Yorkist king. These events overshadowed her life, resulting in her being regarded as a mere bit part player in England's history, but this was far from the case and the role she played should not be underestimated. Her first marriage sealed her father's fate, her second financed Richard III's reign, and the rumours surrounding her death contributed to his downfall.

Richard III would not long survive his wife, dying at Bosworth Field in a final, legendary cavalry charge. However, it is not my intention here to dwell too long on Richard's life; plenty of academic ink has already been spilt on his reign and his guilt or innocence regarding the events of his life. I intend only to tell his story where it influences that of his wife, for I hope to take a fresh look at the life and times of Anne Neville:

Daughter, Heiress, Wife, Widow and Queen.

Chapter 1

Childhood

> So God help Warwick, as he loves the land,
> And common profit of his country!
> *Henry VI, Part 2*, William Shakespeare

It can be argued that few queen consorts of England were more destined for such a role than Anne Neville. Anne was born on 11 June 1456, inside the mighty Warwick Castle, her father's midland stronghold.[1] She was the daughter of Richard Neville, known to history as 'the Kingmaker', and his wife, the heiress Anne Beauchamp. In June 1456, Anne Beauchamp laboured inside a hot chamber; there was a fire burning regardless of the likely summer heat, and as soon as the baby was delivered, the infant was anointed, rubbed in scented oil and swaddled in a cradle before the fire. At a time when life expectancy was only 33 years and nearly half of all children died before their fifth birthday, the fact that both Anne Beauchamp and her daughter survived the birth would have been the cause of celebration and relief. In medieval times, medical understanding of childbirth was in its infancy, and although texts such as the twelfth-century *Trotula* contained some information – such as how to carry out a very basic episiotomy – in reality, most women only had their faith or homemade herbal remedies to rely upon.[2] To this end, many noblewomen like Anne Beauchamp wore a girdle, endowed with religious protection. Analysis of one of these medieval birthing girdles, which was made of parchment and dates to 1500, has revealed that it had been worn during labour, probably around the abdomen or thigh. The parchment contained traces of vaginal fluids, as well as honey, milk, egg and broad beans, which are all known medieval 'treatments' for childbirth.[3] Honey in particular would have been helpful as it is known today to have antibacterial properties. Anne Beauchamp, unlike

Childhood

poorer women, would have easy access to such things from the castle still room, a place where medicines and salves were created from oils, dried herbs and flowers. A great deal of importance appears to have been attached to these girdles, and Anne's niece Elizabeth of York would later pay a lot of money for a monk to bring her a girdle of the Virgin prior to her entering her chamber.[4]

While Anne Beauchamp was sequestered away in the female world of childbirth, the only role for the baby's father, Richard Neville, would have been to pray, or perhaps, as in the manner of Margaret Paston's husband, wear an ornament to try to help ensure the survival of his wife and child.[5]

It must have been a huge relief to her parents that Anne arrived safely and squalling. Her gender, however, would have inevitably been a great disappointment. The baby Anne already had an elder sister, Isobel, who had been born in September 1451. In medieval England, a male heir was always more desirable. The gap in between Isobel and Anne's births suggests that Anne Beauchamp may have had trouble in conceiving or carrying a pregnancy to term so although they continued to try, Anne would prove to be her parents' last attempt for a male heir.[6]

The infant Anne had every material advantage for she had been born into one of the greatest dynasties of medieval England. As was usual at the time, Anne would have joined her older sister's household, which existed separately from that of their parents. Anne Beauchamp would not have breastfed her child and a lady mistress or lady governess would have run the children's establishment, with the help of specially appointed wet and dry nurses. Usually, the lady mistress was a trusted figure, well acquainted with the family. Eighty years later, Blanche Parry, a woman well known to Anne Boleyn, would be appointed as lady mistress to Princess Elizabeth and it was she who was given the task of choosing a wet nurse for the infant baby.[7] Given that Anne had an older sister, it is likely that she was given the same lady mistress. Inside the chamber appointed as her nursery, the infant Anne would have been kept swaddled, with her arms tightly bound, and she would have spent most of her early months in her cradle. Although her parents could have afforded the best quality furnishings, there is a legend that persists today that Anne used the same plain oak cradle that was used for both her sister and mother, although the origins of this rumour remain unclear. The baby Anne would have seen relatively little of her parents – especially her father, Richard Neville. Yet his presence would have permeated every aspect of her life and she would have known from the earliest moments of her consciousness that she was the daughter of a great man.

Richard Neville, Earl of Warwick, was the son of another Richard Neville (died 1460) and his wife, Alice Montagu (died 1464), and he was connected to the foremost families of the kingdom. He claimed kinship to the Beauforts, the leading family of the day, through his father's father, Ralph Neville, the Earl of Westmorland's marriage to Joan Beaufort. Joan was the daughter of John of Gaunt, Duke of Lancaster and third son of King Edward III, by his mistress and later wife, Kathryn Swynford. It was possibly because he had made this connection with the royal family that Ralph was made the Earl of Westmorland in 1397. He was, however, well qualified for a position at the centre of court life, having since a young age 'done good service for the crown'.[8] There was no escaping the fact that Joan was far better connected; she was half-sister to Henry IV, aunt of Henry V, great-aunt of Henry VI, and sister to the powerful Cardinal Beaufort and the Duke of Exeter – her brothers Henry and Thomas Beaufort respectively. Through his marriage, Ralph Neville was therefore practically royal, and Henry IV held him in high favour.

Ralph's marriage to Joan was in fact his second, but no doubt buoyed by the favours that were heaped upon him, he favoured his children with her over those he had had with his first wife. This meant that it was Anne's grandfather, Richard, who inherited the ancestral Neville estates. Unsurprisingly, the children of Ralph's first marriage objected but by 1443, their protests were effectively dismissed. They kept some small lands in Durham but it was Richard who received the bulk of the Neville inheritance, including the vast estates of Middleham Castle, Sheriff Hutton, Penrith, and the wardship of the West March, which made him the North Western English commander against the Scots. This made him one of the most powerful men in England, and when Anne's father was born in 1428, he would have been constantly made aware of his father's importance.

This importance meant that when the time came, Ralph was able to arrange the best marriages possible for his children; after all, he knew better than most the potential advancements possible through marriage. Arguably, the grandest of these marriages was between Anne's grandparents, Richard Neville and Alice Montagu. Alice was the sole heiress of Thomas Montagu, the Earl of Salisbury, and her mother was one of five heiresses to the Earldom of Kent.

Alice in fact could trace her ancestry back to Edward I, a connection she and her husband exploited and emphasised when they in turn sought a bride for their son, Anne's father, Richard. Anne's father was therefore heir to the earldom of Salisbury and all of the Montagu and Neville lands and estates. Consequently, his future marriage was of national importance.

Richard's future wife, Anne's mother (also called Anne), meanwhile, had been born in 1426 and boasted no less a pedigree. Anne Beauchamp was the daughter of Richard Beauchamp, Earl of Warwick, and his wife, Isabel Despenser. At the time of her birth, Anne was not her father's heir; she had an elder brother, Henry (born 1445), and three elder half-sisters, Elizabeth, Margaret and Eleanor. The Beauchamp family was a noble one, and Anne's ancestors included the legendary Guy of Warwick and, more recently, another Guy (de Bauchamp), who had been knighted by Edward I for his services in the Scottish Wars before being in part responsible for the execution of Edward II's favourite, Piers Gaveston. Her father was a tutor to the infant Henry VI and later, a lieutenant in France. Isabel Despenser, for her part, brought yet more royal blood into the equation, being descended from Constance of York, a granddaughter of King Edward III. Their marriage united a large number of estates in the midlands, primarily those of Warwick, Hanley, Tewkesbury and Barnard Castle. The plan initially was to marry the Warwick heir Henry to Richard's daughter, Cecily Neville. Henry was England's greatest heir and Warwick was not enthusiastic initially, but Salisbury (Anne's grandfather) made him an offer he could simply not refuse. He gave Cecily the enormous dowry of 4,700 marks and offered his son Richard as a husband for Anne Beauchamp, an act that would make her a countess. Anne's three elder sisters were all married already and none had made anywhere near such an illustrious match. A double marriage therefore took place around 4 May 1436 between Henry Beauchamp and Cecily Neville, and Richard Neville to Anne Beauchamp in Abergavenny.[9]

Anne Neville: Queen and Wife of Richard III

Henry duly succeeded to the earldom of Warwick upon his father's death; he was later made a duke and rode high in royal favour, having been a boyhood friend of Henry VI. However, in 1446, disaster struck and he died, possibly of tuberculosis, on 11 June. The earldom passed to his 2-year-old daughter Anne, who became the greatest heiress in England, but when she fell victim to childhood illness and died at Ewelme in 1449, at just 5 years old, it was unclear who would profit. Her mother's death a year later took her out of the picture and ultimately, Anne Beauchamp inherited everything. Richard Neville, Anne's father, thus received the earldom and the entire Dispenser and Beauchamp inheritance in the right of his wife. Anne's sisters protested violently, as did their husbands, but to no avail.

Anne Neville's parents had hit the jackpot and in another lifetime, Anne might have lived a very different life, but the England that Anne had been born into was deeply troubled and in many ways, her fate was determined by events that had begun three years before she was even born.

'Good lord, what madness rules in brainsick men.'[10]

In 1453, the Lancastrian king, Henry VI, had been staying at Clarendon Palace – with its amazing gold, grey and pink tiled floor and being a favourite retreat of his – when early in the morning while on his knees in prayer, he suffered a seizure and 'was lifeless as if paralyzed' as well as insensible.[11] The shock was immense; up until then, the king, whilst criticised for his increasing piety, was well respected and considered personally steady. Now England was in uproar, and his panicking physicians helped him to his bed, sent for his formidable queen, Margaret of Anjou, and prayed that rest might restore him. It did not. For weeks, his physicians attended him, but he could not be roused. He was, in modern terms, catatonic. Henry 'had lost control of his body and his wits'.[12] He failed to even recognise his pregnant wife, or his childhood friends, and could no longer determine ally from foe. All of this had to be concealed from the wider court and country, for there were many strong noblemen who would be all too eager to step into the void left by an ailing king.

Today, the cause of Henry's collapse is open to interpretation but modern scholars tentatively offer a diagnosis of catatonic schizophrenia, which is characterised by catalepsy, stupor and mutism. At the time, his doctors – 600 years before any serious understanding of mental illness was possible – studied his urine in line with contemporary Galenic theory and observed him continuously. For the ancient Greeks, on whose theories medieval medicine was largely based, madness was seen as coming from the gods. Hippocrates and Galen attributed the three madnesses of epilepsy, mania and melancholia to a disturbance of the body's humours. In an attempt to balance Henry IV's humours, his diet was adjusted to restore balance, and he was bled to draw dangerous black bile and other matter out of his body. At the root of medieval thinking, however, madness was still considered to be related to religion, or a moral failing, a punishment for sin or a test of one's moral fibre.[13]

Madness also brought with it numerous legal complications. In England, when an ordinary person who owned land went mad, the king used the Prerogative Regis to appoint a guardianship to administer the lands himself. The king would often clash with family members over who should administer lucrative lands. When in 1372 Hugh Mortimer, a marcher lord, died, his lands were left to his 'mad and mentally disabled' grandson, William. King Edward III stepped in and appointed a guardian to run the Mortimer estates efficiently for the benefit of all. This was a system open to abuse yet generally it worked well, but things were very different if it were the monarch themselves who went mad.[14]

As the months rolled by, and Henry VI remained insensible, the kingdom of England ground to a standstill. In desperation, Henry VI's doctors even turned to alchemy to try to cure the king. He was considered phlegmatic, with too many bodily fluids present, and as gold was considered both hot and dry, it was hoped that it could restore balance to the king. However, the rumours surrounding his health could no longer be stopped and in the court and wider country, many began to suspect that the king was being enchanted or bewitched by some evil force. Courtiers formally discussed with his doctors the question of demonic possession. It was, after all, only twelve years since Eleanor, Duchess of Gloucester and wife to King Henry V's brother Humphrey, had been convicted of 'witchcraft and treasonable necromancy'.[15] In response, doctors brought charms and holy relics to the king to try to combat any malevolent presence.

Doctors also, more scientifically, looked to his family history, and not unreasonably feared that his madness was hereditary. His grandfather, Charles VI of France, had been prone to bouts of 'madness'. Charles VI had, according to the monk of St Denis – an eyewitness to his decline – viewed his illness as witchcraft, imposed upon him by his enemies. The doctors treating Henry VI would have been well aware that they themselves could be open to allegations of inciting the king's demonic possession: Charles VI, after all, had banished one of his doctors and executed two more on similar charges.

Family was also on the mind of England's nobles. Henry VI's wife, Margaret of Anjou, was pregnant at the time of her husband's mental collapse. Her pregnancy had come after eight long years of marriage, during which her husband had only come to her bed irregularly, having been told by his confessor that he should shun such earthly pleasures. As a result, there were rumours abroad in the court and country that Margaret was in fact pregnant by the unpopular royal favourite, the Duke of Somerset. His position was not helped by the fact that, given Henry VI's continued indisposition, the council was forced to act as they had during Henry's minority, and issue orders 'by order of the king with the advice of his counsel'. The queen and Somerset were supported by many of the great nobles such as Cardinal Kempe, Chancellor and Keeper of the Great Seal, and Humphrey Stafford, Duke of Buckingham. All were aware, however, that suspicions outside this select group were growing, and that time was ticking. In November, the king would be expected to appear in public when his parliament resumed.

England under Henry VI had been steady but had never been strong; he had come to the thrones of England and France at just nine months old, after the unexpected death of his father, Henry V. He was crowned as King of England in 1429, and that of France in 1431, once Joan of Arc was dead and France considered subdued. During his childhood, his father's two brothers, John, of Lancaster, Duke of Bedford, and Humphrey, Duke of Gloucester, had been appointed as regent and Lord Protector respectively. Under their guidance, Henry had grown, and by sheer force of will (and arms) they had held together the boy king's inheritance despite their own differences. However, by 1447, both men were dead, and trying to keep hold of England's French possessions was proving nearly impossible.

Childhood

One nobleman who played a key role in France at this time was Richard, Duke of York, who claimed descent from Edward III through his fourth son, Edmund, Duke of York. Richard, Duke of York, reached his majority just as England's hold on France was beginning to weaken. In May 1436, following Bedford's death, he succeeded him to the post of commander of the English forces in France, but unlike with Bedford, limits were placed on York's power and he was unable to control the forces' finances or appoint military personnel. This meant that he had to pay the troops largely himself and despite initial successes, he quickly became disillusioned. In spite of his significant successes, when he returned to England in 1437, he was not appointed to Henry VI's council – something he felt was a political snub. However, he was reappointed Lieutenant of France in 1440, with greater powers this time. York was married to Cecily Neville, aunt to Anne's father, Richard Neville, and while in France, she bore him four children: Henry, who died young, Edward, Edmund and Elizabeth. Their eldest child, a daughter, Anne, had been born in England. Once again, though, funding was in short supply and although York was granted an annuity of 20,000 pounds a year, it was not always paid. He was also chronically short of men so when in 1443 Henry VI granted John Beaufort, Duke of Somerset, 8,000 men simply to relieve Gascony, York was less than impressed; the enmity between the families of York and Beaufort had begun.

In 1445, Henry VI had married Margaret of Anjou and part of the marriage settlement had been that Maine and Anjou would be returned to France, something that was considered extremely controversial and not greeted well by the men who remembered the glory days of Henry V and Agincourt. York was personally furious and the council sent him to Ireland to cool off, leaving Somerset at court, where he quickly rose to become the royal favourite.

Worse, however, was to come for both England and York. In 1451, nearly all of England's French territories were lost under Edmund Beaufort, who commanded the campaign, not York. By 1453, when the English were defeated at the Battle of Castillon, the Hundred Years War was effectively at an end, and England no longer had much to show for it. Henry VI was told the news just before his collapse, and some felt the shock of such a humiliation was to blame.[16]

With her king incapacitated, England began to fracture as power-hungry nobles sought to seize control, and no one was better placed to do so than York, alongside his loyal ally, Anne's father, Richard Neville. It was in this context that Queen Margaret went into labour on 13 October 1453 and gave birth to a healthy baby boy. The boy was christened Edward, and known as Edward of Westminster.[17] Though she did not know it, this baby boy would grow up to have a profound influence on Anne's life. His godparents included Cardinal Kempe and Anne, Duchess of Buckingham, and the baby was baptised by William Waynflete, Henry VI's confessor and later founder of Magdalen College, Oxford. More than 500 pounds was spent on Edward's sumptuous christening robes but none of this pomp could completely conceal the curious silence of the king. Cecily, Duchess of York, was one of the first to be invited to view the queen after her confinement, with both women hoping that the birth of a prince would usher in a period of peace.[18]

It was not to be; problems continued as the king failed to recover. The same month as the prince was born, a great council was summoned in London, but the Duke of York was deliberately excluded. Whilst on a personal level this is understandable (he had, after all, tried to overthrow Somerset twice in the last three years), politically it was a disaster. His exclusion had been opposed by many who thought it a critical mistake to anger York further, and so it would prove. Buckingham in particular, who was brother-in-law to Cecily Neville, urged that York be included. Cecily likewise appealed directly to the queen, declaring that her husband was loyal to King Henry. The council, therefore under pressure, summoned York on a day when Kempe and Somerset were conspicuously absent. They claimed that his exclusion had been an oversight, but that fooled no one.

York was strong and everyone knew it. Kempe tried to prorogue the parliament until February in order to weaken York's position, claiming that this was due to threat of plague in the capital, but York, alongside the Duke of Norfolk, now marched into London with clear intent to take down his rivals. Norfolk personally attacked Somerset and with no recourse, Somerset was sent to the Tower.

By 4 December, it was clear to all that Henry VI was completely incapacitated and that York, alongside his key kinsmen, Salisbury and Warwick, Anne's grandfather and father respectively, were in the ascendancy. The royal position was not helped by the fact that when the prince was shown to his father on New Year's Day 1454, the king made no acknowledgement of his son, which some interpreted as his refusal to acknowledge the child as his. Margaret of Anjou wanted to be made regent for her son in the manner of her grandmother, Yolande of Aragon, who had been Regent of Provence during the minority of her son, but the suggestion was dismissed.[19]

The court limped on until 22 March, when Cardinal Kempe died; this was a catastrophic blow to the royal position. Kempe had been called 'one of the wisest Lords in the Land' and his death left quite a void: England now had no king and no chancellor. The appointment of a new chancellor was the province of the king and on 23 March, a party of twelve lords went to see Henry VI at Windsor to ask his opinion. Warwick was amongst them when they 'skilfully, solemnly and respectfully' asked the king who should be the new chancellor. The king made no reply.[20]

In the absence of a royal decision, on 27 March 1454, York was elected as Chief Councillor, Protector and Defender of the Realm, in the same way that Humphrey, Duke of Gloucester, had been during the king's minority in 1422. This protectorate was to last until either Henry recovered his senses or Prince Edward reached the age of majority. Margaret of Anjou was not happy; she had negotiated to maintain power herself but ultimately she had no option but to accept the council's choice of York. However, the council and country were far from united on the issue, meaning that York quickly found himself facing rebellions, including that of his own son-in-law, Henry Holland, whom he defeated and then imprisoned in Pontefract Castle.[21] Throughout these events, Warwick remained loyal at York's side, supporting him both politically and by force of arms where necessary.

By Christmas 1454, to everyone's surprise and the royalists' relief, Henry began to recover; he recognised his wife, his son and his councillors, effectively ending York's protectorate. On 27 December, he was well enough to send a servant to make an offering at the shrine of St Thomas Becket in Canterbury, presumably in thanks for his recovery.[22] He also returned to his religious devotions, and said 'Matins to Our Lady and evensong and hears his Mass devoutly', according to Edmund Clere, a squire in Margaret's household.[23] Somerset was freed from the Tower, most of York's decrees were overturned, and the court was once again split between the royalist/Somerset and Yorkist factions.

York, Salisbury and Warwick now formed an unmistakable political triumvirate along the lines of that seen between Caesar, Pompey and Crassus in Rome, with Warwick fulfilling the role of the ambitious Caesar. Anne's father was at this time 29 years old and strong both in body and in terms of the power he wielded. These three men were no longer open to compromise and in March 1455, Warwick and York left the court without permission. They maintained their issue was with Somerset and not the king, but with Somerset almost entirely dependent on royal favour, the cause was one and the same.

A month later, by royal decree, the 'Yorkist lords were excluded formally from the council of the country and instead were ordered to meet the king at Leicester to explain their actions.' Instead, they raised an army in the north, led by Warwick, who was very much a man of action and who had raced quickly north. By 20 May, the Yorkists had reached Royston, only 40 miles north of London, with a 3,000-strong army and the intention of blocking the king's route to Leicester and meeting him on the road.

Two days later, 22 May 1455 saw the First Battle of St Albans take place. King Henry had set off from Westminster alongside Buckingham and Somerset, their sons Stafford and Dorset, and the king's half-brother, Jasper Tudor. Their force of 2,000 men was at Watford when they heard that York and Warwick, accompanied by York's eldest son, Edward of March, were close by. Henry VI seems to have believed that York would negotiate and he sent Buckingham as his emissary. He was gravely mistaken.[24]

Tired of talking and keen to make a lasting resolution, Warwick led his men into the town. As they forced entry, the bells of the town screamed in alarm. In the ensuing violence, Henry VI himself was injured, and his standard-bearer, likely the Earl of Wiltshire, fled for his life. Warwick attacked to the east of the town, York and Salisbury to the north, with Warwick disposing of his northern rival Lord Clifford on the town's barricades, and later the Duke of Northumberland, but the key target of the day was the Duke of Somerset, who must have known that his number was finally up. He fled into a tavern – according to legend, named The Castle – with his men and son, but when he attempted to leave, he was hacked to death. His son was badly wounded and had to be dragged, bleeding, to safety – it was not a day the young man would ever forget or forgive.

The battle was an overwhelming victory for the forces of York and Warwick; after the battle, they found Henry VI and took him prisoner. Sixty of the king's closest allies lay dead in the town and unsurprisingly, he fell once again into a passive state. Today we might suggest that he was suffering from a form of PTSD, catatonia or shell shock. With the king now in custody, next day the triumvirate marched on London, with Warwick bearing the king's sword in the procession that ultimately saw Henry VI crowned by York in St Paul's on 25 May. This gave the Yorkist regime a thin veil of respectability but in reality, Henry now was little more than a puppet.

Warwick, for his part, took up residence at the manor of Hunsdon after the recrowning. This was a spacious house built recently on the site of an earlier manor, and at the time held by the Duke of York. Meanwhile, the whole of Europe was alight with rumours and reports of the events in London, with the Milanese state papers reporting rather gleefully that 'fresh disturbances have broken out in England … and great part of their nobles have been in conflict and the Duke of Somerset, the Earl of Northumberland and my Lord of Clifford all slain'.[25]

Under York's guidance, the triumvirate now set about consolidating their positions and powerbase. To this end, Warwick was appointed as Captain of Calais, an undertaking that would have a profound impact on his daughter Anne's early life.

Chapter 2

Daughter of Calais

> Foul devil, for God's sake, hence, and trouble us not!
> *Richard III*, William Shakespeare

The Captaincy of Calais has been called 'one of the best offices in Christendom'. The first man ever appointed to the post had been Sir Amery of Pavia, 'a Lombard, who was greatly advanced', by King Edward III when Calais had come into England's possession following the English victory at the Battle of Crécy in 1346. He had later disgraced himself when he made a secret deal with the French, ultimately paying for his treachery with his life.[1] Calais had been occupied since prehistoric times and had evolved into a small fishing village. It was called Caletum by the Romans, and in 55 CE, Julius Caesar used it as the harbour from which to transport five legions and their horses into Britain. Later, in 997 CE, it was made into a walled town and harbour on the orders of the Count of Flanders, and in the twelfth century, Calais was granted a charter, which established it as a city and municipality. The harbour at Calais quickly became a notorious pirate base, from which the coast of England could be raided.[2]

By the thirteenth century, the Count of Boulogne had fortified Calais even further and added towers and additional walls. A hundred years later, it was considered a large and well-fortified town and as such it was coveted by kings and noblemen alike. Men desired it as a potential base from which to both raid into France and to reach England. This placed Calais at the heart of Edward III's French campaign.

According to the chronicler Henry Knighton, in 1346 Edward had sailed with 1,500 ships to Normandy. Today it is estimated that he had with him a force of about 14,000 men. After landing at the harbour of Saint-Vaast-la-Hougue on 12 July, the king and his men 'lodged in the sands' for five days, during which time the English forces were divided into three sections, the right division being placed under the command of Godfrey d'Harcourt, the left under the Earl of Warwick, Thomas Beauchamp, with the centre remaining under the king's direct command.[3] As they marched along the coast they 'ravaged and laid waste … they burned, destroy and pillaged everything'.[4] Edward headed to Caen, Rouen, Poissy and then north towards Beauvais, after which Jean de Bel records that the 'sole aim … was to lay siege to the mighty city of Calais'.[5] Before this, however, he had to gain victory in battle, which he did at Crécy, and by September the English were at the city.

Calais, as we have seen, was not a soft target; it was heavily fortified on the landward side by walls and ditches and in possession of a strongly defended harbour. Edward, though, had come prepared. Jean Froissart tells us that he had 'engines and other instruments of war used in siege to break down the walls'. He also had the harbour blockaded, actions that were counteracted by the French, who built their walls higher and sabotaged the siege engine construction at every opportunity. The English frequently came under attack and *Holinshed's Chronicle* recounts how Edward 'caused a strong castle to be made between the town of Calais and the sea … and therein placed 40 men at arms and 200 archers' to both provide some protection and completely prevent the defenders from accessing the harbour.[6] Thomas Beauchamp, the Earl of Warwick and Anne's ancestor, was a key figure during the siege and frequently raided into France, including on one memorable occasion where he attacked Thérouanne and slaughtered a large number of French before sacking the town and bringing its treasures back to his king at Calais.[7]

By spring 1347, the French inside the beleaguered town were simply starving to death. The French king repeatedly tried to lure Edward away from Calais and into a pitched battle but he would not be baited, and on 4 August 1447, the town formally surrendered after holding out for 335 days. Since that day, Calais had remained in English hands, and with such a history as well as strategic importance had become a 'jewel' in the crown of the kings of England. The city into which Warwick sailed was therefore one with a powerful political and personal history. His role as Captain of Calais meant that he would have a great deal of control over access to both England

and France; any erstwhile noble wishing to return to England would be hard pressed to avoid the gaze of the Captain.

Warwick's wife Anne joined him on his journey; no doubt, he still had hopes of fathering a son and in order to do so, Anne had to accompany him.[8] Even in the medieval period it would have been unusual for female children to have been separated from their mothers for long periods. It is almost certain that the infant Anne, barely a month old, sailed with her parents and her sister Isobel, and it is easy to imagine Isobel running about the ship, eager to catch a glimpse of her new home. If indeed she did, she would surely not have been disappointed by the sight of the mighty walls of Calais, punctuated by tall towers with their flags fluttering in the breeze. We know that Warwick and his countess were residing at Calais Castle in May 1455, meaning he must have set sail soon after his appointment, undoubtedly because violent threats to the Yorkist regime were being made on both sides of the Channel and therefore Calais had never been so important.[9]

For the infant Anne little would have changed. She would still have been largely in the care of her nurses, who would have travelled with her. However, her daily life would now be a rather more static existence than she had experienced in England, where she would have been expected to move between her parents' estates on a regular basis. Calais, on the other hand, comprised only a small area, the perimeters of which were guarded closely. Given this, Anne's formative years would have been influenced by the town's unique culture and the nature of the people who travelled through it. Calais was a melting pot of French, Burgundian, Flemish and English influences. One interesting point to consider is that Anne may have grown up bilingual, able to speak fluently both English and French; she would certainly have been exposed to both languages in Calais, alongside others such as Flemish. The ability to speak French in Calais would have been considered desirable for anyone and indeed might have been a natural consequence for a child growing up there. Has she remained in England she would have learnt French anyway as it was the language of the court but this was a far more organic way for her to gain such a vital skill.

Despite their gender, Isobel and Anne were still their father's heirs, and right from the start, their education would have been aimed at equipping them for their future lives as wives and mothers, as well as women of the court whose presence would be a credit to their powerful father. Life inside the castle at Calais was divided into two spheres – one male and one female. Anne existed in the feminine sphere, where her mother, the countess, ruled. Under their mother's guidance, Anne and Isobel would have learnt to spin and sew, dance and play an instrument, how to run a household, as well as other helpful skills such as an understanding of herbal medicine. Girls were most valued at the time for their piety, good husbandry, thrift, modesty and honesty, according to the 1430 poem 'How the Good Wife Taught her Daughter', and the importance of these virtues would have been instilled in Anne from the earliest moments of her childhood.[10]

Despite a lack of surviving documentation to attest to the fact, Anne must also have been educated in a more formal sense. She certainly learnt to read and write and would have been taught enough mathematics to enable her to read, check and interpret household accounts. Such skills were necessary for even relatively poor women. Margery Paston, for example, who was born in 1448, could read and write fluently – a skill she exercised in both writing love letters to her future husband and in arguing with her family.[11] Anne's early life, however, would not have been entirely serious; there was plenty of time for play and pleasurable pastimes. By the thirteenth century, scholars such as Giles of Rome or Vincent of Beauvais were engaged in discussions on child development and how best to ensure that these 'mini adults', as children were regarded at the time, should be raised. Their ideas quickly filtered through to society as a whole. The royal family as well as many other noble and gentry families would have owned works by Giles of Rome. He argued that even in the womb a foetus was 'something immediately disposed to becoming a man'.[12] He regarded childhood as a time during which the person could be shaped only according to their nature, which had already been shaped by God before their birth.

This increased interest in childhood is reflected in the increasing appearances that children were making in art at the time and it is clear that on top of their studies they also had toys to play with. A near contemporary image of Isabella of Austria as a child shows her playing with a doll or 'poppet' and Anne must surely have had such toys.[13] Perhaps she was also given miniature plates or cups to imitate the adult world around her. She would have been taught her family's history and likely grew up on tales of her legendary ancestors, men such as Guy of Warwick, who was an English and French folk hero. Guy, it is said, fell in love with a lady called Felice, who was from the highest echelons of society and way out of his league. In order to marry her he must therefore prove his courage and valour and so he set about fighting monsters such as boars, giants, dragons and the Dun Cow. The tale reveals that he wins her hand but is overcome by remorse for his violent past and goes on a pilgrimage to the Holy Land before returning to Warwick to live as a hermit.

A daughter's upbringing was under the direction of their mother and given that Anne was apparently living with her mother during this period, Anne Beauchamp probably had a good deal of personal influence over her daughter's upbringing. Young Anne spent three years in Calais, during which time she was largely sheltered from the politics and violence of the Wars of the Roses, but her father was embroiled in events that were increasingly bloody.

> 'Sound drums and trumpets! And to London all: And more such days as these us befall!'[14]

The summer following the Battle of St Albans saw Henry VI fall ill again and he was no doubt still shocked at his new reality. He seems to have recovered gradually and on 9 July 1455, he opened a parliament under York's direction, with Warwick in attendance.[15] The situation, however, was extremely volatile and most people weren't as willing to accept York's second protectorate as easily as the king apparently did. A week after the parliament opening, Anne's father came to violent blows with Lord Cromwell, Treasurer to Henry VI, over the events of St Albans. The situation was so tense that York took to travelling on a barge loaded with weapons. Buckingham in particular opposed the Yorkist takeover, and others who agreed with him, such as Exeter and Lord Dudley, were summarily imprisoned. To diffuse the situation, on 19 July, Henry VI declared that Warwick was his 'beloved kinsman' and 'faithful liegeman', and five days later, all the nobility, both Yorkist and Lancastrian, swore fealty to the king at a parliament called under York's direction.[16]

It was not enough; hatred and thoughts of revenge were simmering throughout the whole country. In the West Country in particular, serious violence broke out, and by February 1456, York's regime was in serious jeopardy. Margaret had been garnering increased support in the name of her husband and later the same month it was strong enough that the Lancastrian lords felt able to dismiss York. Margaret, it is said, was now a 'great strong laboured woman for she spareth no pains to sue her things to an intent and conclusion of her power'.[17] The government of England was now firmly in her hands.

It is interesting here to consider, given their later relationship, what Anne Neville may have heard during this time about Margaret of Anjou. She is viewed by Shakespeare as a 'foreigner, white devil, shrew, virago, vengeful fury'. Contemporary opinion, however, offers us a very different Margaret. She is described by Raffaelo De Negra in 1458, writing to the Duchess of Milan, as 'wise and charitable', but there is no doubt that she was also the power behind the throne.[18] *Gregory's Chronicle* writes that the lords knew 'well that all the workings [of London] were done by her, for she was wiser than the king'.[19] Those around Anne, as we have seen, were no fans of Queen Margaret, but inevitably, Anne would have been exposed to the idea that a woman, for better or for ill, could wield a huge amount of influence and power, though there would have been little chance for a 3 to 4-year-old to be exposed to Margaret's political opinions.

We know that Warwick and York attended a great council held at Coventry in October 1456 in which York and presumably Warwick were 'greatly distressed'.[20] They were called to answer to the king for their actions over the past eighteen months. In a statement that speaks more of Henry VI himself than of Queen Margaret, they were told that if they swore loyalty to the king, all would be forgiven. Both did so and swore oaths on the gospel that bound them to 'good behaviour'. For the king it seems all was once again well, but no one else was as willing to forgive and forget. Soon afterwards, Warwick was the subject of an ambush and assassination attempt by Henry Beaufort, who, blaming Warwick for his father's death, had intended to ride out and attack him with 400 men. Fortunately for Anne, her father was forewarned and managed to escape by the skin of his teeth. Given the demotion of York, Warwick might have expected to lose his position in Calais, but luck was on his side. In 1457, the French mounted a raid on England's south coast at Sandwich, which led to a brief period of political unity. Given the importance of Calais, it simply made sense to keep the powerful Warwick in his post.

During his time as Captain of Calais, Warwick had faced mounting difficulties, not least in the fact that the parliament in 1454 failed to grant the 40,000 pounds in wages owed to the garrison. This left Calais weak and exposed to French attack; indeed, in May 1455, Calais had come under French fire. The army in Calais was really the only standing army maintained by the English and it seems that Margaret feared what Warwick could again do with a force loyal to him. By withholding pay, she was perhaps attempting to introduce discord into the garrison. The blocking of proper pay and funding for weaponry weakened Calais and the surrounding area.

It is not known precisely how much Anne and Isobel knew about the troubles in England, the tensions with the French or the role that their father was playing in them, but living in Calais, they were better placed than most to catch snippets of gossip, and they would have been naturally curious about their father's frequent absences.

In 1457, the French struck, launching an attack on the English port of Sandwich. Fearing it was merely a precursor to a full-scale invasion, Margaret decided to trust Warwick's patriotism as well as his military expertise. He was given the position of Lord High Admiral and ordered to keep the seas peaceful and free of the French for three years. Also, he was finally given some money – 1,000 pounds – to cover his expenses. Warwick was now charged with protecting England's coastline, by any means necessary, including acts of piracy. In 1458, two cases concerning his defence appear in the Close Rolls. One concerned a Portuguese ship, the *Saint Mary de Elizabeth*, which had anchored at Dartmouth and not been permitted to leave. The second involved a fleet of Calais ships at Tilbury under Warwick's overall command, which had taken by force three Dutch vessels. All these activities were carried out right on the edge of the law, and Margaret objected to them, making it clear that she still did not trust Warwick completely.

On 25 March 1458 (on the day of the year that was then widely celebrated as Lady Day, the day on which the Archangel Gabriel appeared to the Virgin Mary and told her that she could be the mother of Jesus Christ, the son of God), at a meeting held in London, Henry VI made the latest in a long line of reconciliation attempts. York was still threatening and England's court remained fractured, but all parties, including York, Warwick and Salisbury, were invited to the meeting, which had been organised by the Archbishop of Canterbury, Thomas Bourchier. After the meeting, all parties were to attend Mass. The Mass on this day, known as 'Loveday', was traditionally one of reconciliation at which enemies would walk together. Each man had attended with a large number of retainers; York had an estimated 400, Salisbury 500, whilst Anne's father brought 600, swelled by extras from his garrison at Calais, all dressed in Warwick's splendid red livery emblazoned with the bear and ragged staff. Somerset, meanwhile, had 800 men and the northern lords brought 1,500 combined. The peace held for now, no doubt helped by the fact that the Yorkists and Lancastrians were housed separately and the city itself posted armed guards at the gates.

The whole of London held its breath as, emerging from the cathedral, the queen walked with York and Warwick walked arm in arm with Henry Holland, who hated him for having taken 'his' post of Lord High Admiral, and Henry Beaufort, who would never forgive Warwick for his father's death.[21]

The service was followed by a magnificent jousting tournament in honour of Queen Margaret. In spite of everything, the mood was optimistic amongst the people. Positive and popular ballads were issued, including one that declared:

> In York, in Somerset as ye understood,
> In Warwick also ys love and charity,
> In Salisbury also and in Northumberland,
> That every man may renounce the concord and unite.[22]

It is not certain whether Warwick was personally invited to the meeting, but there was no chance that he was going to leave York and his father without the protection that his 600 men offered. His presence meant he was presumably able to grant his assent for his younger brother John's betrothal to the queen's ward, Isabella Ingaldsethorpe, during the festivities. In theory, the Percy–Neville feud also ended when Salisbury and Warwick agreed to forgo money that Lord Egremont owed to them. Warwick also agreed to pay Lord Clifford 1,000 marks in compensation for the death of his father at St Albans, a tacit admission of guilt. This was intended to be both a legally binding and a symbolic reconciliation, with heraldic posturing and promises made by both sides.

False promises, as it turned out. Warwick returned to Calais and to his duties as Lord High Admiral, but Germanic merchants now appealed to the king and queen to rein him in. It was the opportunity that Margaret had been waiting for and she now began to try to remove him from his position at Calais. Later, she attempted to have Warwick arrested for piracy. Meanwhile, Somerset, it was said, was ready to ransack Warwick's properties in London – with the intent to cause the earl harm if they found him.[23] Warwick was furious and accused Margaret of making nothing but fake promises of peace at Loveday, with the aim of reigniting their quarrel. Warwick was summoned to court and according to his own later account, only narrowly avoided death by assassination when he fled an ambush in the Westminster kitchens. His men, meanwhile, ran amok in London. In November at a council meeting, his men again clashed with those of the queen and Warwick had to fight his way out. With little time to spare, he reached the Thames, where a barge was waiting to take him back to Calais. Public opinion, however, was now on Warwick's side. His piratical actions had made him something of a national hero to patriotic Englishmen, who were always disturbed by, and distrustful of, Margaret because of her French birth.

Anne's father and his retinue now returned to Calais, furious and not likely to obey any more summonses from the king. Naturally, neither the countess, nor Anne or Isobel would have travelled with Warwick, and there is no evidence that they left Calais during this period.

It must have been clear to all that tensions were mounting and not even the infant Anne, by now 2 years old, could have failed to pick up on it. Warwick's escape had proved once again the weak position of the king. He had not been able to hold his nobles, or even his wife, to the Loveday agreement. Crucially, the attack on his son had also hardened Salisbury's position and he now threw his weight behind York. There would be no more concessions on the Yorkists part.

Civil war was now inevitable.

Chapter 3

Daughter of a Traitor

> though those that are betray'd
> Do feel the treason sharply, yet the traitor
> Stands in worse case of woe.
> *Cymbeline*, William Shakespeare

Did Anne notice the increased tension as her father and the whole of Calais prepared for war? Surely, she must have, for no part of the city was free from activity as Warwick set about raising an army capable of facing the forces that Queen Margaret was building in England. Matters came to a head in 1459, when a royal council was summoned. It was one from which Anne's father, grandfather Salisbury, and York were excluded, because its purpose was to deal with the Yorkist 'enemies of the king'. In response, Warwick continued to rearm in Calais. Salisbury, who had up until now been reluctant to take up arms, formally vowed allegiance to York at Middleham Castle.[1] Soon Warwick was back in England, landing in the south-east, from where he planned to move north-west towards York. Salisbury, meanwhile, marched to York's stronghold of Ludlow Castle to meet up with the duke and his other allies with the plan then to turn towards London. Mighty Ludlow had legally come into York's possession in 1425, after his uncle, Edmund Mortimer's, death and it was a potent symbol of his power and authority. York had used the castle as a base from 1432, when he took physical possession of it. Historian Ralph Griffiths suggested that he lived there for most of the late 1440s and 1450s, during which period he rebuilt the Great Tower.[2]

Queen Margaret, however, was one step ahead; she was well placed at Eccleshall, and ordered that Lord Audley raise 8,000–14,000 troops and stop Salisbury from reaching York at all costs. Her forces intercepted Salisbury on 23 September, and the two armies met at Blore Heath. The Yorkist forces were heavily outnumbered but Salisbury was an experienced commander, and the veteran of many a Scottish skirmish and episode of the Percy–Neville feud. Both sides initially tried to avoid open battle, and sent messengers back and forth, but Salisbury wished to be prepared and he positioned his forces just above a partially hidden shallow valley where he could wait for the Lancastrians to come to him. The Lancastrian army under Audley were hampered severely by marshy ground but they launched the first key attack, a major cavalry charge. Salisbury then ordered his men to trap the Lancastrians as they tried to cross a stream. There is no evidence that Audley himself gave the order for this ill-conceived cavalry charge but regardless, it proved disastrous. Intense fighting saw Audley killed and John Sutton, 1st Baron Dudley, take command, and the failure of his initial actions saw 500 Lancastrians defect to the Yorkist side. It only took about ninety minutes for the Lancastrian army to collapse and flee for their lives. One contemporary chronicle records that the Lancastrians were pursued for many hours. Modern estimates suggest that 3,000 men were killed at Blore Heath, nearly all of them Lancastrian, and local legend tells how the local brook flowed red with blood for three days. Afterwards, Salisbury marched on to join Warwick and York at Ludlow. He moved quickly, fearing that there were further Lancastrian forces nearby, but although Blore Heath – the opening battle of the Wars of the Roses – was a resounding victory for the Yorkists, the question of whether they would be able to capitalise on their advantage remained to be seen.

At this point, the Yorkists were still insisting that they were acting to protect the king from his 'evil advisors' and following Blore Heath, the *Brut* chronicle tells that 'the Duke of York and the Earls of Warwick and Salisbury saw that the governance of the realm was exercised mostly by the queen and her council ... [they] proclaimed throughout the realm that these Lords should be utterly destroyed.'[3] In October, to confirm their loyalty to Henry VI, Warwick, Salisbury and York all knelt before the altar of Worcester Cathedral and swore oaths of loyalty to the king. The Bishop of Worcester took careful note of this and his account was handed to the king as proof of the Yorkists' loyalty. No one, however, was convinced, and on 9 October, Warwick was formally dismissed from the Captaincy of Calais and replaced by Henry Beaufort, Duke of Somerset.

Daughter of a Traitor

Whatever the truth of the Yorkist intentions, the fact was that the majority of Lancastrians did not believe their claims despite some such as Jean de Wavrin calling York a 'valiant and loyal prince'.[4] The royal army marched on Worcester while the Yorkists tried to return to Ludlow, having sent a letter to the king again protesting their loyalty to him. This letter never reached its destination and it seems certain that on Margaret's orders, a reply was forged whereby battle was to be joined.

Given this, the Yorkists took up position at Ludford Bridge on 12 October, expecting their reinforcements to arrive at any minute; without them, they were massively outnumbered. Across the fields, the royal standard could be seen fluttering in the breeze, signifying that Henry VI himself was present at the battle. Unlike at Blore Heath, the Yorkists could be under no illusion that they were fighting anyone other than their anointed king. With this in mind, 600 of Warwick's men defected overnight and the Yorkists commanders chose to remove themselves from the field rather than face what they felt would be inevitable defeat.[5] York, alongside his second son, Edmund of Rutland, headed to Ireland via Wales. Meanwhile, Anne's father, alongside Salisbury and Edward of March, York's eldest son, headed for Calais. When they fled, they left behind their entire armies and families, including, crucially for Anne's later story, York's wife Cecily Neville and her two younger sons, George and Richard, who had been inside the castle keep. They were taken as hostages. *Gregory's Chronicle* tells us how, after the Yorkist flight, Ludlow was devastated but that Cecily was 'humbly granted grace' by Henry VI and placed in the care of her sister, Anne. Richard, son of York, was just 7 years old; it would certainly not be the last time that children were used as pawns in the bloody conflict.

There is no evidence as to where Warwick's family was during this time, but as we have seen, Warwick liked to have his wife close by if possible. However, given the political turmoil it seems most likely that they remained in Calais, safely out of the way, where they could not be taken and used as political leverage. There was no advantage to their being in England. We do know that Anne and presumably her two daughters were in Calais when Warwick arrived there on 2 November, bloodied and exhausted following Ludford Bridge, with his equally sorry looking allies. Only the help of a local knight, John Dynham, and his mother had enabled them to get to safety.⁶ What the young Anne, who was not yet 5 years old, thought of the battered Edward of March is unknown; likely he was to her just one of many figures that she glimpsed on occasion from the windows or walking about the castle. Nevertheless, this was Anne's first prolonged period in the vicinity of her future king and brother-in-law.

Meanwhile in England, as the Crowland chronicler relates, 'parliament [was] summoned to Coventry, the Duke and the earls were attainted and their goods and inheritances transferred to new owners.'⁷ This parliament, held on 20 November 1459, has been known ever since as the 'Parliament of Devils'. It was held in the chapter house of the Priory of St Mary's (founded by Leofric of Mercia and his wife Godiva in 1043), which was packed with loyal Lancastrians. It was held with the sole purpose of attainting twenty-nine Yorkist rebels, including York, Salisbury and Warwick. The petition of the attainder had been carefully drawn up by the queen's lawyers and it accused York of inciting or encouraging rebellion, of breaking his oath of loyalty to the king, of conspiring with Salisbury and Warwick to wage war, and of 'levying war' against the king at St Albans, Blore Heath and Ludford Bridge. Unsurprisingly given that they were not there to defend themselves, the Yorkist lords were found guilty and the bills of attainder for high treason were passed by the king.⁸

The parliament marked a turning point in the Yorkist approach. Henry passed the bills, proving once and for all that he was either unable or unwilling to overthrow his advisors. It was probably at this point that York determined that the king must be replaced in order to ensure the safety and proper governance of the realm. In addition, by disinheriting the Yorkist heirs as well as the Yorkist lords themselves, Henry and Margaret now ensured that York, Salisbury and Warwick had nothing left to lose.

Anne was now the daughter of an attainted traitor, although whether she was aware of the fact immediately is unclear. Warwick, however, despite the Act replacing him, was still firmly ensconced in Calais and he would not be easy to dislodge. Henry Beaufort, who wanted nothing less than Warwick's head on a spike, began to plan an attack on Calais. Warwick was well aware that if Beaufort's forces landed he would likely attract French support from the queen's allies. He therefore attacked first at Sandwich, where Beaufort had been assembling his forces. He caught Beaufort completely off guard and was able to take prisoners and destroy the Lancastrian ships. Even now, though, Warwick still insisted that he 'was disposed to be devoted and obedient to your majesty and desirous to maintain and augment the commonwealth of the kingdom', as Francesco Coppini, the papal legate, wrote to Henry VI.[9] Nevertheless, he was planning an invasion.

Perhaps Anne's first taste of real danger came over the next few months as Beaufort continued to try to take Calais; strangers in the city were treated with increased suspicion and arrests took place. Calais was now a Yorkist bastion; any new arrivals might have come with the purpose of sending information back to the Lancastrian queen. Calais held out but Beaufort did establish a base at the nearby castle of Guînes, something that would certainly have made those in the city uneasy. However, Warwick had a plan: soon after his success at Sandwich he sailed for Ireland, where he met with York to discuss how the invasion should be carried out, and it was determined that Sandwich again would be his landing site. He informed the garrison of this when he returned two months later. He brought with him someone who would have soon become an everyday presence in Anne's life: his mother, Countess Alice.[10] Alice was by now in her late fifties and was possibly already in poor health (she would die in 1462). Alice would have slotted into the feminine world in which Anne existed, and no doubt, the older woman would have been pleased to find her two granddaughters safe and healthy.

In June 1460, Sandwich was defended by a force of about 400 heavily armed men under the command of Osbert Mountford. The intention was not for this force to defend the town but rather to join Beaufort in Guînes. When Warwick made his move, Exeter had tried to intercept Warwick's ships before they could land but his poorly provisioned and largely unwilling sailors refused to fight the earl. Despite the fact that Mountford's men were not prepared when Warwick landed, he and his central corps put up a stout defence of the town. But they were ultimately no match for Warwick's troops under the command of William Neville, Lord Fauconberg, Warwick's uncle: Mountford paid for his defiance with his life. By 26 June, Warwick himself was in Sandwich alongside Salisbury, Edward of March and 2,000 troops. From Sandwich, the Yorkist lords headed to Canterbury and then to London, where they were welcomed, their forces now having swelled to between

20,000 and 30,000 men. They had encountered no opposition; the king was at the time still in the midlands, and Buckingham, although charged with the defence of the south coast as Warden of the Cinque Ports, had stayed at his king's side. The Lancastrian nobles still in London, including the Duke of Exeter's wife, Anne of York, herself a daughter of the duke, took refuge in the Tower, which was commanded by Lord Scales. Meanwhile, the Yorkists took up residence in nearby Smithfield, the site 155 years earlier of William Wallace's execution.

These events were witnessed, and reported, by the papal legate, Francesco Coppini, who accompanied Warwick. He had arrived in England in June 1459 as a nuncio appointed by pope Pius II to help bring about peace in England, and to persuade him to fight against the Turks. By December 1459, he had been made a papal legate to bolster his position. When Queen Margaret rebuffed his entreaties, he opened negotiations with the Yorkists and by now, he was firmly on the Yorkist side. His account is therefore valuable but not without bias.[11]

When the Yorkists moved to take the Tower, Lord Scales opened fire whilst at St Paul's, the Yorkist Convocation of Canterbury continued to insist that they would respect the king and protect him. With Londoners now largely on their side, Fauconberg set out to face the king, followed soon after by Edward of March and Warwick, leaving Salisbury to besiege the Tower with the aid of militia raised from the city. Warwick and Edward met the king's forces at Northampton on 10 July, where the king had taken up position at Delapré Abbey with some field artillery and about 5,000 men. The Lancastrians were commanded by Humphrey Stafford, Duke of Buckingham, who, when Warwick sent a messenger to negotiate with the king, simply replied, 'The Earl of Warwick shall not come to the King's presence and if he comes he shall die.'[12] At around two o'clock, the Yorkists began their advance in vicious rain, which, crucially, largely neutralised the artillery the Lancastrians had brought into the field. It appears they did fire at least a cannon at the start of the battle, though – a 3-inch cannonball recovered from the site in 2015 testifying to the violence of the Lancastrian intent.[13] However, in the face of the Yorkist advance, Lord Grey of Ruthin, who was commanding the king's left, lay down his arms, having promised at some point to switch sides if Edward of March would support him in a quarrel he was having with his cousin, the Duke of Exeter.

The fighting itself lasted barely half an hour; the Lancastrians with their left flank exposed had no hope of winning the day and many fled. Buckingham, Shrewsbury, Egremont and Beaumont all died trying to protect the king, who, according to legend, was peacefully captured by an archer called Henry Mountfort.[14] The Yorkists took the king to Northampton, where historian Lauren Johnson suggests Henry VI became unwell, something that delayed their departure by three days.[15]

It was, however, York and not Henry who now journeyed through the country in royal estate and when he rode into London, he and his supporters were bedecked in his blue-and-white livery and proudly displaying the arms of Lionel of Antwerp, York's ancestor and second son of Edward III. Cecily of York rode out of the city to meet her husband dressed in blue velvet and arrayed like a queen. Anne did not witness this; she was still in Calais, but surely, messengers would have been flying across the Channel bringing news of such events to the women left behind. Perhaps she was told of her great-aunt's power and appearance that day. Any news was followed swiftly by the triumphal return of Anne's father, for we know that Warwick was back in Calais on 7 August, and that soon after, Countess Anne and their daughters came back to England, landing first at Sandwich before heading for Greenwich.[16] Once there, they rendezvoused with Henry VI.

England must have seemed an alien place to Anne as she looked out on her surroundings. Whilst her sister Isabel would have remembered Warwick and her parents' other great houses, Anne would not have, and the violence of the past few years would have meant that any visits Anne had possibly made could only have been fleeting. Hence, the journey from Greenwich to Warwick Castle was probably the first time that Anne had seen her birthplace at an age where it could have made an impression.[17] While Anne was at Warwick, becoming acquainted with the castle and exploring it with all the curiosity possible at 5 years old, her father rode on to meet up with the Duke of York at Shrewsbury. Then he went to London, and shortly afterwards was joined by the duke, who now made his bid for the throne. A parliament had been called and was sitting on 7 October. Three days later, York arrived at the Palace of Westminster and strode into the great hall with a sword drawn and held aloft before him in regal fashion. He walked towards the throne and placed his hand upon it, intending no doubt to sit, but the assembled audience did not cheer. Instead, there was silence and palpable tension. Shakespeare has the Earl of Warwick declare at this moment:

> 'I'll plant Plantagenet, root him up who dares – Resolve thee Richard claim the English throne!'[18]

In reality, it was the Archbishop of Canterbury, Thomas Bourchier, who quietly asked York if he wished to see or speak with the king, who appears to have been somewhere in the palace. York responded by stating that he had the right to the throne, but it seemed that no one else agreed. York and Warwick had massively miscalculated. Whilst London liked and respected York, they had no desire to see another king usurped, and though they joined York in his opposition to 'evil counsellors', they did not oppose the king himself. Vergil, a Tudor historian, states that at some point during the proceedings, a crown either on Henry's head or suspended from the ceiling fell to the ground – a worrying omen in such a superstitious age.

The parliament withdrew to Blackfriars, to discuss what they were going to do, whilst according to Wavrin, York went so far as to begin to plan his coronation, which was rumoured to be taking place on either 13 October or 1 November. No one wanted to make a decision and England held its breath while first the king's justices, then the serjeants at law and even the king's attorney tried and failed to reach a consensus. Eventually, an agreement was reached whereby an Act of Accord stated that until Henry VI laid down the crown or died, he would reign as king, with York acting as Lord Protector, but upon Henry VI's death, the crown would be inherited by either York or his sons, disinheriting Prince Edward by virtue of York's superior genealogical claim through descent from Lionel of Antwerp. On 31 October, virtually all nobles in the land swore, or were forced to swear, oaths to abide by the Act of Accord. This included the king, whom Warwick now called a 'dolt and a fool', all pretence of loyalty gone.[19]

The treaty might have held were it not for the indomitable Margaret of Anjou, who immediately wrote to the council objecting to her son's disinheritance. She had been able to raise large amounts of support in Wales, under Henry VI's half-brother, the ever-loyal Jasper Tudor, and the north under Northumberland. Margaret also hoped to draw support from the Scots. The Yorkists realised they had to act quickly and whilst Warwick remained in London to watch over the city and the Lancastrian king, York, his second son, Edmund, and Salisbury headed north to face Margaret's forces. York and his followers spent Christmas 1460 at Sandal Castle, whilst in London, Warwick oversaw Henry VI's participation in the Christmas Day festivities.

Sandal was a magnificent Norman motte-and-bailey castle lying about a mile away from Wakefield, but York found it badly provisioned and by the end of the year, supplies were running low. Despite this, had York and his men remained inside they would have been safe from the Lancastrian army, but York now made a miscalculation and he left the castle. Current thinking has it that because the castle had not been expecting his arrival that there simply weren't enough provisions for York and his retinue of a couple of hundred men and so they were forced to leave in search of provision. A Lancastrian force surprised him when he was far enough away from the castle for easy retreat to be impossible. Wavrin claims that they lured the Yorkists out by false promises of negotiation. Even if this was the case, for a man who was so experienced as a military commander, this decision seems inexplicable. Historians have suggested that perhaps John Neville had betrayed the Yorkists or that they were ambushed while out hunting for supplies. Whatever the cause, York found himself vastly outnumbered by the Lancastrian army under the command of the Dukes of Somerset and Exeter and Lords Clifford and Roos, all of whom were intent on revenge for their slaughtered fathers, brothers and sons.

Trapped, the Yorkists tried to fight their way out, but to no avail. York was killed in the fighting whilst his younger son, Edmund, was killed by Lord Clifford as he fled. His youth should have protected him from such a fate but Lord Clifford sought revenge for the death of his own father at St Albans. Both York and his son were decapitated and their heads sent to make a grisly spectacle atop York's Micklegate. In a final insult, York's head was adorned with a paper crown. They were soon joined by the head of Anne's grandfather, Salisbury, who had been captured and taken to

Pontefract Castle, where the next day he was dragged outside by the mob and summarily beheaded.[20]

Margaret had won the day and Prince Edward, at just 7 years old, was now paraded into York at the head of the Lancastrian army in a livery clearly bearing the ostrich feathers that marked him out as Prince of Wales and heir to the throne. In London, Henry VI was said to be 'much moved' when he heard of York's death.[21] Warwick likewise was 'much grieved'. Meanwhile in the Welsh Marches, Edward of York vowed vengeance on those who had slaughtered his father and brother. London remained under Warwick's control but its citizens were terrified that the Lancastrian army would wreak its revenge when they arrived at the gates. The *Crowland Chronicle* reported that 'all the lords of the north … [it is thought, would] destroy the south county'.

Warwick did not panic; he knew that Edward was mustering men in the west. Indeed, he would win the battle at Mortimer's Cross, a skirmish mostly remembered today for the fact that Owen Tudor, stepfather to the king, was executed after it. Until this moment, Edward had largely practised mercy and indeed, Tudor expected it, but the bloodshed at Wakefield had hardened his heart; there would be few pardons now issued by Edward of March. Unfortunately for Warwick, Edward had been forced into the engagement earlier than intended, meaning that his journey east to meet with Warwick was delayed.

Warwick, realising that the Lancastrian forces were closing in, took the king north to St Albans, where he began to fortify the city having been informed that the queen's forces were still over 40 miles away. He intended to block the road at Dunstable and prevent the Lancastrian army from even reaching the town. This time, however, it was Anne's father who had miscalculated. He decided to move his forces outside St Albans, where supplies might be found more easily. He also followed his well-established tactic of dividing his army into three and facing north. This time the Lancastrians were prepared and it was Warwick who was taken by surprise; Dunstable had in fact fallen easily and the army bypassed him, heading straight into the town unopposed. The fighting was brutal and bloody. John Neville, commanding the Yorkist vanguard, was smashed into by the Lancastrian cavalry before they could form up and he himself was captured.

Daughter of a Traitor

Warwick frantically tried to reorganise his men but it was hopeless, and fearing treachery, he fled alongside most of the Yorkist commanders. The king was left behind and was soon reunited with his wife and son. He knighted his son that evening, and the next day, young Edward oversaw the execution of two loyal Yorkists, Bonville and Kyriel, who had remained at their posts when Warwick and the others fled.

The deaths of such loyal men, whilst seemingly insignificant in relation to the deaths of men such as Tudor or Salisbury, in fact proved to be very important because it was soon reported that the king had promised them pardon but then broken his word and executed them. Both men had switched sides, having begun life as Lancastrians, but then so had half the men in England by now, and their execution sent waves of unease throughout the land. After all, if a king's word could not be trusted, whose could?

Victorious, Margaret, Henry and Prince Edward now planned to march towards London, but they hesitated, and London did not welcome the proclamation that announced the Lancastrian victory. Edward of March was still at large, and some reported he was making his way there at the head of 10,000 troops. The rumours weren't wrong. Warwick had met up with Edward in the Cotswolds and with this in mind, London rebuffed emissaries sent from the king.

They had thrown in their lot with the Yorkists and when Warwick and Edward reached the capital, they were welcomed into the city. Once there, Edward publicly accused Henry VI of breaking the Act of Accord, and said that by doing so he had forfeited all right to the throne. Then, on 4 March, the Yorkists asked the masses of London in Westminster Hall whether they would have Edward as their king instead, to which they shouted 'Yea!'

Anne's cousin, Edward of March, whom she knew from Calais, was now King Edward IV of England.

Chapter 4

The Kingmaker's Daughter

> No longer Earl of March, but Duke of York;
> The next degree is England's royal throne ...
> For York in justice puts his armour on.
> *Henry VI, Part 3*, William Shakespeare

There was one more bloody act to take place before Edward could reign. On 29 March 1461, Palm Sunday, the forces of York and Lancaster met on the battlefield at Towton. It was to prove a final denouncement – for now, at least. The Yorkist army was headed by Edward, alongside Anne's father and Lord Fauconberg, whilst the Lancastrians were under the command of Somerset, Trollope, Percy, and Henry Holland, Duke of Exeter. Anne's father was not present at the battle, having been wounded the day before at the Battle of Ferrybridge, where the Lancastrians had destroyed a bridge, effectively cutting off Warwick's vanguard. Warwick's men had set about constructing a bridge out of planks of wood but on the morning of 28 March, they were caught off guard and Warwick was wounded in the leg by an arrow. The fifteenth-century chronicler Edward Hall tells that Warwick personally rode to inform the king of the impending battle and then tells that he nobly cut his horse's throat so that he could not flee to demonstrate his loyalty.[1] In reality, it is very unlikely that Warwick did anything of the sort; he was probably carried to safety by his men, and then dispatched a messenger to Edward. But *Hall's Chronicle* does demonstrate just how loyal to Edward Warwick was considered to be. Edward's men quickly constructed a bridge and crossed the river ready to do battle the next day.

It is doubtful that Anne or her mother would have been informed of her father's injury. We don't even know for certain where Anne, her sister and mother were during these events. Perhaps they were still at Warwick, but given the castle's proximity to the Lancastrian forces, it seems unlikely. It is much more probable they had returned to the relative safety of Calais, especially following the death of Anne's grandfather at Wakefield, when the stakes for the Neville family had been immeasurably raised. It is interesting to think that if Warwick had died that day, Anne would likely have been little more than a footnote in history. Warwick would certainly have been buried by Edward with all the honours due to him as his greatest supporter, and Edward would no doubt have subsequently taken Anne into his royal household, once he had married, in reward for her father's loyalty. Perhaps Anne would have eventually been given in marriage to a great nobleman or even to one of Edward's future sons, although as Kim Harding of the Richard III Society points out, there would have been an age discrepancy: Anne would have been in her early twenties before any sons of Edwards would be of marriageable age. Either way, ironically, had Warwick died at Towton, Anne's future would have likely been far more settled than it would prove to be.

However, Warwick did not die and would have been brought constant reports throughout the next day when Edward gave battle. *Gregory's Chronicle* claims there were hundreds of thousands of soldiers on each side but historians today estimate that a figure of 50,000 to 65,000 is more likely, which still amounted to between 1 and 2 per cent of the entire population of England.[2] The majority of the men making up the armies were in their twenties and thirties, and their skeletons testify that for most, this was not their first battle. They were veterans of this 'cousins' war'.

The day opened with a volley of arrows being fired by the Lancastrians into the Yorkist ranks, but the weather was horrific, with driving snow, meaning the Lancastrians did not see that their arrows were falling short. When the Lancastrian volleys ceased, having failed to hit their target, Hall tells us: 'The Lord Fauconberg marched forward with his archers, who not only shot their own whole sheaves, but also gathered the arrows of their enemies and let a great part of them fly against their own masters.'[3] This left the Lancastrians little choice but to advance into the Yorkist line, which although initially fell back, was immeasurably strengthened by the presence of Edward himself fighting in the fray. Strengthened by the presence of their king, the Yorkists held the line until reinforcements under Norfolk arrived and the Lancastrians began to break. Many fought on, in the near blizzard conditions, possibly because communication on the battlefield was poor, but the day belonged to the Yorkists. Both sides had ordered that no quarter be given, and now the Yorkists hacked down the fleeing Lancastrians. The fighting at Towton was famously the bloodiest of any battle fought on English soil, so bloody in fact that the river ran red, and the snow was streaked with blood for miles around. The fighting was also particularly vicious, with men's skulls being smashed in by battle hammers and necks impaled on halberd spikes.[4] Contemporary reports, including one issued by Warwick in the aftermath of the battle, claim that 28,000 men died at Towton. Today, though, most consider these numbers to be exaggerated. Of the Lancastrian elite, the Earl of Northumberland, Lords Welles, Mauley and Dacre, and Sir Andrew Trollope lay dead on the ground at the end of the day, whilst the Earls of Devon and Wiltshire were executed shortly afterwards. Only Somerset, Ros and Exeter escaped the slaughter and headed north to join Henry in exile along with his queen and Prince Edward.

For Anne, the Yorkist victory at Towton meant that she and the rest of Warwick's family could now return to England on a more permanent basis. On 28 June 1461, Edward was crowned King Edward IV in a splendid ceremony at Westminster. His new Yorkist regime, however, depended largely upon the continued support of Anne's father, and Edward knew it. He rewarded Warwick for his loyalty with the position of Admiral of England and King's Lieutenant in the North.[5] Such a position meant that Calais was now largely irrelevant and Warwick duly made plans for his household, and his daughters, to return to England. The packing up and removal of their household would have taken place under the supervision of Anne's mother, Duchess Anne, and Anne would no doubt have watched, perhaps with some trepidation, as her belongings and clothing were all packed up into crates for transportation to England.

Anne's return to England coincided roughly with Edward IV's coronation, but we don't know exactly when she travelled. Alongside Anne, many other Yorkist exiles, including Edward's two younger brothers – George, by now 11 years old, and Richard, 8 years old – who had been until now safely ensconced at the Burgundian court where they had been sent following their father's death at Wakefield, returned to England. Upon their return, they were made the Dukes of Clarence and Gloucester, respectively. If Anne went first to Warwick Castle she did not stay there long. After 1461, the Earl and his family seem to have rarely visited there – something that makes sense when you consider that Warwick's power base had now shifted north, where he had vast lands to govern.[6]

While the world changed around her, the one constant in Anne's life would have been her mother and her sister. Anne's mother largely comes down to us today in the words of John Rous, a Warwick cantarist who knew the countess chiefly during the years 1449–57. John Rous (Rows) was a cleric who spent most of his life in the service of the House of York. He was a canon of the Church of St Mary, in Warwick, and chaplain at the chapel of Guy's Cliffe during the reign of Richard III. He was a learned man, having been educated at Oxford, and is most famous for having been responsible for the creation of the Rous Roll, which gives us a Yorkist's version of history, and for the Warwick Roll, which largely focuses on the life of Richard Beauchamp, the 13th Earl of Warwick. He also wrote a number of other accounts regarding the history of Warwick, the area and its nobles. Rous was therefore very much part of Anne's world. Rous describes Anne's mother as 'a full devout lady in God's service' and notes that she attended services regularly. She was also 'companionable and liberal … seemly and beauteous'.[7] Rous also notes that she took particularly good care of her servants and women who were pregnant in her household. Hers was, after all, a woman's world where pregnancy, labour, children and infants were all common sights. Despite all this, it was, as Tudor historian Michael Hicks writes, her father's power that was Anne's reality.[8] It was Warwick's power that meant Anne was cared for and respected. He was the public face of Anne's family and her 'most famous, and dread and beloved Lord'. It was Warwick's presence that could have permeated every corner of her world, even though he was absent more often than not.

Anne spent the next few years at Middleham Castle, at the heart of her father's northern domain. The castle lies 45 miles north-west of York, and John Leyland, a Tudor antiquary, calls Middleham 'a pretty market town and standith on a rocky hill, on the top whereof is a castel meately well dyked with the castle joyneth hard to the town side on the south'. Middleham

Castle was founded around 1190 by Robert FitzRandolph to defend the road between Richmond and Skipton. It had come into the Neville family in 1270 through marriage and Anne's great-grandfather had undertaken a large programme of rebuilding and refurbishment. During his time, the castle had been extensively modernised.

Life at the castle was centred on a massive central square keep, which had a great hall on the first floor and kitchens and storerooms beneath. The great hall would have been accessed by an external staircase, which climbed up the keep's eastern wall. Above the hall, there were two chambers, the Great Chamber to the south and a more private one to the north. Each of these had a fireplace, cupboard, closet and latrine. Anne would have known these rooms very well. At first-floor level, there was also a chapel, which could be accessed from the lord's first-floor chamber. Outside the keep along the north, south and west walls there was accommodation for the lord's retainers and other family members. This range was connected to the keep by a wooden bridge linking them with the family's rooms there. There was also a tower, which had been converted before Anne's time into a gatehouse. Interestingly, a 1538 survey of the castle lists the south-west tower of the keep as having been a nursery. By now, Anne was too old to need one, but it could possibly have been kept in readiness in case her mother should bear another child, or perhaps it was a favourite room of Anne's, which she later used as her own child's nursery.

There were great improvements made to the castle during its time as a Neville stronghold, which reflected the importance of the household of which Anne was part. In 1466, when Warwick himself stayed from July to Michaelmas, we know that a master carpenter made beds, benches and trestle tables in preparation, and that during this period, forty oxen and 200 sheep were consumed, alongside beer, sea fish, hens, wildfowl and quantities of expensive mustard – all of which helps to give us a picture of the sort of diet with which Anne would have been familiar. Likewise, we know that she would have walked on floors that were strewn with rushes and herbs, as the account books note that they were purchased alongside timber faggots for the fires.

Anne's time at Middleham would not have been idly spent; she had much to learn from her mother about running a great English household. This was management on a scale that Anne had not experienced before in Calais, and her mother was an expert at it. Anne would have learnt to perform such feminine household duties as managing access to luxury items like wax, salt, honey and spices, ensuring that they were obtained, restricted and consumed in an appropriate manner. In addition, Anne could have had to learn skills such as managing the household finances, gardening, how to order from the butcher's, and how to instruct cooks and other servants appropriately. A glimpse into Anne's likely daily life can also be found in the 1493 book *The Orders and Rules of Princess Cecill*, which records the life and routine of Anne's great-aunt, Cecily Neville, Edward IV's mother and widow of the Duke of York. This potentially offers us clues as to the basic framework of a medieval noblewoman's life. Cecily, it tells us, would rise at seven, then she dressed, and heard Mass before attending chapel. All this took place before she took her 'dinner; at about 11am she ate whilst listening to religious texts being read to her which focused on the lives of the female saints'. Cecily's ordinances give us a list of books that Cecily read from, and from which she was read to. These included Walter Hilton's *The Epistle on the Mixed Life,* Bonaventura's *Meditationes Vitae Christi* (*Meditations on the Life of Christ*) and *Infantia salvatoris* (the *Legenda aurea*), and works associated with Catherine of Siena and Birgitta of Sweden.[9] All of these texts were available by the mid-1400s and so it is perhaps reasonable to assume that Anne would have read such religious works, all of which were written in Middle English. We know from her will that Cecily Neville also treasured other books including many liturgical texts, three of which were found in her private closet upon her death.[10] In particular, in keeping with nearly every woman of the time, she kept a book of hours, and it is almost certain that, following the example of her devout mother and aunt, Anne would have had one too.[11] A book of hours contained the prayers to be said throughout the day, at the eight holy hours. Some also contained calendars, gospel lessons and suffrages, which were prayers to specific saints.[12]

    Cecily's ordinance goes on to say that after dinner she would have held an audience with members of her household or estates who wished to speak with her, before resting and returning to her prayers until supper at five. During supper, the household would have to a certain extent eaten together and afterwards the women would have undertaken recreational activities such as sewing, and playing of the virginals or other instruments, with wine and sweetmeats on offer. The ordinance then says that Cecily retired to pray in her closet until it was time for bed.

Nevertheless, this should not be regarded as a blueprint for the pattern of the young Anne's life; Cecily was, after all, an elderly widow when it was written, a pious woman buffeted by death and beset by tragedy. Yet it does give us valuable clues as to the reality of a noblewoman's life, her duties and the emphasis placed upon piety and prayer. The range of Cecily's books moreover give us a taste of the literary offerings with which Anne would have been familiar.

There is one text in particular that we know Anne later owned, a Middle English translation of the Latin text *Liber specialis gratiae*, a collection of the revelations of Mechtild of Hackeborn, written in the mid-thirteenth century by nuns at the convent of Helfta, possibly by Gertrude the Great. Cecily also owned this text but Anne seems to have owned a different copy.[13] Anne of York also owned a copy, so it seems to have been widely held and popular amongst noblewomen. The book was designed to inform men and women how they should ensure the health of their souls through prayer and self-discipline. It tells how the dead depend on the living to offer them good works and prayers. It is an engaging and energetic text, an attribute that probably appealed to the young Anne. At some point, Anne signed the flyleaf of her own copy, and underneath, her future husband, Richard of Gloucester, also signed his name. Dr Teresa Halligan suggests that these signatures are not genuine but acknowledges that Anne possessed a copy of the book, even if not this copy. Today it is generally thought that the book was primarily Anne's and possibly in her possession from the years of her childhood, and her later life shows she listened to its message to carry out good works and patronise charities, as well as to pray.

When not reading, Anne would have undertaken other suitable pursuits such as needlework and dancing – equally necessary accomplishments for future noble wives as the more practical skills of household management. By now, Anne would have been able to read and write in English, Latin and perhaps French. She would also have learnt about her family's illustrious history and the nobility of the bloodline to which she belonged. Anne would also have learnt to ride. The idea that women could only have gently walked on horseback, however, is something of a myth; riding was considered necessary and feminine courage in such pursuits was prized. Middleham Castle was flanked by two parks, Sunskew to the south and West Park and Cotescue Park to the west, where she could ride and hunt. Middleham had kennels, stables and rabbit warrens for this purpose. In addition, Middleham Castle also had both fish and ornamental ponds. There were also gardens at Middleham in which Anne would have walked and picked the herbs necessary for the stillroom. These gardens, which by Anne's time were walled, dated to the time of Ralph, 1st Earl of Westmorland (1364–1425), and possibly contained fruit trees, running water and rose-covered bowers in which to sit.

Anne and Isobel, alongside their mother, would have also been expected to present a united and elegant front; they were, after all, the visible face of Warwick, the Kingmaker. When not at Middleham it seems likely that they, like Cecily, would have been present at many court events such as Edward IV's coronation, where their appearance would surely only have been second to that of the royal family itself.

Anne would have forged close female friendships, for women who lived surrounded primarily by other women, friendships with their sisters and female friends would be the deepest and most enduring. After all, 'women lived in circumstances that allowed them to nurture and support other women',[14] as we have seen with Countess Anne, who took such care of the women in her household. Skill-based connections were particularly valued in medieval literature. Anne may have learnt embroidery at the feet of her mother. She could also have learnt skills such as how to make basic herbal remedies, and through such activities, she must have forged relationships that are lost to us. The idea that she was living in rarefied isolation therefore is simply not true. One specific female relationship that Anne may have forged during her childhood is worthy of more consideration – that with her half-sister, Margaret Neville, who was most likely a regular visitor to Middleham during Anne's childhood. Margaret Neville was the illegitimate daughter of Anne's father who had been born around 1450 to an unknown mistress while he was likely still in his teens. Warwick acknowledged Margaret as his own and she was therefore accepted by the family. Evidence for a warm relationship between Anne and Margaret is found by the fact that in her later coronation, Anne would give Margaret precedence over many other women of far more noble birth. Margaret was also given a special gift from the king and the chronicles refer to her as the honoured 'Dame Margaret'. Perhaps, then, Anne and Margaret's relationship was warm and Margaret was a half-sister with whom Anne grew up alongside and loved. The lack of men in the female household also would have created a space where Anne could have talked freely. That is not to say that men were entirely absent, of course. Male servants, workers and those who came to conduct business with the countess would all have been familiar sights for the young Anne, although she and her sister were taught to resist any temptation offered by handsome young men, not to avoid it entirely.

Warwick's position would often have kept him away from his family at Middleham, but when he did visit, the chroniclers took note, telling us that his household was very large and that the earl and his countess were extremely hospitable.[15] The stature of Warwick and of his wife's household at Middleham was such that it was deemed a suitable place for one of the king's young brothers, Richard, to be placed. It was normal practice for noble children to be placed in houses of similar rank in order that they may be educated and forge connections for the future. Young men would be trained together in the arts of war and the childhood bonds forged at this time were often lifelong, as can be later seen with Henry VIII and Charles Brandon: it is doubtful that Brandon would have been forgiven half his offences had he not been a boyhood friend of his king.

Given that Anne must surely have attended court fairly frequently, she and her sister would probably already have known Richard fairly well. Exactly when Richard joined the Warwick household is unclear, but it seems unlikely that it was before 1464. By this time, Richard's elder brother, George, had begun his chivalric military training and was already head of his own establishment at Greenwich.

Warwick was now charged with performing this task for Richard, who was about 12 years old. The Role of the Exchequer records that at Michaelmas 1465, the king paid Warwick 'for costs and expenses incurred by him on behalf of the Duke of Gloucester, his brother'.[16] In addition, at the same time, Warwick was also given the ward and guardianship of

Francis Lovell, whose lands were being held by the king on account of his father's support of the Lancastrians. Lovell, though he was younger than Richard, would play an important part in Richard's later life, becoming what we today would call his best friend, and as such, he would play a key role in Anne's later life too. Warwick also was entrusted with the care of other young men such as Richard Ratcliffe and Robert Percy, who would display unshakable loyalty to Richard, even if they did not always agree with him.

We know that Anne sometimes travelled the country; it seems certain that in February 1463 she was at Bisham Priory when her grandfather, Salisbury, and their uncle, Thomas Neville, both killed after Wakefield, were reburied alongside her grandmother, Alice, who had died in December 1462. Bisham Priory was home to the family mausoleum and many of Anne's ancestors rested there, with Masses being said regularly for their souls. In 1464, she is recorded as being present alongside her parents at St Mary's in Warwick, where they made offerings in the presence of the king, and they were almost certainly present at the marriage of their aunt, Margaret, to John de Vere sometime during the early 1460s. John de Vere was restored to his lands in 1465, following his father's Lancastrian treachery.

Anne again comes into view, briefly, in September 1465, when she is recorded as attending, along with the rest of her family, the enthronement of her uncle, George Neville, as Archbishop of York and the feast that followed. Leland, an antiquary who toured England in the 1530s, tells us that Warwick acted as steward and sat in high estate. Anne, meanwhile, sat alongside her sister near to Richard and was watched over by no less than three countesses, those of Suffolk, Elizabeth, one of Richard's sisters, Westmorland, and Isabel of Northumberland, whilst Anne's mother sat in another chamber. At about 9 years old, Anne was already considered by the standards of the time as mature and well behaved enough to participate in the adult part of the proceedings. The feast was at Cawood Castle, and the chronicles record that it was of almost epic proportions. Thousands of birds, including 4,000 pigeons, 4,000 mallards, peacocks, 1,000 capon, 1,200 quails, 200 pheasants, 400 swans, 204 bitterns, 400 woodcocks, 1,000 egrets, 204 cranes, 2,000 geese, 400 herons, 100 curlews, 400 plovers and 2,000 chickens were served alongside 2,304 pigs, 1,000 sheep, 6 bulls, 304 calves, 204 goats, 4,000 rabbits and apparently even 12 porpoises. There was also fish – salmon, pike and bream, to name just a few. In addition, there were 6,500 venison pasties, plus breads, cakes, custards, sweetmeats, alongside wine and ale. Sixty-two cooks were engaged to ensure that everything was prepared to perfection. Clearly, Warwick and his brother were determined that none of their nearly 6,000 guests would go home hungry.

Anne would have been right at the heart of this excess, choosing the choicest meats and perhaps indulging in a 'dish of jelly'. Surely, Anne cannot have but been impressed at such an event over which her own father presided; it was the sort of event that was talked about for years to come and it was the name of Warwick that echoed around the palace walls. Anne's future must have seemed utterly secure.

Chapter 5

Uncertain Times

Hasty marriage seldom proveth well.
Henry VI, Part 3, William Shakespeare

For all the pomp and ceremony of the Cawood feast, events in England were not progressing in quite the way that Anne's father wished. Warwick had recently spent a good deal of time abroad in the kings' service. In 1464, he had been sent to the French court to conclude an Anglo–French peace treaty, a key part of which was to be Edward IV's marriage to Bona of Savoy, Louis XI's sister-in-law. Warwick had taken the negotiations very seriously and appears to have struck up something of a rapport with the French king.[1] At a meeting in September of that year at the monastic complex of Reading Abbey, during the Council of the Peers, he presented his plan to the king as an almost fait accompli, and asked for his approval to proceed with arrangements for his marriage to Bona.[2] Warwick seems to have been extremely confident and no doubt did not expect any serious issues to be forthcoming; after all, he had been acting on Edward's orders, or so he thought. *Gregory's Chronicle* relates how Edward instead of agreeing told Warwick and the other men assembled that he could not marry Bona because he was already married. Edward IV's new wife was Elizabeth Woodville, and by the standards of the day, she was a very unsuitable match. She was a relative commoner and already a widowed mother, having been married to John Grey of Groby, a Lancastrian knight who had been killed at the Second Battle of St Albans.[3] After her husband's death, Elizabeth had been left with two young sons to raise, Thomas and Richard, and little money on which to do so. She was not entirely without connection, however; her father was John Woodville, Baron Rivers, who had started life as the Duke of Bedford's Chamberlain, but had married Elizabeth's mother, Jacquetta of

Luxembourg, the Duke of Bedford's widow. Jacquetta was the daughter of Peter I of Luxembourg and sister Louis of Luxembourg, who by the time of Elizabeth's marriage ruled the principality. Richard and Jacquetta's marriage had caused a huge scandal but it proved to be both happy and fruitful, as Elizabeth was one of fourteen children.[4] In Warwick's mind, however, these connections were not desirable ones. He had already quarrelled with the Woodville clan early in 1460, when Elizabeth's brother Anthony, one of the great men of the age who started life, like Elizabeth, as a Lancastrian, had attempted to raise forces with which to attack Warwick in Calais. In addition, the Woodvilles were known to be in favour of a Burgundian alliance rather than supporting Warwick and promoting a French one.

None of this mattered to Edward, who, as the Milanese ambassador at Louis' court wrote from Abbeville to the Duchess of Milan, 'has taken to wife an English lady, out of love'. According to legend, he and Elizabeth had met near Grafton, Northamptonshire, when she had determined to meet him on the road and ask for his help in securing her son's access to their paternal inheritance. Upon seeing her, the king was struck by her beauty and was determined to have her. Elizabeth, though, was made of stern stuff and with all of her mother's pride in her bloodline, refused to submit to the king unless he offered her an honourable marriage. Exactly when and where Elizabeth and Edward were wedded and bedded is unclear, but two weeks after the council was held, Edward IV presented his queen at Reading Abbey. The new queen, splendidly arrayed, entered the church on the arm of George, Duke of Clarence, and of Warwick. However, Warwick had been humiliated; not only had his time in France been wasted but it was also abundantly clear to all that the king had chosen not to confide in his 'Kingmaker' regarding his marriage. The Milanese ambassador expressed his bewilderment that the king had so 'frequently caused representatives' to speak with the king regarding the marriage of the queen's sister when he knew full well nothing could come of it. It is difficult to escape the impression that Edward was beginning to chafe under Warwick's 'guidance' and was seeking to strike out on his own. Perhaps the timing of his marriage, with Warwick safely out of the country, was not coincidental.

It is apparent that Edward was now, as Crowland puts it, 'relying entirely on his own choice without consulting the nobles of the kingdom'. In fact, there is a clear suggestion that part of Elizabeth's attraction lay in the fact that she and her family were completely independent of Warwick, and that they would help Edward to end his reliance on the Nevilles. However, the idea that there was widespread disquiet in England in response to Edward's marriage isn't true; the nobles were shocked but they were not, as later historians would try to claim, already 'up in arms' about it.

The fact that Warwick was not present at Elizabeth's coronation on 26 May 1465 should also not be regarded as an intended slight. For Warwick was again off on the king's business, this time in Burgundy alongside Lord Hastings. Given his absence it seems unlikely that Anne, her mother or sister attended the queen's coronation but the fact that the countess was absent from Middleham for most of 1465 does suggest that perhaps she had a role to perform in assisting with the establishment of the queen's household as one of the senior countesses in England. Perhaps she and her daughters were amongst the unnamed 'attendants' who accompanied Elizabeth Woodville when she entered London via London Bridge on 24 May, the thoroughfare having been cleaned and new embellishments, including highly decorated model figures, commissioned for the occasion.[5] Alternatively, she may simply have been absent while attending matters in other parts of the Warwick estates.

The marriage of Edward and Elizabeth had one clear and material effect on Anne's world: Elizabeth came from a large family; she had many sisters and brothers who now required marital matches that were appropriate to their newfound status as the family of the Queen of England. Anthony Woodville was made Lord Treasurer but he had married sometime previously Elizabeth de Scales, the sole heiress of Thomas de Scales, becoming Lord Scales in right of his wife, so at least he didn't require a high-born spouse, but pretty much all of the queen's other connections did. So followed a spate of high-profile and political Woodville marriages. Elizabeth's sister Anne was married to William Bourchier, the son and heir of the Earl of Essex and Isabel of York, sometime before 1467. Mary Woodville, another sister, was married in 1467 to William Herbert, 2nd Earl of Pembroke, 'amid profuse magnificence'. John Woodville, one of Elizabeth's brothers, was married in January 1465 to Warwick's aunt, Katherine Neville, Dowager Duchess of Norfolk – something that angered Warwick greatly as it took his aunt's inheritance away from the Neville family.[6] Last in these great marriages for the Woodville siblings was that of Catherine Woodville to Henry Stafford, 2nd Duke of Buckingham, which took place just prior to Elizabeth's coronation. Henry was aged 10, Catherine only 8. Stafford had been a ward of Edward IV's since the death of his grandfather at the Battle of Northampton, and this marriage in particular caused some consternation, being seen, correctly, as part of Edward's plan to tie Stafford's great inheritance to the crown. As the marriages rumbled on, to include that such as Anne of Exeter to the queen's son by her first marriage to Thomas Grey, Warwick's 'great secret displeasure' was becoming increasingly apparent.

All of this meant that for Anne and her sister, and indeed Warwick's wider relations, there was a distinct lack of suitable future spouses on the horizon.

Marriage was the destiny to which Anne and Isobel were born and for which their early lives had prepared them. Child marriages, such as that of Henry Stafford and Catherine Woodville, were not unusual. Anne's parents themselves were aged only 7 and 11 when they were wed. Yet there seems to have been no attempt to make an early marriage for either Anne or her elder sister. If there was such an arrangement, no records have survived, but given that there is no reference anywhere at all, it seems unlikely. By the time of the Neville feast, Isobel in particular, at around 14, was at peak marriageable age. The delay seems to have been simply that Warwick was determined that his daughters would not be married to anyone other than those from the highest echelons of the nobility, matches that as we have seen were now increasingly thin on the ground. In addition, of course, the political instability in England had not left Warwick much time to decide such matters. He would also have been hesitant, at a time when loyalty was often so easily bought and sold, wanting to be sure that they were married to men on the right side of the conflict. He would not have wished them to find themselves in the position of Anne of York, whose brother later annulled her marriage, to everyone's relief.

Another reason for his hesitation was that his daughters were in the almost unique position of having no material concerns for their future. Also, it had become apparent by the mid-1460s that they were going to be their father's only heirs. Their husbands, therefore, would inherit the Warwick lands and titles in right of their wives. Thus, it was even more crucial that Warwick chose correctly. Without a son, the vast Warwick inheritance would have to be broken up upon Warwick's death. The question of why Anne's father did not now seek to cast off his wife and remarry is one that deserves a moment's consideration. The simple fact is that he and Anne Beauchamp could not have just divorced a la Henry VIII, as divorce really wasn't an option at this time, except in extreme cases of non-consummation, obviously not applicable here, or of previous legal pre-contract, again not applicable. In addition, even if they had found grounds for divorce, any future sons would have inherited only the Warwick lands, the Neville and Salisbury inheritance, but Countess Anne's lands would have gone to her daughters, so their combined estate would have been broken up anyway.

For the time being, therefore, Anne and Isobel remained unmarried, but they were also becoming increasingly visible in society. By 1465, Elizabeth Woodville was pregnant, and it is almost certain that they attended the baby Elizabeth of York's christening and Elizabeth Woodville's churching in February and March 1466 respectively. Their father presided over these events and we know that at the christening there were in attendance eight duchesses and thirty countesses, who all stood as the queen was seated on a throne of gold.[7] Warwick also stood as Elizabeth of York's godfather, alongside Jacquetta of Luxembourg and Cecily Neville, who stood as her godmothers. There seems no reason at all, therefore, why Countess Anne and her daughters would not have been in attendance. Assuming they were, they would have stayed at the Warwick house of L'Erber, which was situated in the heart of London, between Newgate and Old St Paul's Cathedral. It was a house with which Anne Neville would likely already have been very familiar. L'Erber was one of London's great medieval houses and it boasted a great garden and a small or 'lytell' one for Anne to walk in. It also had a brewhouse, stables and tenements. Warwick was known to keep an extravagant table. At another of his houses located nearby in Warwick Lane, it is recorded that there were 'oftentimes six oxen eaten at breakfast and every tavern was full of his meat', and that any man who was permitted to enter through the gates could leave with as much meat as he could carry upon a long dagger.[8] It is logical to assume that such extravagance and generosity was also witnessed at L'Erber. The house had a long association with the Neville family. It was said to have been built by a knight called Pont de l'Arche before passing into the possession of Geoffrey le Scrope and then into the hands of John Neville of Raby. From there it would pass to Ralph Neville, the Earl of Westmorland, and then to Warwick's father, Salisbury, before becoming part of Warwick's vast property portfolio.

Edward IV's younger brothers, George and Richard, joined the royal family at the celebrations that followed the christening, and again, Anne and Isobel were almost certainly also present although their names are not specifically mentioned. It was reported that the feast went on for three hours, late into the night, and that there was wild dancing that saw Margaret of York take to the floor with her brother Richard. Margaret of York was one of the leading ladies of the kingdom; she emerges from the historic record at the coronation of Elizabeth Woodville and afterwards she joined the queen's household. She does not seem to ever have been described as beautiful but she was educated, gracious and full of energy. An image of her dating to around this time in Nicholas Finet's *Dialogue de la duchesse of Bourgogne* shows her to have a plain but soft face, and dressed in a sumptuous gown of gold with black floral decoration and trimmed with white fur. She also wears a high headdress, trailing a fine white veil, fashions that Anne would have been familiar with.[9] Like her brother, she was tall, nearly 6 foot, and would have towered over many of the other ladies at court. Anne certainly would have known her, and perhaps emulated her energetic dancing. Though at the time of Elizabeth of York's christening she would not have known it, Anne of York would play a key role in the widening rift between Anne Neville's father and the king.

Warwick had continued to push for a French alliance, even after Edward's marriage, but the Woodville clan, under Anthony Woodville, were beginning to urge more forcefully an alliance with Philip of Burgundy. Their persistence paid off and in 1467, Anthony had led a party to Bruges, and shortly afterwards, a peace and trade treaty had been signed with Philip. With peace now established, in June of 1467, Philip's son Anthony, the Comte de la Roche, came to England. He was commonly known as the Bastard of Burgundy, being the illegitimate half-brother of Charles the Bold.[10] To mark his visit a great tournament was held at Smithfield on 11 and 12 June 1467. Called the most spectacular tournament of the age,

Edward IV declared the days as public holidays, but whilst it might have looked like entertainment, the tournament had a serious political aim, for Edward hoped to seal his alliance with Burgundy through a marriage treaty between his sister Margaret and Charles the Bold. Edward also wanted to prove that his court was quite as rich, glamorous and beautiful as anything Burgundy could muster. The court of Burgundy had for decades been the epitome of chivalry; now Edward wanted to show that England had put her troubles behind her and could devote herself to chivalry, romance and the purity of honour and glory. It was Warwick's old foe Anthony Woodville who took the part of the English challenger, representing the king in his manly vigour. He fought with the Bastard and was clearly determined not to give any quarter. On the first day, he unhorsed his opponent, to the great delight of the crowd. The next day, Woodville and the Bastard fought on foot with various weapons, and the fight, according to one account, was so vicious that each sliced with their blade into the other's armour. At this point, Edward stepped in and ended the fight before one or both were killed. He declared a draw and both men left the field as friends, with their honour intact… and with the marriage treaty as good as signed.[11] Chroniclers again do not mention whether or not Anne and her sister were present but it seems almost certain they were. If so, they would have likely been involved in the distribution of prizes, whereby as one tournament observer records, 'noble and rich prizes will be given by ladies and damsels'. They would also have taken part in other elements of the festivities such as dancing and feasting.

With the death of Philip of Burgundy in 1467, and the accession of Charles the Bold, the marriage became even more desirable. Despite his opposition to the match, it was behind Warwick that Margaret rode as she left London on her way to rendezvous with her future husband. Warwick, however, left her when she took a ship to cross the Channel, when Earl Rivers escorted her onwards. Jean de Wavrin, a French nobleman in the service of Philip the Good, chronicled Margaret's marriage. He tells us that Margaret stayed first at Sluis before the wedding ceremony took place in Damme, and then she made her triumphal entry into Bruges. Anthonis de Roovere has also left us an account of the event, and both men tell us that the wedding was spectacular, with symbolic pageants, music and fireworks taking place all over Bruges. Margaret entered the city in a golden litter at the head of a procession. She was met at the gate of the Holy Cross by four more processions whose job it was to welcome her officially to the city, and she was presented with gifts including a gold vase and a statue of St Margaret. John Paston would write that it was the best event of its kind that he had ever seen.[12] Nevertheless, the glory and excess of the occasion could not quite disguise the fact that the marriage, as Wavrin acerbically states, took place 'in spite of Louis XI, Warwick and nearly all the people of England'.

It is at this time that Wavrin has something of even greater importance to say. He tells us that the delay in promoting marriages for Anne and her sister was in fact because Warwick had been plotting, secretly or otherwise, to make the most spectacular alliance available and to marry his daughters to the king's brothers as early as 1464. In 1464, however, Anne would have been just 8 years old and it seems unlikely that her father had given it serious thought at that stage, although there is little doubt that it had already implanted itself in his mind.

By 1467, the Pseudo-Worcester chronicle tells us that Warwick had actually broached the idea of a match between Anne's sister Isobel and George, Duke of Clarence, but that the king had refused to countenance it.[13] The question of why is an interesting one; Isobel was, after all, a great heiress but it is clear that Edward was seeking to loosen, not tighten, his ties to the 'Kingmaker' – plus, of course, Clarence was an attractive carrot to dangle on the international marriage market and Edward needed all the international capital he could get. In March 1466, Edward had proposed that George marry Marie of Burgundy, heiress to the dukedom at the time. The fact that she was just 9 to George's 14 was unfortunate, as was the fact that the proposal came to nothing because had George married her, his ambitions would surely have been fulfilled as he would have inherited the dukedom of Burgundy. The prospect of this match was likely another reason why Edward was not keen on Warwick's plan, particularly as Queen Elizabeth had yet failed to produce a son. As such, George was next in line to the throne in an age that would not have accepted Elizabeth of York as queen.

George, Duke of Clarence, was the second of the three sons of York. George's character has been forever set by Shakespeare as 'false fleeting perjured Clarence', but whilst he was not yet false, there is good evidence that he was already considered to be rather an arrogant young man. In 1463, for example, on a visit to Canterbury, George entered the cathedral carrying his sword pointing upwards rather than down in a traditional show of respect.[14] He also, in the words of historian Michael Hicks, was immature enough to point out publicly that the Lord Mayor had 'fallen asleep whilst presiding over a treason trial at the London Guildhall'.[15] He was loyal to his brother, though, and in 1466, when he had come of age, he paid homage to him and set him up his own household at Tutbury Castle. George increasingly appears in the historical records, usually incidentally, suggesting that he was not active at the centre of power. We know that he owed John Howard money and that Rous thought him 'witty'. George had never lived in Warwick's household but now he seems to have come into regular contact with Anne's father as he grew estranged from his brother, for a reason that Vergil 'cannot tell what cause'.

Warwick was also becoming estranged from his king. On 8 June 1467, the king demanded the Great Seal be surrendered by his chancellor and Anne's uncle, Archbishop George Neville. He was to be dismissed from office – something that Warwick only learnt of when he returned to England having been in France. Upon his return, it was notable that not a single member of the king's household greeted him.[16]

It is clear that Warwick had decided to press ahead with the Clarence match. Technically, Edward IV could not refuse his consent; it was not yet illegal to marry into the royal family without the monarch's permission, but he continued to vehemently object to it. This widened the gulf between Warwick and Edward, as well as between Edward and George. The marriage was not a straightforward proposal because as first cousins once removed, George and Isobel were within the prohibited circle of relations. To marry, they would need a papal dispensation. Warwick was determined that everything was to be done by the book. The Pope, however, was not inclined to go against the King of England in the matter. When Warwick sent an envoy, Master Lacy, to press his suit with the pope, Edward blocked his access and no audience was granted. Furious, Warwick then used Edward's man, James Goldwell, to get what he wanted. Eventually, the dispensation was granted but a clearly worried Warwick sought permission from Cardinal Bourchier for Isobel to be married in Calais, by his brother, Archbishop George Neville.

What Isobel or Anne thought of this match is not recorded but George was an illustrious match by any standards, the sort of match for which they had prepared their whole lives. They would also have been aware, however, that their father had quarrelled with the king in making it. Their journey to Calais would thus have been riddled with tension.

Chapter 6

Isobel's Sister

> A ministering angel shall my sister be.
> *Hamlet*, William Shakespeare

When Anne set her feet down on Calais soil, it was probably the first time in eight years that she had seen her childhood home. She had left as a child and was returning as a young woman, but she would certainly have wished the circumstances were different, and that her father's position was more secure. It is unlikely that Anne and her sister were fully aware of the details of Warwick's defiance of the king, or privy to Clarence and Warwick's machinations, but they would have known that the king had objected forcefully to Isobel's marriage. The question of why Isobel made no objection is sometimes raised today, but for Isobel, refusing was simply not a possibility. Their father's will was law, and neither Isobel nor Anne had any real scope for disobedience, either in law or in fact. It is also likely that the match held some attraction for Isobel; quite aside from his rank, she already knew George of Clarence, although how well she knew him is not clear. In an age when she could have been married to an elderly widower, sent abroad to an unfamiliar country, or even married to a child, Clarence being of age and reasonably attractive was not a bad proposition at all.

Although Warwick took great pains to make sure this wedding was not clandestine, the fact it was held in Calais rather than in England certainly raised a few eyebrows internationally. Warwick, it seems, wanted the marriage to take place in 'his' territory, where he believed the men were loyal to him as well as, or perhaps even more than, to the king. Isobel and Clarence were married on 12 July 1469, although where exactly is not certain.[1] As we have seen, a papal dispensation was necessary for the marriage to take place and the required paperwork had been issued on 14 March 1469.[2] There are two likely locations for the marriage. The first is the Église Notre-Dame, which, with its stunning paintings, comprising a woman standing in front of a fortified city, is considered by some the front runner.³ The second is the chapel dedicated to the Virgin Mary that stood within Calais castle. Perhaps, given the fact that she would have been familiar with it, this might have been Isobel's preference. The decision, though, would not have been hers and arguably, Warwick would have wanted the celebration to be publicly visible, given Edward's disapproval, in order avoid any question of invalidity. To this end, there were also celebrations, which lasted for between two and five days and at which Anne attended, always at her sister's side.

Interestingly, it has been suggested that Cecily Neville, George and Edward's mother, attended that marriage, as she is listed as having been with them at Sandwich. However, the chronicle of John Stone makes it clear that whilst 'she departed from Canterbury towards Sandwich to her son, that is to say the Duke of Clarence', she was back in Canterbury soon after, when 'she was at Vespers [and on Sunday] attended High Mass'. It therefore appears that she spent five days in Sandwich with the party but did not sail to Calais with them. Whether or not she was there to support the marriage or to try to prevent it from happening is unclear.⁴

The recorded ordinances tell that apart from immediate family, 'five knights of the garter and many other lords and ladies and worshipful knights well accompanied with wise and discreet squires in right great number' also were present at the marriage.⁵ This suggests that despite the king's displeasure, some felt it worth the risk to attend. The marriage ceremony itself was conducted by Isobel's uncle, George Neville, Archbishop of York, and Isobel would have sworn the traditional woman's oath to be 'bonny and buxom at bed and at board', and to obey her husband in all things, as generations of women had done before her. At that time, wedding dresses were not white. A picture of a wedding of around 1470, attributed to the Rambures Master, shows the bride in a deep crimson gown trimmed with gold and with her long hair flowing loose to symbolise her virginity. Her groom, meanwhile, is also bareheaded and dressed in purple, crimson and gold. Red seems to have been a popular colour for marriage dresses at the time, but we should not picture Isobel contrasting it with any white roses; the device of Edward IV was not widely adopted by Yorkist supporters. Anne, at her sister's side, would also have been dressed in her finest clothing; after all, a daughter of Warwick was marrying into England's royal family. Her dress would likely have been of velvet, which was very popular in England at the time and was often paired with cloth of gold. She would likely have also worn a tall pillbox cap with a veil suspended over it. Dresses with deep backs were also the fashion, as were long, deep sleeves.[6]

This, however, would be the last time that she was truly at her sister's side. From this moment on, their relationship would change, and for young women who had spent all their lives together up to that point, perhaps even sharing a bed, as was usual for maidens, the wrench would have been considerable. Isobel was leaving her father's house and Anne was being left behind … only she wasn't, not just yet. Wavrin tells us that Isobel's honeymoon period was exceptionally short, and that just five days later, her new husband and her father set sail for England. Isobel's marriage had the effect of greatly elevating Anne's own status. She was now both an unmarried heiress, daughter of a mighty magnate, and a member of the royal house of England. More importantly, however, with the marriage signed and sealed, Warwick and Clarence were now as bound together as firmly as Isobel and her husband were, for this was, first and foremost, a political alliance.

It seems unlikely that Warwick would have confided his plans to his daughters, but perhaps George – by all accounts a far less discreet figure – shared his dreams of coup and kingship with his new bride. We shall never know. What we do know is, for now, the Warwick women were left behind in Calais while the earl and Clarence sought to remake the politics of England by deposing Edward and putting Clarence on the throne, with Isobel as his queen. It is clear that Warwick had been fermenting rebellion in northern England, where discontent with Edward's regime was growing. In Richmondshire, Warwick's men began to rebel, at the same time as a force rose under the leadership of Robin of Redesdale, who today is considered to have been an alias for Sir John Coyners and/or his brother Sir William Coyners, to whom Warwick was conveniently related.[7] They claimed that they were protesting against 'taxes and abuses of power' but in reality they were supporting Warwick's power grab, no doubt thinking they would do better if Warwick rather than the Woodvilles were influencing the king.

When the revolt broke out, Edward headed north to deal with the rebels. This proved to be a serious miscalculation: it left London open. Warwick and Clarence landed at Sandwich, where they attracted a good deal of local support. They headed for Canterbury before turning their attention towards the capital. In London, 'they waited for their men and sometimes got news of the progress of the northerners' as well as to raise money, before heading north to meet the king.[8] Edward, meanwhile, was awaiting reinforcements in the shape of Pembroke and Devon, who were riding to join him. It was these reinforcements that the rebels under Robin of Redesdale had first encountered, and a Warwick cousin, Henry Neville, was killed in the violence. Pembroke and Devon had the advantage but there appears to have been a falling out between the two men, which led to Devon withdrawing from the field. This meant that the next day, when they faced the rebels properly on the morning of 24 July, they were weakened and Pembroke was deprived of his archers, which left him dangerously exposed. Despite this, Pembroke fought like a 'true liegeman of his king' and his brother, Sir Richard Herbert, 'twice by fine force passed through the battle of his adversaries and without mortal wound returned'. They might have won the day had not his men panicked when they saw the first Warwick reinforcements arriving crying, 'A Warwick! A Warwick!', and in the end, 4,000 royalists were killed. Pembroke was captured, later to be executed alongside his brother, and within days, Edward IV was taken prisoner by Warwick at Northampton. His chief allies, the queen's father, Richard Woodville, and brother John, were also captured and were executed at Coventry. Both men had long been enemies of Warwick, but by executing them, history would show that Warwick had passed the point of no return, for there is no evidence that Edward or the queen ever truly forgave this act. The battle had been political but these executions were personal.

The King of England was now in the hands of Anne's father, and he was held at Warwick Castle while Warwick decided what to do next. It appears that he didn't intend to depose Edward immediately; instead, he ordered that Edward's government continue in London but under the direction of the Archbishop of York. Edward was moved to Middleham Castle while Warwick turned his attention to depriving the queen of her mother; Jacquetta of Luxembourg was accused of witchcraft, something designed to invalidate the king's marriage.[9] Once Edward's marriage was invalidated, so were his heirs, and then George of Clarence was once again first in line to the throne. The allegations against Jacquetta of Luxembourg were carefully constructed and naturally could not appear to have come directly from Warwick, although he no doubt endorsed them. Jacquetta was accused of having made lead figures of the king and her daughter Elizabeth to bring about their marriage and later of using witchcraft to try to bring about Warwick's death. However, Jacquetta acted quickly and wrote to the aldermen of London, reminding them that it was she who in 1461 had used her friendship with Margaret of Anjou to save the city from Lancastrian destruction. It worked, and the mayor wrote to Clarence himself to intercede on Jacquetta's behalf.

Warwick was now confident enough to recall Anne and the rest of his family back to England, where they made for Warwick Castle. The party would have been tired and anxious for firm news. No doubt, the whole family were also hoping that Isobel had managed to fall pregnant during her very short honeymoon; if so, this would indelibly strengthen their position. If she had not, then it was imperative that she and Clarence be together again in order that they might regularly sleep together.[10] Anne now assumed the position of second lady in the Warwick household, and would have become her mother's chief support and assistant as Isobel re-joined her husband. Meanwhile, the courts of Europe were in a frenzy trying to predict what Warwick would do next. The Milanese ambassador in France wrote that 'everything remains in the hands of the said Earl of Warwick, the conqueror' and that Edward himself was dead.[11]

The king, however, was very much alive. Fatefully, Warwick now hesitated and the parliament he summoned never met. Edward IV was moved to Pontefract, from where he was allowed to escape when Warwick realised that he had lost popular support. Edward quickly resumed control of both the kingdom and its parliament. Whatever his private feelings might have been, reconciliation was foremost in Edward's mind. To this end, he, Warwick and Clarence were all together at a council held in London at the beginning of December, and both sides celebrated Christmas and New Year in London. With little choice, Warwick and his allies had submitted to the king and pledged once again their allegiance. Anne was almost certainly present at these Christmas festivities, along with her mother and her sister, who by now was indeed pregnant. After her return to England, Isobel and Clarence had set up house at the monastery of Waltham in Essex, and they likely also spent time at one of the Clarence properties in London, Coldharbour House, considering how frequently they later used it.

However familiar Anne was with court life, this Christmas celebration would have been unlike any other she had ever attended. She was now the daughter of a traitor, despite the king's pardon, and the king and queen were ever watchful. Their eyes must surely have fallen more than once on Anne, who now stood in prime position to make a valuable marriage alliance – one upon which her father could capitalise or on which he could even base further rebellion.

In an attempt to bind Warwick to him, in January, George Neville, Anne's cousin, was betrothed to 3-year-old Elizabeth of York. George was also created Duke of Bedford the same day.[12] In effect, Edward was dangling George Neville's marriage as a carrot, promising future Neville advancement through George Neville instead of Clarence, should the Neville brothers remain loyal, of course. As well as George being made Duke of Bedford, his father, John, was made Marquis Montagu. Whilst this might seem like a promotion, in reality, it sent John Neville south, breaking up the Neville hegemony of the north. Edward had graciously accepted the submission of his wayward lords but this and other evidence suggests that he was merely biding his time. It is clear that he was quietly taking action to replace his executed Woodville allies with loyal men, but not Warwick supporters. Pembroke's death saw Richard of Gloucester and not Warwick assume the power vacuum in southern Wales. The Percys – long-time rivals of the Nevilles in the north – were also restored to favour, and George Neville was removed as Edward's chancellor. When the council met in February, Jacquetta Woodville complained to them that Thomas Wake had slandered her and accused her of witchcraft. The council cleared her of all charges and 'pray[ed] that the same may be enacted off record'.[13] The fact that the two brothers of York had not fully reconciled is suggested by the fact that their mother, Cecily, evidently felt it necessary to try to arrange a personal reconciliation between her two sons at her London house, Baynard's Castle, in March.[14]

Isobel's Sister

Anne and her mother had, at some point at the beginning of the year, returned to Warwick Castle, where they would have picked up the rhythms of their lives again – hearing complaints from those on the estate, dealing with household accounts and ordering supplies. When the Warwick women were in residence we know that there was a good supply of meat and wine for the table. Anne would also have taken up her needle to stitch fine cloth for Isobel's baby. At the time, babies would have been swaddled because, in line with Plato's teachings, during the medieval period it was believed that if they were not, their limbs would grow crooked. It would have been common, therefore, for noblewomen to embroider the swaddling cloth in preparation for the infant's first few years. Anne's dresses would have been trimmed with blackwork, gold and gemstones; a child's clothing would have been similarly decorated to demonstrate the infant's status.

Isobel's pregnancy was advancing and she was back with her mother and sister sometime before 7 March, when Warwick and Clarence arrived at the castle. Perhaps she was happy to be back at her mother's side, and to have the support of her sister at this time. Warwick, meanwhile, was chafing under the insults, as he saw it, being heaped upon him by Edward, and was increasingly unhappy as the king consolidated his own, more independent, position. Warwick wanted power and once again began to plot, with the aim of directly putting Clarence on the throne with no prevarication. This time it was in Lincolnshire that he fermented rebellion, which was orchestrated by another Warwick puppet – Sir Robert Welles. In an echo of the previous year, Edward IV marched north to deal with what we now call the 1470 Lancashire Rebellion. Anne and her mother remained at Warwick Castle while Warwick and Clarence marched their men eastwards. Despite her advanced stage of pregnancy, however, Isobel did not stay with her mother and sister; it is recorded that she accompanied Clarence to Exeter – a journey that must have been very uncomfortable.

These moves by Warwick and Clarence were ostensibly to support Edward but in reality, captured correspondence proves that they really intended to support the rebels. The rebels, records one chronicler, were shouting 'A Clarence! A Warwick!' on the field, leaving no room for misunderstanding. The rebellion was almost over before it started; just one volley from the royalist cannon was enough to break the rebel lines. The leaders, Sir Robert

Welles and Richard Warren, were executed on 19 March, but the ordinary men, who according to legend threw off their Warwick and Clarence liveries as they fled, were allowed to live. Before his execution, Welles confirmed that Warwick and Clarence were behind the rebellion.[15] Edward, it seems, was not surprised.

Warwick now had no choice but to flee and he picked up Anne and the other Warwick women on the way. Traditionally, the now heavily pregnant Isobel would have been expected to withdraw and rest quietly for a month before the birth of her child, but she was afforded no such luxury. Although their flight was not quite as desperate as has later been suggested – for example, Warwick was able to drop off some of his artillery at Bristol on the way – it would still have been terrifying. They first tried to reach Warwick's newest ship, the *Trinity*, which had attempted to dock at Southampton or had been impounded there, but Earl Rivers prevented it from either docking or leaving. The *Trinity* had been blessed on 12 June 1469 by George Neville in the presence of Warwick, Clarence, the Prior of Oxney and three Christ Church monks, raising the interesting question of how complicit Christ Church might have been with Warwick's rebellions.[16]

When Warwick realised the *Trinity* would not be permitted to dock, their flight took on a far more serious energy and they quickly fled westwards, with Edward by now in pursuit. They finally managed to take ship at Dartmouth on 7 April, where Anne is specifically mentioned as having been, along with her parents, Clarence and Isobel.[17] The atmosphere on board must have been unbelievably tense. Perhaps Anne ran up on deck to watch the coastline of England retreating. Warwick must have done his best to assure them all that they would be heading towards shelter at Calais. Perhaps they even looked forward to returning there, where Isobel could give birth in the castle's warm and familiar Great Chamber, but as Calais approached, Warwick was both shocked and furious when his deputy, Lord John Wenlock, refused to allow them to land. Edward had sent express orders that the Earl was now a traitor to his king and was not to be admitted.[18]

Wenlock had long been a friend of Warwick's, and would have been a familiar figure to Anne, who must have struggled with his treachery. Perhaps it was at this point that the true scale of her father's treason and the reality of their perilous position became apparent. Wenlock has rather unfairly been called the 'Prince of Turncoats', because his decision to turn away Warwick made sense. Even if he wished to disobey the king, he could not be sure of the Calais garrison's loyalties and Warwick could have effectively been walking into a trap. Whatever his motivations, the delay was disastrous. As the ship lay at anchor, Isobel went into labour, possibly triggered by fear, shock or physical distress. Her pregnancy was likely at term already – it was almost exactly nine months since her wedding night – but equally, the circumstances might have caused her to go into premature labour. Isobel's labour was long and violent; sailors on deck reported hearing her screams. Rous tells us that the countess was well experienced in childbirth and she, alongside Anne, attended Isobel. At 14, it would have been unusual for the unmarried Anne to witness the birth of a baby but it could hardly have been avoided in the cramped conditions on board ship. Childbirth in the fifteenth century was dangerous enough even in luxurious conditions on dry land; aboard ship, Countess Anne would have had few of the supplies she was accustomed to using such as herbs, honey or warmed spice wine to dull the pain. She may have had time to grab a religious girdle or relic – in an age of deep religious faith, it was common for women to clutch relics during childbirth hoping that they would offer them and their child some protection. Perhaps Isobel simply prayed.

There was little more any of them could do. Anne and her mother must have watched helplessly as Isobel laboured, no doubt losing a lot of blood. Warwick again begged for permission to land, likely evidence that he had been advised that by now, Isobel was in mortal danger, but Wenlock would have been guilty of treason if he had allowed it. Instead, he sent flagons of wine and advised Warwick to try to land further along the shore.[19] At some point over the next few hours Isobel was delivered of her child, which was either stillborn or died shortly after birth. There is some debate as to whether the child was a boy or a girl but Philippe de Commines, writer and diplomat in the courts of Burgundy and France, claims that it was a boy, and if that was the case, then George, Isobel and the House of Warwick was now deprived of its heir. Anne was also deprived of her niece or nephew, and for her it was the most brutal introduction possible into the adult world of childbearing.

Over the next few days, as Anne reeled from the shock and tended to her weak sister, surely the idea would have crossed her mind that if Isobel had laboured at Warwick Castle or another of their residences, warm, rested and with a midwife in attendance, then the outcome might have been different. She would not have been human if it did not. There is no evidence that in an age when belief in the will of God was absolute that any of the women ever blamed Warwick for the position in which they now found themselves, but then again, they would hardly have put such thoughts to paper even if they had them. Anne and her family finally came ashore in Normandy sometime around 1 May, and Louis XI of France offered shelter to the ladies. He specified that this included the Countesses of Warwick and Clarence, plus their entourage, which included Anne. Louis' treaty with Burgundy meant that he could not openly assist Warwick, but women were exempt from such political considerations. Despite their exhaustion, however, the women did not go to Louis' court; instead, they stayed with Warwick himself. It was an insecure and uncertain existence, not helped by the fact that news quickly reached them that back in England, Edward had wasted no time in declaring Warwick and Clarence traitors.

Chapter 7

Princess of Wales

> Thy friends suspect for traitors while thou liv'st,
> And take deep traitors for they dearest friends.
> *Richard III*, William Shakespeare

The penalty for treason was death – and this is the fate both Anne's father and her brother-in-law now risked if they were to return to England. It was therefore further into France that they went. Louis made his allegiance clear when he ordered that his navy protect Warwick's ships from those of Burgundy and the Low Countries. Warwick was now preparing to invade England. This was really the only option open to him. His lands and possessions were now forfeit and Edward was in no mood this time to be understanding. Anne's privileged life was at an end and she was facing an uncertain future. She was now entirely dependent on the grace and charity of others such as Louis to maintain her and allow her to remain. Anne's exile resembled that of the woman in the mid-fourteenth century romance *Emaré*, which was also very much a family affair. The woman in *Emaré* does not choose exile but she does make the best of it, and ultimately returns home not through force of arms but by political machinations. Her survival requires her to remain utterly royal, even when 'that web of loyalties [around her] is tangled to breaking point'.[1] This may well have been a book that Anne herself had read, and if so, maybe she adopted such a stance. There is evidence that Anne's mother, the countess herself, now engaged in these sorts of 'political machinations' when she wrote to her relations in England, seeking to garner support and gather information from which they could begin to judge the prevalent English mood.

Anne's fate was utterly dependent on the actions that her father took next, but more immediately, there were things to be done, primarily helping Isobel to recover, and organising their servants and those who had accompanied them on their flight into an exile. According to the register of Thomas Bourchier, by 12 May, Warwick had not only resolved to invade England but had also realised that he would have to ally himself with the exiled Lancastrians in order to have any chance of success. This would mean the restoration of Henry VI as king, and abandoning the plot to put Clarence on the throne. When Isobel had married Clarence, her whole life had become entangled with his, and it was a knot that could not be undone. Her political usefulness was therefore limited, but Anne's marriage was a card that Warwick could still play and sometime in May, the idea of marrying Anne to Prince Edward of Lancaster, the son of Margaret of Anjou and Henry VI, was tabled. By 2 June, it had been agreed, in principle, at least.[2]

Louis was very keen to broker this alliance; he rode to meet with Warwick and Clarence in France, where they greeted each other warmly and familiarly. Louis' Queen Charlotte was also there and we know that Warwick and Clarence at least were taken to see her at Amboise; it is natural to assume that Anne, her mother and sister accompanied them. There was entertainment laid on for them, including four days of feasting and jousting, and it was a chance for them all to rest and catch their breath in safety.[3] Queen Charlotte of Savoy was educated, known for her excellent library and exceedingly virtuous. Having endured Louis' near constant infidelities for years, Louis eventually repaid her devotion by swearing he would remain faithful, an oath that Philip de Commines, his chronicler, tells us that he kept. Charlotte would go on to act as a regent of France in September 1465. If Charlotte and Anne did in fact meet, it is likely that Anne was greatly impressed by the notoriously serene and controlled Charlotte. Her life at Amboise has been described as both 'monotonous and secluded', and she spent her time stitching, attending to her devotions and listening to the lute – a favourite instrument of hers. She had come to be queen of France by a very dangerous and circuitous path, which saw her first betrothed to Frederick, Duke of Saxony, upon the death of his first wife. Louis had asked his father several times for permission to marry Charlotte in order to cement an alliance between France and Savoy, and was each time denied, leaving her already in a perilous and difficult position at just 9 years old. Louis eventually took matters into his own hands and they were married in 1451, at ages 12 and 9 respectively. Charlotte chose to overlook her husband's infidelities and the fact he abandoned her at the court of his father on one occasion, and she carved out her own life as a studious and educated woman almost independent of her husband. Her devotion paid dividends in the end; Louis returned to his wife and she prospered. Perhaps Charlotte saw echoes of her own situation in the teenage Anne. Louis offered to assist Warwick in his invasion plans, should he forge this alliance with Margaret. To this end, he waited in Vandoma with Louis while Anne, and the rest of the party including Warwick, went north into Normandy. It is notable that by this point, Anne was being referred to as 'the future princess' of England.[4]

This plan made sense for Warwick on many levels; not only would it make Anne into Queen of England, it would also take the marriage of Edward of Lancaster off the table in any future alliances. There had been rumours that Margaret was planning to marry him to Princess Mary of Scotland, which, whilst this no doubt would have caused numerous problems for Edward IV, it would also have sidelined Anne's father, something he was obviously keen to avoid. More immediately, of course, Henry VI was not expected to live long once restored to the throne, and Anne would be queen consort of England and the mother of future generations of Lancastrian kings of England. There was also the consideration that Edward of Lancaster and Anne would have claim to lands in Provenance, Maine, Jerusalem and Sicily through Margaret of Anjou's bloodline, even if England proved to be beyond their grasp.

Margaret was by all accounts far less pleased by this alliance proposal; she was 'right difficult' about the prospect of such an alliance and even went so far as to claim that there was the prospect of a match being made between her son and Elizabeth of York. She said that in the alliance between her son and Anne Neville, 'she saw neither honour nor profit for her nor her son' and that 'she should find a more profitable party and of a more advantage with the King of England'.[5] Margaret produced a letter that apparently was evidence for this proposed marriage but no other evidence exists for it and indeed, the whole idea makes no sense at all. Elizabeth of York was, after all, still intended for George Neville; upsetting his father, John Neville, would hardly have helped Edward's cause. Ultimately, Margaret came to see, like Warwick, the need for their alliance; she was an eminently practical woman, but she certainly did not trust Warwick and she steadfastly refused to send her son into his care because, as the Milanese ambassador tells us, 'she mistrusts him'.[6] She clearly suspected, possibly correctly, that Warwick was hoping to have Edward of Lancaster's effects in his possession as a back-up, which he could surrender to Edward as a bargaining chip for his freedom if the invasion went badly.

Anne's father and Margaret of Anjou met at Angers Cathedral, where it is said that she made Warwick kneel before her for twenty minutes and then 'swear upon the veney [true] cross ... that without change he shall always hold the party and quarrel of King Henry and shall serve him and the Prince as a true and faithful subject oweth to serve his sovereign Lord'.[7] Louis joined in the oath-taking and sometime before 30 July, he and his brother, the Duke of Guienne, took an oath to protect their 'very dear and beloved cousin Anne', and any issue she might bear.[8] Warwick now published a pamphlet to help rally support in England. Naturally, he did not admit that he had been wrong but instead he presented himself as a hero who had, in the words of Michael Hicks, 'won the hand of the Lancastrian heir for his daughter'.[9]

Meanwhile, a chronicler at Cambridge tried to give events an almost biblical theme by claiming:

> when the said Duke of Clarence and the Earl of Warwick were in France here appeared a blasting star in the west and the flame thereof like a spear head the which divers of the kings house saw it, whereupon they were full of sore dread. And then in France where the said lords were there took their counsel about what best for to do; and they could find no remedy but to send to Queen Margaret and to make a marriage between Prince Edward King Henry's son and another of the said Earl of Warwick's daughters [Anne].

It is difficult to get an impression of Anne's betrothed. In terms of politics, he had been disinherited in 1470 by the Duke of York, and he had spent most of his life in his mother's company, going with her to Scotland in 1460 and the court of Mary of Guelders. He had been knighted by his father at only 6 years of age, but following the defeat of the Lancastrians at Towton, he had followed his mother into exile in France. In exile he was tutored by Sir John Fortescue, who wrote many treatises. One of these, the *De laudibus legum Angliae*, which takes the form of a dialogue between him and the prince, tells us:

> the Prince as soon as he became grown up gave himself over entirely to martial exercises and seated on force and half tamed steeds urged on by his supra he often delighted in attacking and assaulting the young companion attending him, sometimes with a lance sometimes with a sword, sometimes with other weapons in a warlike manner and in accordance with the rules of military discipline.[10]

Fortesuce wished that he would study the law 'with the same zeal as you are to that of arms'. He did, however, approve of Edward's military training, remembering that Edward had known from an early age that he would have to grow up and fight for his rightful throne. This description ties in with the tradition whereby he is thought of as a cold, uncaring youth, largely owing to the 1467 description of him by the Milanese ambassador who wrote that he 'talks of nothing but cutting off heads or making war, as if he had everything in his hands or was the god of battle or the peaceful occupation of the throne'.[11] However, George Ashby, another man who knew Prince Edward in exile, suggests a slightly softer side to Edward's education. He wrote a work, which he dedicated to the prince, in which he entreats Edward, amongst other things, to learn from history – which can teach circumspection, be moderate, choose your servants well, pay your debts, be decisive but hear counsel patiently, be just, moderate in rhetoric and music, pray, do not favour traitors and rather ironically, beware of reconciled enemies.[12]

We know that Anne was at Volgenes near to Barfleur on 8 July alongside her father, and it was likely then that she was told that her marriage to Edward of Lancaster was almost certain.[13] What she felt can only be guessed at, but as we have already seen, she simply had no choice in the matter. In theory, women could refuse a match but in practice, they did not. Now aged 14, Anne's consent would have been asked for, but it was a mere formality. Anne would have been aware that this alliance was quite possibly her family's only chance of salvation – a responsibility that surely weighed upon her. There were personal advantages to contemplate for Anne as well: the prospect of her own royal household, of riches and jewels, and perhaps the idea that she would now take precedence over all her family was also attractive. For the past few years, she had been sidelined as Isobel and Clarence took centre stage; now it was her turn.

Anne and Edward were betrothed, likely by proxy, at Angers Cathedral on or around 25 July 1470. Beneath its stunning windows, Anne's father and Edward's mother swore on a fragment of the true cross to be faithful allies. The marriage, however, was conditional on Warwick holding up his end of the bargain; betrothals, after all, could (and had) been broken before.[14]

On 31 July, Anne set off towards Amboise in the company of Edward and Margaret of Anjou, where Warwick believed that the marriage would be celebrated under the watchful eye of King Louis. What Anne felt, we do not know, but she must have been grateful that her mother still accompanied her, though it is unclear whether or not Isobel was with them. This is indicative of the status in which Anne was now regarded. Up to this point, she had been the obscured second daughter; now it is Isobel who slips out of view. She was not forgotten entirely, however, and Warwick negotiated that Clarence should become Duke of York and heir to the throne should Edward and Anne fail to have children. Despite this, there was a gulf opening between Clarence and his father-in-law. In an attempt to exploit this, Edward IV, expecting an invasion any day, sent a lady as a messenger to France to speak with his brother. This messenger 'won over the Duke of Clarence who promised to join his brother the king as soon as he came back to England'.[15] The truth of this is unclear but the discord between Warwick and Clarence must surely have been a source of worry and pain between the sisters.

Anne might have confidently expected her marriage but there appears to have been a hitch. Edward and Anne were related by blood, distantly in the fourth degree, both being great-great-grandchildren of John of Gaunt, but this still required a papal dispensation and, as many a monarch would later find, papal dispensations took time. Louis sent one of his men, Matthew Fontenailles, to the papal ambassadors in France to secure the necessary paperwork.[16] While this was taking place it was determined that Anne would remain in the care of Margaret of Anjou and that her marriage would not be consummated until the dispensation had been obtained. In the end, three dispensations were issued to cover every eventuality. Anne now began her life in Margaret's care. Despite later accusations of cruelty, there is no evidence that Margaret of Anjou was ever anything other than kind to Anne. There was, after all, nothing to be lost and everything to be gained by being a welcoming mother-in-law. Anne was to be the broodmare of the new Lancastrian dynasty, and maintaining her welfare was necessary to ensure this. Perhaps in her dealing with Anne, Margaret also remembered her own marriage, where she had been betrothed at 14 – the same age that Anne was now – and sent to a foreign land to be married to a stranger.

For Anne, Margaret, whom she had only known as her enemy, must have been a formidable figure, but necessity makes for strange bedfellows and all the women seem to have determined to make the best of it. Initially, Anne and the exiled Lancastrian court stayed at Razilly Castle rather than Amboise, where they had expected to be. On 29 September, Louis sent some medicinal herbs to Razilly, suggesting that either Edward or Anne were sick.[17] Louis, meanwhile, continued to apply pressure for the dispensation, including writing to the Bishop of Beauvais to find out whether or not he could authorise the marriage between Anne and Edward himself. The response was no. It is clear, though, that Anne was already being treated as if she were in fact Edward's wife, and from August to October 1470, she was given financial provision in keeping with her position 'as wife of said prince'. It was in October that the dispensation finally arrived, but it was problematic because it authorised the marriage of Edward of England, layman of London, to Anne de Warwick, damsel of Salisbury – but Edward had been in exile for years and Anne never lived in Salisbury.[18] It was back to Rome and it was not until 28 November that the vicar of Bayeux finally issued the correct dispensation. The delay had the advantage of allowing Anne and Edward to get to know each other. They were together at Amboise and we know that they were permitted to be in each other's company, with a chaperone, of course. Perhaps they walked the beautiful gardens together or played cards to pass the time. Did this period of courting breed affection between them? We simply do not know. What we do know is that news from England came regularly and that Anne's father appeared to be holding up his end of the bargain, to everyone's apparent satisfaction. As reports of Warwick's favourable actions reached France, Louis clearly felt that the Lancastrian chances of success were increasing and accordingly, he began to spend more money on Anne's accommodation and entertainment. In November and December, an enormous 3,830 pounds was spent on the Lancastrian court.[19]

Despite everything, Anne must have been relieved to end all uncertainty and finally marry Edward, on 13 December 1470 at Amboise.[20] Warwick was not present, nor was the groom's father, but Margaret was, as were Anne's mother and Isobel. After their marriage, Anne and Edward went to bed in order that their union be properly consummated. Anne could have had few illusions about the reality of the marriage bed by that point, and perhaps she feared pregnancy, given Isobel's ordeal, but it was nevertheless her duty. The primary purpose of her marriage was for the procreation of children, specifically, to provide a male heir for the House of Lancaster.

While Anne was in France, Warwick had sailed for England. On 9 September, he sailed along with Clarence, Jasper Tudor and the Earl of Oxford. They landed in the West Country four days later and they issued a proclamation declaring that they invaded on behalf of the true king, Henry VI, and that Edward IV was a 'usurper, oppressor and destroyer'. As they marched eastwards, they were joined by 'a great number of men', including the Earl of Shrewsbury and Lord Stanley. Margaret of Anjou had feared that her alliance with Warwick would have cost her their support but her fears proved to be unfounded. Edward IV, meanwhile, was in the north, having been lured there once again by a rebellion orchestrated by Warwick. Edward hurried south when he heard of Warwick's arrival, but at Doncaster, he learnt that Warwick's brother, Montagu, had betrayed him (yet again) and intended to support his brother.[21] London mounted its defences, but ultimately dissolved into chaos, and Elizabeth Woodville was frightened enough to leave the royal apartments in the Tower with her children and flee into sanctuary at Westminster. She was right to; her husband, faced with the defection of Montagu and other supporters, had little choice but to flee to King's Lynn, where he took a ship to Holland, along with his loyal brother, Richard, Duke of Gloucester.

On 3 October, Henry VI was released by William Waynflete and the Constable of the Tower, and he was moved into the royal rooms recently occupied by Elizabeth Woodville and her family. Three days later, Warwick was in London and he immediately went to pay homage to Henry VI, who was 'entirely conciliatory'.[22] Warwick went on to parade Henry VI through the streets of London in a blue gown. Warwick carried the king's train, and the ever-loyal Earl of Oxford his sword of estate. The party rested that night at the Bishop of London's residence. Anne's father now acted quickly and decisively, perhaps having learnt from the consequences of past hesitations. He summoned a parliament in the king's name on 15 October and restored his brother as chancellor. According to the *Chronicle of London*, the papers of this parliament do not survive, but Edward IV was declared a traitor and Warwick was made the king's Lieutenant of England. In addition, Warwick was made Captain of Calais once again.

It was clear to all, however, that Henry VI was not himself capable of ruling, although he was ostensibly king. With Warwick firmly ensconced in power, and Margaret in France, it was now imperative that Edward, Prince of Wales, be in England to act in his father's interests, and perhaps as regent against Warwick should their alliance fail. They did not, however, leave as soon as some expected and the ambassador Bettini records that the 'Queen of England and the Countess of Warwick with their children [are still in France] as it appears that the king [Louis] will detain them until a reply has come from his ambassadors who have gone to England'.

This delay can be explained by the fact that Louis desired Warwick's reassurance that he could support Louis in declaring war against Burgundy but it must have been very frustrating for Margaret left back in France. For Anne, however, the delay had little consequence; she was where she was supposed to be – at her husband's side. On 15 December, two days after her wedding, we know that Anne, now styled as Princess of Wales, left Amboise for Paris, where Louis had laid on a lavish reception for them. She rode through the streets, which were hung with tapestries, and was entertained by music and song. They stayed at the royal residence, the only place now suitable, as Louis had already proclaimed Henry VI's restoration throughout France on 19 October.[23]

Before they left, Margaret and Prince Edward formally agreed that they would support Louis in his war against Burgundy and on 13 February, Warwick stated that he would personally lead the troops. Three days later, the Anglo–French truce was announced in the parliament and John Langstrother was sent to escort Edward and Anne, alongside Margaret, back to England. They took with them Louis' many presents of wine and money.[24] It was not, however, until 24 March 1471 that the party finally arrived at Harfleur, where for seventeen days the winds remained stubbornly uncooperative, meaning that Anne, who could have had no fond memories of her last sea voyage, had to wait around in nervous anticipation. In a document written by John Fortescue, who was Queen Margaret's chancellor and had shared her exile, it is clear that Margaret was envisaging upon their return to England a royal council governing England, ruled over by Prince Edward as his father's lieutenant or as Protector of the Realm, but as we have seen, Warwick had already firmly taken charge. The role Fortescue played in Margaret's life is interesting as not only would he have got to know Anne, his relationship with Margaret would also have given Anne a glimpse into the sort of working relationship that a queen could forge with a well-qualified advisor. While in exile he had written his *De laudibus legum Angliae*, commendation of the laws of England, which was not published until 1543 but was widely discussed in Margaret's circle. It mused on such lofty ideals as goodness and justice, and famously declared, 'one would rather, much rather, that twenty guilty persons escape the punishment of death, than that one innocent person be condemned, and suffer capitally.' Perhaps Anne imbibed such views, when she heard them debated. They were eminently compatible with the sort of religious teachings with which we know she was familiar.

Clarence, meanwhile, had taken up residence at L'Erber House in London. He did not really have a role in the new government and instead he was left to rot, and to plot. We know that during this time both Cecily Neville and his sister, as well as the Duchess of Exeter, contacted him and tried to win him back to the Yorkist side.

> By right covert ways and means were good mediators ... the high and mighty princess my lady their mother, my Lady of Exeter, my Lady of Suffolk, their sisters, my Lord Cardinal of Canterbury, my Lord of Bath, my Lord of Essex and by mediations of certain priests and other well disposed persons.[25]

It was something to which he was growing increasingly receptive, no doubt hammered home by the fact that the lives of his brothers and sisters would have been effectively over if Henry VI remained on the throne.

Margaret likely had spent the time between December and March schooling Anne in the part she was to play in her vision of England's future. As Princess of Wales, Anne would have been stepping into the shoes of the last woman to bear the title, Joan of Kent. Joan was said to have been 'the most beautiful woman in the realm of England'.[26] In the medieval period, how one looked was thought to be reflective of a person's inner soul, and physical disfigurements were considered to be symptoms of impiety or an evil mind. Anne would have been well aware of the need to appear at all times every inch the virtuous and pious princess and she would have dressed accordingly.

As well as appearing virtuous, a Princess of Wales had to also *be* virtuous; her behaviour had to be above reproach. Joan seems to have fulfilled this role magnificently and is described as being 'pious, loving and faithful'. No hint of scandal could attach itself to a princess. Scandal was not something that Anne could avoid but we know that her father's government took great pains to attempt to legalise their actions in order to minimise any legal consequences for Edward and Anne. There was, however, little they could do about the reality of Warwick's widely perceived duplicity.

Privately, it was a princess's role to keep out of politics and to create close and harmonious relationships with her husband's family. Again, Joan excelled at this; so much so that when it became clear that the Black Prince, her husband, was dying, there was no hint of removing her son from her care because she was 'held in such a position of respect and trust'.[27] But for all her virtue, Joan was not passive. Letters exist in which she clearly was forging the political connections that she could need, and she created her own power base. Anne also had the example of many powerful women around her – Cecily Neville, Anne of Exeter and her own mother, to name but a few – who, as we have seen, were far from impotent, and plotted and schemed to influence their menfolk, operating within their own sphere and frustratingly, largely hidden from view.[28] There is no evidence that Anne did anything but follow their example.

Sometime before her departure for England, Anne had lost the company of her sister as Isobel journeyed on ahead to join her husband. Isobel certainly cannot have been ignorant by now of Clarence's fluctuating feelings. We know she was with her husband at this time and probably was a witness to the visit of his mother and sisters. Did he confide in his wife? It seems unlikely. Did she have an inkling of what her husband was thinking? We simply cannot know, but we do know that she does not appear to have sent any warning to Anne or to anyone else.

While Anne was awaiting a favourable wind in Harfleur, Edward IV landed on the Yorkshire coast, alongside his brother, Richard of Gloucester. If Isobel did not already believe the situation to be deadly serious, she was now proven very much mistaken. Clarence had by now been entirely won back into the Yorkist family fold but he still had hopes of persuading Anne's father to join him. Wavrin records:

> The Duke of Clarence being right desirous to have procured a good accord between the King and the Earl of Warwick, not only for the Earl but also for to reconcile thereby into the king's good grace many Lords and noble men of his land of whom many had largely taken part with the Earl. He made therefore his motions as well to the King as to the Earl by messages sending to and for both for the well above said as to acquit him truly and kindly in the love he bears unto him and his blood where unto he was allied by marriage to his daughter.[29]

Edward might have been open to reaching such an accord and he offered Anne's father forgiveness, but Warwick remained implacable. It seems likely that Anne was his primary concern in doing this; she was Princess of Wales – the living embodiment of all his ambitions – and more to the point, she and her mother were still in France with Margaret of Anjou. Should Warwick turn his coat yet again, they would be considered hostages. Clarence's physical betrayal of Anne's father occurred when he was, in theory, en route to join Warwick with his men, when he persuaded Edward to make one more offer of forgiveness to Warwick – an offer that was rebuffed.

Meanwhile, we know that in Harfleur, Anne finally, after seventeen days of contrary winds, set sail for England. She sailed separately to her mother but alongside her husband.[30] The Countess of Warwick ended up landing at Portsmouth, whilst Anne landed at Weymouth, on 13 April. This separation is symbolic of Anne's new role; her place was now at her husband's side, not her mother's. Although Anne did not know it, the events of the day after she landed perhaps determined her fate. They certainly rewrote England's future.

Chapter 8

Wife of Lancaster

> they breathe truth that breathe their words in pain.
> *Richard II*, William Shakespeare

The next day was Easter Sunday, 14 April 1471, and it dawned cool, damp and crucially, foggy. Warwick, we know, had been personally gathering as much support as he was able. In a letter to Henry Vernon, in which he entreated him to support his Lancastrian cause, he added a postscript in his own hand.[1] Edward IV was marching south, towards Warwick, who was at Leicester, where his forces numbered about 6,000 men, but he apparently hoped to gather more support before battle was drawn and so he retreated to Coventry. Edward, meanwhile, marched on London, which was still apparently loyal to Warwick, and in an effort to attract more support, Henry VI was paraded through the streets – a plan that failed spectacularly and the city instead opened its gates to the forces of Edward. Edward gave thanks for this at Westminster Abbey, freed his wife and children from sanctuary, and took Henry VI into custody once more.[2] In the meantime, Warwick had raised more men and now marched south to confront his king. With a force now numbering 15,000 men, he took up position just north of Barnet on 13 April. Edward arrived later that day, with a slightly smaller force of 10,000–12,000 men. It was dark by the time he arrived but he chose to deploy them anyway, very close to Warwick's lines. There has been considerable debate as to whether or not Edward chose to deploy so close to his rival by accident or deliberately, but given that we know he issued an order that silence was to be maintained and no fires lit, suggests he knew exactly what he was doing. By this time, Edward IV was, after all, a very experienced soldier and he had the foresight also to bring with him Henry VI, no doubt hoping he could use him as a bargaining chip should the day go ill. Deploying so close to the position of Warwick's men worked and when the Lancastrians formed up the next day and loosed a violent artillery volley, their shots flew over the heads of the Yorkists, completely missing their intended targets. Historian Phillip Haig suggests that the Yorkists did not return fire at this point so that their precise location would remain unclear.[3]

Battle was quickly joined on the morning of 14 April and opened with volleys of arrows and cannon fire. The fog was very thick and the Lancastrian Earl of Oxford, de Vere, was able to overwhelm Lord Hastings' Yorkist flank very quickly. Oxford's men would have given chase to the fleeing Lancastrians but he rallied them and swung them back into the fight. The weather conditions, however, meant that neither Warwick nor Edward had actually been able to see what was happening, and Oxford's victory was not capitalised upon nor did it disadvantage the Yorksists. In the middle, Anne's uncle, Montagu, was giving a fierce fight against the centre of the king's forces. Edward's brother, Gloucester, however, was able to beat back Exeter's men, something Warwick noticed, and he immediately sent reinforcements.

Oxford, meanwhile, had swung back to rejoin the battle but when he arrived at the back of Montagu's forces, his badge, the star with rays, was mistaken for the king's Sun in splendour, and Montague's men launched a ferocious volley of arrows straight at them. *Warkworth's Chronicle* explains, 'But it happened so, that the Earl of Oxford's men had upon them their lord's livery, both before and behind, which was a star with streams, which [was] much like King Edward's livery, the sun with streams.' Oxford's forces shouted treachery – after all, Montague was not the most reliable of Lancastrian bedfellows – and the cry of traitor was taken up by the Lancastrian ranks. Panic quickly spread and men broke their line in anger and confusion. With the fog having lifted by now high enough for Edward to be able to see what had happened, he called his reserves into the action to weaken yet further the Lancastrian line. Anne's father and uncle had decided to fight on foot so as to bolster the morale of their men. This was not unusual in an age when it was often a decided tactical advantage to be able to see for yourself what was happening in the front line of battle. It was at this point that the *Arrivall* chronicle tells us that Anne's uncle was killed 'in plain battle'.[4] *Warkworth's Chronicle* implies that he had in fact tried to change sides and was slain by one of his brother's men when he put on Yorkist livery but as this is the only source that mentions this, it seems unlikely, and Sir John Paston, a Lancastrian ally fighting in the retinue of Oxford, praises his conduct and bravery.[5] With his brother dead, Warwick realised that the day was lost. *Warkworth's Chronicle* tells us that upon hearing of his brother's death, Warwick tried to flee. *Holinshed's Chronicle*, however, states that Warwick had been killed before Montagu, who had been trying to come to his aid. Whatever the exact circumstances of his death, we know that Warwick was dead by the time Edward IV arrived at the scene, perhaps having intended to try to prevent the slaughter of his one-time friend and ally, or perhaps hoping to do the deed himself. Warwick's body was stripped of its armour and laid out on the bloodied grass. As for his allies, Exeter was left bleeding on the battlefield for nine hours before he was dragged into sanctuary. Oxford managed to escape.[6]

Anne's father was dead, though she did not yet know it. Indeed, word had initially reached London of a Warwick victory, when the men who fled Oxford had arrived. This mistake was quickly corrected when Edward marched victoriously back into his capital immediately after the battle. He placed the banner of Warwick upon the altar of St Paul's. A day later, it was joined by the bodies of Warwick and Montague, which were placed upon the pavement of the cathedral in order that everyone could come to see that they were dead as 'fained seditious tales' were already circulating that they had escaped the field with their lives.[7] Edward did not rejoice at the brothers' deaths, although Grafton says this was for Montague's sake and not Warwick's. Both men's bodies were spared the fate of being quartered and their head mounted on Tower Bridge. Instead, they were packed off for quick, if honourable, burial at Bisham Priory.[8]

News of her husband's death reached Anne's mother when she was still at Southampton and she chose not to join her younger daughter at Weymouth. Instead, she travelled quickly to Beaulieu Abbey, which belonged to the Cistercian order, and claimed sanctuary. She seems to have feared that she had been, in the words of Michael Hicks, 'too deeply impacted in her husband's plots that she might herself suffer an attainder for treason as Warwick's mother had in 1459'.[9] The Latin name for Beaulieu is *Bellus Locus Regis*, meaning the beautiful place of the king, and it had been founded by King John as penance after he quarrelled with the Cistercian order. As a royal foundation, it was richly endowed and it seems likely that Anne Beauchamp was accommodated in one of the many guesthouses that surrounded the church and monastic establishment. Beaulieu was an extremely safe place to flee to as it had been decreed an Exempt Abbey, which answered to the Pope alone. It also bore special privileges of sanctuary, which covered an area of nearly 24 hectares. Its sanctuary rights were therefore the largest and most strictly enforced for miles around. Had she not fled to sanctuary, Edward would likely have forced her ensconcement in a nunnery, but he would not allow any harm to come to her once there. After all, his own wife and children had relied more than once on the protection that religious sanctuary offered them to preserve their lives. He ordered that she be kept safe or risk his displeasure: For now, at least, Anne's mother, though grieving, was physically safe.

The same cannot be said for Anne, and she perhaps now felt abandoned by her mother. She would not have the support and physical presence of the countess as she faced what was to come. We must not forget that Anne was still only 14 years old. This period appears to mark the end of Anne's physical and emotional closeness to her mother and she would later hesitate to act in her mother's interests, perhaps bearing her continued resentment.

News of Warwick's defeat at Barnet reached the Lancastrian camp very quickly, but it seems likely that initially, Anne still held out hope of her father's survival. Nothing was certain and rumours were flying about, with the Milanese ambassador reporting that Warwick had been only severely wounded and that he 'had withdrawn to a secret and solitary place to get well of his wounds sickness'.[10] Soon, though, the truth became clear, and both Anne and Margaret were 'right heavy with sorrow'. Margaret, one report states, actually 'swooned for fear … distright, dismayed and tormented with sorrow', indicating that perhaps she had grown to hold Warwick in real affection, or far more likely that she realised what a blow his death was to their cause. Anne was pale and wan with grief, and filled with worry for the future. Unlike her mother, however, she had no chance here to decide what action to take; her fate was bound to that of her husband. There were some in the Lancastrian camp who now felt that their position might in fact be stronger without the presence of the Warwick brothers to confuse the issue and potentially switch sides yet again. Surely, such feelings reached Anne's ears and they must have alarmed her; she was the living embodiment of her father's legacy. Whatever her private feelings, her place was at Prince Edward's side. It was there she remained, and if Margaret was temporarily overcome by grief, she soon rallied, buoyed by the renewed enthusiasm of Somerset and Devon, who were happier to fight for her now that Warwick was dead.[11]

We know that after landing at Weymouth, Anne accompanied her husband and mother-in-law to Cerne Abbey.[12] Physically, it was a fairly easy journey, on good roads, of just over 15 miles. At Cerne, Anne would have found sanctuary and peaceful gardens, noted for their beauty. The south gate and guesthouse, which still stand today, are buildings that Anne would have recognised, with their large windows, fireplaces and spacious accommodation. Records indicate that she stayed in the guesthouse along with her husband and Margaret.[13] The abbey had been founded in 987 by Æthelmær, a leading thane under Æthelred the Unready, and it dominated the landscape. It seems likely that John Morton, the Lancastrian Bishop of Ely, who had accompanied Margaret on her French exile and who had been educated at Cerne, suggested to Margaret that this would be an ideal location to set up the Lancastrian base. Anne would surely have prayed for her father's soul but there was little else she could practically do except watch as surviving Lancastrians made their way to join them at Cerne. Amongst them were the Duke of Somerset, Edmund Beaufort, Devon, Dorset and Exeter. Some were one-time allies of her father; others, such as Edmund Beaufort, his implacable enemies. Men like Beaufort had no desire to see Warwick's daughter prosper through her marriage to Henry VI's son and it seems unlikely that they welcomed her presence. Anne was well and truly alone amongst her enemies. These men, alongside Margaret, now sought to mobilise support in the West Country. Without Warwick, Zannotus Spinula claims, the queen's 'prospects were [more] favourable..because she [now] ought to have many lords in her favour who intended to resist her because they were enemies of Warwick, Northumberland amongst others'.[14] The absent Clarence, now firmly back on Edward's side, was likewise not much lamented.

From Cerne Abbey, Anne travelled with the Lancastrians to Exeter, to raise troops, and then north towards Bath, but the Lancastrians were still outnumbered and knew that they had to try to meet up with the forces being raised by Jasper Tudor in Wales before any decisive battle could be joined. King Edward, meanwhile, was following their movements with interest and now determined that he must take on Margaret's forces before they could join with those of Tudor. There followed, according to the Yorkist annals, a period in which both sides sought to outmanoeuvre the other, culminating in a desperate flight north. The *Arrivall* specifically mentions that the Lancastrian women were seen on horseback riding at breakneck speed. Anne rode at the side of Margaret of Anjou, tearing through the countryside.[15] Her hair no doubt worked its way loose and sweat would have made her clothing cling to her skin. It was a ride of 36 miles and must have been utterly exhausting, even for a teenager who had been in the saddle regularly since infancy. Yorkists blocked the route across the river Severn and into Wales, and so the party headed towards Tewkesbury. Anne was familiar with the lands through which they were now riding and perhaps it was she who suggested that they lodge in her family's nearby manor house at Gobes Hall, which had been built in 1438 and was a handsome timber building. According to tradition, it would be here that Anne spent the night before the battle. Anne was very familiar with Tewkesbury; her grandmother was buried there alongside her De Clare and Despenser forebears. Her mother was also a foundress of the abbey and perhaps she had a desire to stand on familiar ground.[16] Given that Prince Edward took leave of his mother very early on the following morning, it seems likely that she lodged there with the young couple. They were joined by other wives of the Lancastrian party such as the Countess of Devon.

Battle was now inevitable and Anne bid farewell to her 17-year-old husband on the morning of 4 May. Her personal feelings can only be guessed at; there is nothing to suggest whether she did or did not have affection for Edward, but that was simply an aside to the political work that needed to be done that day. Anne had seen her mother watch her father go to battle often, and experienced this terrifying wait too many times before for it to have been completely unfamiliar. Inside the rooms, the atmosphere must have been thick with tension and utterly claustrophobic as the anxious women's servants packed up any possessions they had used overnight. Perhaps the Lancastrian women prayed together. By nightfall, Anne would know if she was the wife of the unchallenged Prince of Wales or once again a traitor by association.

At a distance from the fighting, Anne and Margaret could not have seen the Lancastrian lines taking up a defensive position to the south of the town. The Lancastrian forces were split into three formations, as was common at the time. The right flank was commanded by the Duke of Somerset, the centre by Lord Wenlock, and the left by the Earl of Devon. Anne's husband took up position in the centre; his presence was considered essential for Lancastrian morale but he had little actual battle experience and so was not in command.[17] Arrayed against him and commanding the Yorkist vanguard was Richard, Duke of Gloucester, whilst King Edward took command in the centre, where Clarence was also placed, and Lord Hastings commanded the rear. Traditionally, the vanguard was placed upon the right, but it seems that Gloucester was actually fighting on the left at Tewkesbury. Perhaps this was because there was a wooded area to the left of Edward's army and fearing that this could be used to conceal in part, although the king also sent 200 mounted spearmen into the woods to defend them. With the battle lines drawn, Edward then 'displayed his banners, did blow upon the trumpets, committed his cause and called to Almighty God to our own blessed mother the Virgin Mary the glorious Saint George and all the saints and [then] advanced directly upon his enemies'.[18]

The two sides exchanged arrows and artillery fire in the smoke. Somerset determined that he could travel down 'evil lanes' and outflank Edward on his left side. Edward's men resisted and the 200 spearmen that he had previously positioned in the woods now stepped forward to trap Somerset, and Gloucester quickly entered the fray to support them. Somerset's men were routed and as they tried to flee, they were cut down in the field that leads to the river Severn – a field that today is still known as the Bloody Meadow. Somerset fled to the abbey in search of sanctuary. The Lancastrian forces collapsed and many of their nobles were killed in the fighting, including John Beaufort (Dorset) and the Earl of Devon, whose wife was with Anne.[19]

There are conflicting reports as to how Anne's teenage husband died. The *Arrivall* tells us that he 'was taken fleeing to the town and slain in the field', which agrees with the Tewkesbury and Warkworth chronicles, which also say that he was 'slain on the field'. Soon, however, a much darker tale was circulating. *Hall's Chronicle* states that Prince Edward was dragged still alive from the battlefield and when he was before the king, he was killed by the king's brothers, Clarence and Gloucester. Shakespeare, of course, will later put into Anne's mouth the words that Queen Margaret saw Gloucester standing in a 'murderous fashion, smoking in his [Prince Edward's] blood'.[20] This would make Anne's second husband the murderer of her first. Although this idea has long been considered, Tudor propaganda historian Michael Hicks points out that there is a contemporary French account that does show and describe Prince Edward being struck down before the king and he believes that 'Hall's account may [therefore] be authentic', describing this image of Anne's first husband standing still defiant before Edward IV as fitting one of a 'spirited, arrogant, fearless adolescent'.[21] Ironically, this is an image reminiscent of Anne's 'spirited and arrogant' father. Perhaps she had found something familiar and admirable in her husband.

> Here lies Edward, Prince of Wales,
> Cruelly slain while a youth
> Anno Domini 1471
> Alas the savagery of men
> Thou art the sole light of they mother
> The last hope of thy race.[22]

Chapter 9

The Prince's Widow

His soul thou canst have; therefore be gone!
Richard III, William Shakespeare

While battle raged, Anne and Margaret withdrew 'early that Saturday morning for the surety of her person to some poor religious places on the Worcester road'. Historian Alison Weir suggests that they travelled to Paynes Place when news of the Lancastrian defeat began to filter through and that they were sheltered there by some loyal supporters.[1] On their way there it is said that Margaret fainted and had to be carried into a litter by her ladies, of whom Anne would certainly have been one. Others accompanying them included the Countess of Exeter and Katherine Vaux.[2] Back in Tewkesbury, those Lancastrian Lords, including Somerset, who had sought sanctuary inside the abbey, were dragged out. Some were killed immediately, others were executed on 6 May, Somerset meeting his fate in Tewkesbury marketplace. With him died the direct male Beaufort line and promoted a girl by the name of Margaret Beaufort to the last surviving direct Beaufort descendant.[3] This time, no quarter would be given and barely a nobleman of Lancastrian blood was allowed to live after Tewkesbury, although Edward pardoned all the common soldiers.[4]

It is not known exactly where Anne was when news reached them of the Lancastrian defeat and her husband's death, but the sheer horror with which it was greeted surely cannot be overstated. They fled to Birtsmorton Court, a fortified medieval manor house near Malvern, in Worcestershire, where Margaret and presumably Anne were housed in a fine chamber. However, evidently fearing that Edward was closing in, they removed to Little Malvern Priory.[5] It has been suggested that Anne and Margaret had travelled to Evesham Abbey instead and the abbey chronicle there does record that the ladies were there but the exact chronology remains unclear. The *Arrivall* records that it was at Evesham that Margaret and Anne were found and that the 'Lady Anne Princess' and Margaret were taken from there and were to be presented to the king.[6] The fact the *Arrivall* states that they were taken somewhere raises the possibility that they were taken to Tewkesbury, perhaps deliberately, to witness the horrific reality of their total defeat. If so, they could not have avoided seeing the quartered remains of their family and their allies.[7] The full effect that such a sight might have had on Anne is hard to comprehend but at the very least, it would have brought home the danger that she was now in. The idea that Anne saw her husband's body at Tewkesbury cannot be entirely discounted either, although she could not have attended any service for him because the church had been deconsecrated by the violence it witnessed, when Edward and his men dragged Lancastrians out of sanctuary. Edward did, however, grant Anne's husband a dignified burial. His body was 'placed in the midst of the convent choir', where it remains.

Anne and Margaret now travelled to Coventry, where they submitted to the king, who then pardoned them alongside the Countess of Devon and Katherine Vaux.[8] Alison Weir suggests that when Margaret saw King Edward, she 'screamed abuse and curses at him', but whether or not Anne shared her mother-in-law's sentiments, she could not voice them.[9] Hers was now a fight for survival and to survive, she could not ally herself with the defeated Lancastrian cause. One thing that must be considered is that Anne might have been with child at this time; historian J.L. Laynesmith suggests that she was. However, the fact that Edward pardoned her indicates that he considered her no threat, which suggests that he assumed that she was not pregnant. Likewise, the later murder of Henry VI would have been pointless if Anne were carrying the legitimate Lancastrian heir.

In her mind, she was likely now dowager Princess of Wales, but England was now Yorkist, and there were no Lancastrian champions left alive to take up the cause. Prince Edward, it had been declared, had had no claim to either Wales or the crown. Since he had never been in possession of either, he had no lands for Edward IV to confiscate or widow's portion to deprive of Anne. She was nevertheless now entitled to half of her inherited lands – the great Montagu and Salisbury inheritance. Theoretically, as a widow she had the right to manage her own affairs but in practice, her ability to act was severely restricted. There was no one to champion her, or indeed to help her, as even her own mother was unable to assert her own legal rights at this time.[11]

Whether or not she harboured ideas of independence or of managing her own affairs, Anne was now placed by the king in the custody of her brother-in-law, Clarence, and her sister, Isobel.[12] The alternative was that she be placed in the care of her mother, but this would have isolated her completely from society and the court – something that at just 15 years of age, she is unlikely to have wanted.

There is a suggestion that Clarence took Anne into his protection at Tewkesbury but this is not certain. Clarence, however, did not have the wardship of Anne, something that would have entitled him to arrange her marriage and to manage her affairs. She was a widow and of age; there was no legal way for this to be the case, so it was in the eyes of the law, at least, an informal arrangement. At around this time, Anne would have been reunited with Isobel, but there is reason to doubt how cordial their relationship now was. Clarence's betrayal had, after all, led to the deaths of Anne's father and husband. Anne would have had to have been made of stone not to have struggled with the reality of that, however grateful she might be at that time for Clarence's protection. Isobel's feelings at this time would have been equally complex.

Meanwhile, Margaret of Anjou was taken to London, where she was paraded through the streets, twenty-six years after she had first entered the gates of the city, before being taken to the Tower, where Henry VI was being held, though they were most likely imprisoned separately.[13] Henry met his end there on 20 May. Traditionally it is said that he was killed by a blow to the head while he was at prayer. This murder would have been utterly pointless if Anne was indeed pregnant with a Lancastrian heir.[14] The circumstances of Henry VI's death have long been debated. The *Arrivall*, which presents the official Yorkist view, maintains that he 'had been overcome with melancholy after learning of recent events' and died.[15] The *Crowland Chronicle*, meanwhile, made it clear that Edward had had Henry VI put to death.[16] In relation to Anne's story, the most crucial account comes down to us in *Warkworth's Chronicle*, which as historian Laura Johnston states, was 'written no later than 1484 ... and completed early in the reign of Richard III'.[17] It tells us that Richard, Duke of Gloucester, was present at the Tower on the night Henry VI met his end. Other men were there too, but it is plausible though not certain that the act was carried out by Richard himself as Constable of England, on his brother Edward's orders.[18] Henry VI's body was embalmed before being displayed through the streets of London before being laid on the pavement of St Paul's.

Where exactly Anne was for the next eight months cannot be proven with certainty, but most likely, she was simply absorbed into Clarence's household and accompanied her sister in society and at court. Clarence and Isobel spent a good deal of this time at Coldharbour, their London house. The 1543 Wyngaerde 'Panorama of London' shows Coldharbour House to have been a sizable dwelling with a garden between it and the riverbank. It was situated near to L'Erber House in the parish of All-Hallows-the-Less or All-Hallows-in-the-Hay, named after the adjoining wharf. It was an area and possibly a house that was familiar to Anne. The house had been built sometime in the thirteenth century and by 1319, it was already known as 'Coldherghe', when a draper named Henry de Tower paid a rent of 33*s* 4*d* to Robert de Hereford. From 1370 to 1377, it had been the home of Alice Perrers, the mistress of Edward III, and she added to it a structure known only as le Toure, the exact nature of which is unclear. Henry IV met with ambassadors from Burgundy there in 1412; it later came into the possession of Henry V and it is likely that he spent a good deal of time there. It had numerous royal connections and Henry IV's sister, Elizabeth, died there in November 1426.[19] There is also the intriguing possibility that some right of sanctuary was granted to the manor house, with Sir Robert Cecil later calling it a privileged place, when he was unable to search it without legal difficulty.[20]

When the manor was later refurbished, and granted to Margaret Beaufort in 1485, extensive records were left, from which we can deduce that there were a lot of windows, which in 1485 needed replacing. There were many secure rooms, given that a large number of locks were removed and went missing. Numerous walls were also recoloured red, suggesting that they had been red ten years earlier, during Anne's stay there, but had to be repainted as they had faded. There were forty rooms in total and a great hall with an adjoining little hall, which possibly was a private dining room. The hall led to a garden where, much in the manner of Hampton Court today, a great vine grew, a sight that must have been familiar to Anne. It also had as many as twenty chimneys, suggesting a large number of heated rooms. What emerges therefore from the records is the definite impression that Coldharbour was a splendid and lavish manor house and one that was virtually impregnable. There is a record in the *Crowland Chronicle* that Anne was kept there concealed as a maid by her brother-in-law and forced to work in the kitchens. However, this seems extremely unlikely, not least because women would rarely have been employed in the kitchen of great houses at the time. It seems a later invention to set up Richard of Gloucester as the knight errant who saved Cinderella from domestic drudgery. It is much more likely that Anne spent her time with her sister. Thanks to a number of records that survive regarding the set-up of the Clarence household at Waltham Abbey, where Clarence and Isobel had lived eighteen months earlier, we know that Isobel had six personal ladies who attended her and who in turn each had their own servants. She also, as was usual, headed a smaller version of her husband's household whereby she had a treasurer, chamberer, almoner, chaplain, yeoman, servers, and other necessary staff. She also had extensive modes of travel, which included carriages, palfreys, litters and chariots, one of which must have brought Anne to Coldharbour.[21]

The household was well ordered, and Isobel, like her mother before her, had a good deal of authority over her own domain. We know that in summer the household dined at 10 am and 5 pm, with the household gates being opened between 5 am and 10 pm, and in winter, at 9 am and 4 pm, with the gates open from 7 am until 9 pm, and that a great range of food including meats was served. At Waltham Abbey, they had spent an enormous sum on running their household. Historian Amy Licence estimated that their household in 1469 consumed:

> 650 quarters if what, 41 tonnes of whine and 365 tonnes of ale, 2700 sheep, 420 pigs, 2 barrels of honey … pepper saffron, ginger, calves, mace, cinnamon, dates, liquorice, sugar, raisins, currants figs and rice … as well as salt.[23]

All in all, this would have been a return for Anne to the pattern of her younger years; the routine of the Clarence household was markedly similar to that which had governed Middleham. Anne's position now, though, was very different, and there were those who had their eyes on her inheritance – not least of whom was Clarence himself. It may be that Clarence and Isobel now suggested that Anne should retire to a nunnery, which certainly would have been the ideal outcome for them, but as we have already seen, neither they nor the king could legally force her to undertake such a course, even if they had wished to. There is no evidence that Anne ever seriously considered it. Given this, there was only one realistic option open to Anne: that she would remarry. Anne would have known this and considering the speed with which she was later to act, it seems she actually sought it. Clarence, however, vehemently opposed this and whilst Anne was not kept locked in the kitchen, there is the suggestion that the very secure Coldharbour had been chosen to house her because access to it could be tightly controlled, and indeed, we know it was. Something definitely happened to Anne, although where 'Clarence caused her to be concealed' is open to debate, and Crowland claims that she was found in the clothing of a maid. Porters manned the gates and any man found smuggling out goods or breaking locks or windows would lose his wages and probably his position. We cannot be certain of the pressures that Clarence and Isobel brought to bear on Anne. Did they cajole, reason with or try to bribe her? That Anne would grasp the first chance she had to escape the household of her sister suggests that she was unhappy and not willing to continue as she had been. This was a clear indication of her desire at least to manage her own affairs and this time perhaps even to have a real say in her future.

At some point during the year, it became apparent that Richard, Duke of Gloucester, wished to marry Anne. Shakespeare has Anne react 'with curses in her mouth and tears in her eyes', but this seems to be nothing but dramatics.[23] The real Anne, it seems, was far less emotional and far more practical. In the manner of her mother, she began to explore the options that were realistically open to her. She wrote to Queen Elizabeth asking that she be allowed to apply to the court to press her claim to her half of the Warwick inheritance. The claim was denied, shutting off one avenue for Anne as she tried to assert her independence. A new marriage must have begun to look more appealing. It was, after all, the state to which she had been brought up to aspire, and she was not yet 16; she still had plenty of time to secure her family's bloodline.

It seems that Richard had already raised the issue of their marriage with Edward as early as the summer of 1471, and that Clarence had been forewarned of the plan. What Anne felt at the prospect of Richard as a husband can only be guessed at; he was a prince of the realm, a duke – a catch by any standards, and exactly the sort of husband her father had sought for her. On the other hand, it is looking increasingly likely, via evidence such as the Burgundian illumination, that he was actively involved in the death of her first husband, and even if he hadn't been, he had still fought against her father, husband and uncle in the battles in which they were slain. With so much history, there would be no fresh start for Anne with Richard as her husband. If Anne were to marry Richard, she would have to swallow all distaste or any desire for revenge that she may be harbouring. As the new year of 1472 broke, Anne had a lot to think about while walking the rooms of Coldharbour.

Thanks to the 2012 discovery of the skeleton of the man who was now wooing Anne, we know a good deal about his appearance.[24] Richard had been born on 2 October 1452 at Fotheringhay Castle. He was the youngest surviving child of the twelve that Cecily Neville bore Richard, Duke of York. He was now 19 years old, bloodied and battle-hardened, with a strong jaw and light blond hair, and likely had blue eyes. We know he was suffering from adolescent onset scoliosis, meaning that he would have probably walked with a distinctive gait and his right shoulder was higher than the other. It is also clear that scoliosis did not inhibit Richard's physical abilities, as has sometimes been suggested. He could and did ride well and wielded a sword to deadly effect. Richard was also a relatively tall man, standing at approximately 5' 7", with the Silesian visitor to Richard's court in 1484, Nicolas von Poppelau, describing him as being 'three fingers taller' than himself. Whatever Anne's personal feelings about Richard might have been, she knew that she needed a powerful husband to press for her birthright in her stead, having been refused the right to do so herself. There was no man in the kingdom more powerful than her current protector, Clarence, except the king, and Richard, Duke of Gloucester. Richard was therefore the ideal and possibly the only candidate she felt was realistically open to her if she wanted to challenge for her inheritance.

The details of how and when Richard and Anne agreed to marry, and Anne agreed to allow him to 'abduct' her from Coldharbour, are simply not known but we do know that the decision was reached quickly. Richard had had an eventful year dealing with various uprisings, and we know that he was in the north as late as 11 December 1471. Therefore, as Michael Hicks calculates, their whole courtship, if that is what it can be called, took place over a period of only eight weeks as we know that Anne had been removed from Clarence's care by Richard before 16 February 1472.[25] We do not know if she snuck out or if she simply bribed her way out, but we do know that when she left Coldharbour, Richard was waiting for her and took her straight to the sanctuary of the College of St-Martin-le-Grand.[26] What is absolutely clear is that despite the use of terms such as abduction being wrongly applied by later historians, Anne had made the decision herself not to remain where she was. She had chosen not to stay with her sister and brother-in-law, not to remain passive or seek a quiet religious life. Anne had instead chosen to allow Richard to take her from Coldharbour. Her choices as a woman were limited but here we see her exercising her right to choose for herself within the limits that society imposed. Whatever her reasons, Anne chose Richard.

St-Martin-le-Grand had long been a controversial place, lying within the city walls but not subject to its jurisdiction. Previously known as a refuge for thieves and murderers, by 1457 it had become well known as a sanctuary, where people were registered with the dean and were searched for weapons before entry. Every night it pounded out the curfew bell – a sound that would have become very familiar to Anne over the next few months.

What were Anne's thoughts as she waited in sanctuary? Her first husband was barely cold in his grave, and now here she was planning to marry his enemy. Survival seems to have been her primary thought, how she could best survive and prosper. England had been remade and there was no point in clinging to what had gone before. Some subscribe to the idea that Anne's marriage with Richard was a true love match, that they had fallen in love as children and were now reunited at the first real opportunity. However, there is no evidence that either Anne or Richard viewed this as anything other than a political match. That they were not strangers and knew each other fairly well was not necessarily an advantage, given their shared history. Anne needed Richard as her champion to regain her inheritance and to escape her sister's household. Richard wanted Anne's inheritance and preferably, her mother's too. This is clearly shown in the negotiations that followed Anne's fleeing from Coldharbour. Clarence, John Paston reports, 'conceded her [Anne's] person but not her livelihood' quickly.[27] Richard, however, had no interest in Anne without her inheritance and he declined this compromise proposed by Clarence. He had Anne already, and he would fight his brother for Anne's inheritance to the bitter end.

Richard was a royal duke but now he wanted the land to go with it, as well as practical power on the ground. For his loyalty to his brother, he had been well rewarded, and Edward IV had effectively given him everything he could of the lands forfeited by various treasonous nobles, including Anne's father, whose Neville estates at Penrith, Sheriff Hutton and Middleham had been granted to him.[28] He had also been given former de Vere lands in the east of England. Despite this, however, as Michael Hicks points out, his wealth did not match that of Clarence or Buckingham.[29] To make it so, he needed to marry well, and Anne offered him more potential wealth and power than did any other woman in England.

Anne remained at St-Martin-le-Grand until July, while Richard sought to deal with any impediments that might prevent their marriage from proceeding. Despite her consent, he could not simply take her into his household; to do so would make him guilty of unlawful abduction or rape, by the standards of the time. Anne could be placed under no one's legal guardianship and would not be free to marry him unless she were located independently and beyond his control, which is why she was moved to a sanctuary. Clarence would later question the degree of freedom that this afforded Anne. As the *Crowland Chronicle* records:

> as a result of Anne's placement in sanctuary so much disputation arose between the brothers and so many keen arguments were put forward on either side with the greatest acuteness in the presence of the king, sitting in judgement in the council chamber that all who stood around even those

learned in law marvelled at the profusion of arguments which the princes produced for their own cases.[30]

Leaving this issue to one side for a moment, the most obvious and immediate difficulty appears to be that Anne and Richard were related within the prohibited degree of affinity. Marriage was prohibited between anyone sharing common ancestry from a great-great-grandparent downwards. It was also the case that, as historian Marie Barnfield states, 'the church took the view that sexual intercourse created a relationship with the parent. This relationship is known as affinity and it impeded marriage with the partners' kindred over four generations.'[31] However, since the 1215 Council of Lateran, it had not been considered that the relatives of the couple became blood relations. Anne and Richard were related within the prohibited degree and both would have known this. Richard's mother, Cecily Neville, was the sister of Anne's paternal grandfather, Richard Neville, Earl of Salisbury, both of whom were the children of Ralph Neville and Joan Beaufort. In addition, Richard's great-grandfather, Edmund of Langley, was also Anne's great-great-grandfather. There is also the suggestion that Cecily Neville may have stood as Anne's godmother; she was Isobel's, and the godparents' children were regarded as becoming the spiritual siblings of the baptised child.[32] This impediment was frequently dispensed with but it did require a papal dispensation. As such, Clarence had required a dispensation to marry Isobel, which had been acquired with difficulty by Warwick on 14 March 1468, and as we have seen, Anne and Prince Edward's marriage had also required one. Richard and Anne were also brother and sister-in-law already, which related them to the first degree of affinity. Therefore, they were related in the first through to the fourth degrees of affinity. A dispensation was definitely sent for and duly issued in April 1472, probably reaching England one to two months later, but this only covered their ancestral third and fourth degrees of affinity. As we have seen, they required a much more wide-ranging one that also addressed their affinity as siblings-in-law and as cousins once removed. Consequently, Michael Hicks believes that by pledging themselves to marry, both Richard and Anne were willing, and required, to reject contemporary standards of morality and that they married 'in defiance of canon law'.[33] Kim Harding, however, would disagree and suggests that given that they applied for one dispensation strongly suggests that they also sought one for their nearer blood kinship, and that just because we don't have the document doesn't mean that they didn't.

We don't know exactly when Anne and Richard married but historian Annette Carson suggests it is most likely to have taken place early in 1472. It must have been a small and private ceremony; if not, surely a record would exist. One suggestion is that they married at Richard's mother's London home, Baynard's Castle, or equally, the church at St Martin's itself could have served. It is not until 1474 – well over a year after Anne had left Clarence's household – until we find the first official and undisputed reference to Anne as Richard's wife, theoretically meaning that they could have arrived at any time during the intervening twenty or so months. Realistically, though, a date of summer 1472 seems likely, probably shortly after the dispensation arrived. Unfortunately, the birth of Anne's son Edward, which was traditionally considered to have been in 1473 and therefore used to date the marriage, is now thought to have been later – possibly not until 1474–6. We know that they were married before June 1474, as the legal settlement regarding Anne's inheritance made provision for her should she and her husband divorce.

The Warwick inheritance and what should happen to it was foremost in the minds of everyone during this period. Clarence had fought on numerous grounds to keep the bulk of it for himself. As stated earlier, he argued that Richard had coerced Anne forcibly and that therefore his actions had been unlawful. Richard was supported in his opposition to this view by the king, who declared that the whole Warwick inheritance should be divided. This was a decision that surely thrilled Anne but infuriated Clarence, who had wanted to keep control of the entire Neville inheritance, all of the Beauchamp, Despenser and Montagu lands. It was decided that Richard and Anne would have everything in the north, with Clarence and Isobel having the lands in the south midlands, including Warwick Castle. Clarence was also made Earl of Warwick and Salisbury. The parliament of October 1472 drew up the initial settlement, the only fly in the ointment being that Anne's mother petitioned from Beaulieu Abbey to be granted her jointure and inheritance. This was refused. Clarence was furious, fearing correctly that Richard would try to claim it, and he 'objected to the implementation [of the settlement] by refusing to give up what he held'.[34] Later, Richard's man Sir James Tyrell, in June 1473, removed Anne's mother from Beaulieu (to what degree the countess went willingly is unclear), and took her to Middleham in Richard's custody, and it was reported that she was going to be granted her inheritance by the king in order that she might now grant it to Richard and Anne.[35]

Chapter 10

Wife and Mother

> Short summers lightly have a forward spring.
> *Richard III*, William Shakespeare

Anne was now married for the second time and she was to spend a good deal of her life over the next few years at her childhood home of Middleham Castle. She now assumed the role of duchess and wife of England's greatest northern magnate. It is known from surviving documents that initially Richard spent much of his time at Middleham with Anne, perhaps both of them hoping that she would quickly fall pregnant. At Middleham, Anne could finally assume the role that she had been born to and for which she had been educated: that of a great duchess. She seems to have performed it brilliantly – so well, in fact, that she often deputised for her husband when he was away. She also fulfilled her primary function as a wife and she bore her husband a son. Anne of course was not a virgin when she married Richard and they would have no doubt started sleeping together in the fullest sense of the word immediately after their marriage. We do not know exactly when Anne gave birth but it seems that she did not fall pregnant immediately. The most likely date of the birth of Anne's child is sometime from 1475 to 1477. Historian Charles Ross dates it to 1476, also the date considered by historian Peter Hammond to be the most likely.[1] John Rous, in 1483, records that the child was then 7 years old, but Rous was not with Anne's household at the time. Vergil, meanwhile, says that he was 9, but he would not have seen the child either.[2]

From 1472 to 1474, the Middleham household records do not contain anything that might suggest a celebration or food ordered especially for Anne while she was pregnant. The baby is mentioned in the *Chronicle of Tewkesbury* as having been born in 1476, and on 10 April 1477, was listed alongside his parents as one of those whose soul was to be prayed for.³

Whatever the precise date, Anne gave birth to a healthy baby boy, whom they called Edward, presumably after the king. Anne would have been 17–19 years of age and the Rous Roll suggests that her mother attended her during her confinement. This does not imply that it was a sentimental decision by either Anne or the duke; the issue of the Duchess Anne of Warwick jointure and inheritance was still rumbling on when Richard took her from her sanctuary at Beaulieu Abbey in May 1473. Rous reported that she remained confined in the north 'with the greatest strictness', at Anne's own direction. Perhaps she had not yet forgiven her mother's abandonment in her hour of need, or perhaps she simply wanted her with her. Likely, it was a mixture of both. Either way, though, it was greatly to Anne's advantage to keep her mother confined so that she could not remarry someone who would be able to help her recover her jointure and inheritance. As we have seen, Clarence knew that possession of the duchess's person greatly strengthened Anne and Richard's position, and he remained furious. It is also possible that Cecily Neville travelled north to attend Anne at the birth of her child. Unfortunately, we cannot be certain, as details of her precise whereabouts during this period are sporadic. If she did, we can be sure that she would have prayed for Anne and her child in the castle chapel. By this point, religion had become extremely important to Cecily Neville and she had developed a deep interest in the Benedictine Order. In August 1475, for example, Margaret Paston wrote that the duchess was in Norfolk with her entire household at St Benet's Abbey.⁴

Like her mother before her, Anne would have given birth in a specially prepared birthing chamber, richly draped, with a fire burning and all draughts excluded. She would have entered the exclusively female world of confinement, reading and resting while she awaited the birth of her baby. We sadly know nothing of the celebrations that surrounded Edward's birth and there surely must have been some. For Anne, this was the high point of her life; she had fulfilled every duty that was expected of her and the future of her dynasty was now secure. The baby Edward was Anne and Richard's heir and the embodiment of all their hopes for the future, as Prince Edward of Lancaster had been for Margaret of Anjou. However, both must have now felt little more than a distant memory to Anne as she gazed upon her healthy son, by Richard, Duke of Gloucester, in his cradle. By July 1477, Edward was already beginning to make an appearance in the records of England when he was described as the Earl of Salisbury, a title that was confirmed upon him seven months later by the king.[5] King Edward called him 'our most dear nephew Edward Plantagenet, first born of our most dear brother Richard Duke of Gloucester'.[6]

The baby would have had his own household at Middleham. As a duchess, Anne would not have fed the baby Edward herself and we know that his wet nurse was a woman called Isobel Burgh, who was well rewarded for her service.[7] The Burghs were clearly a family with whom the duke and duchess were on good terms. In 1474, an Alice Burgh, who is referred to as having been Richard's 'beloved gentlewoman', was granted £20 a year for life for 'special' reasons. Hicks implies that she was Richard's mistress and this is a decided possibility. Perhaps it is on her recommendation that her relation Isobel was selected as wet nurse for baby Edward. We know that Richard had illegitimate children and he would later acknowledge two of his bastard children – a daughter called Katherine and a son, John. Richard took great care of his illegitimate children. He organised Katherine's marriage and John would later be appointed as titular captain of Calais. Katherine was almost certainly born before Richard's marriage, likely in 1470, but John, according to Michael Hicks, was most probably born after it.[8] Amy Licence, however, suggests that John was more likely to have been conceived when Richard was at Pomfret (Pontefract) Castle in 1471, meaning that his birth predated Richard's marriage.[9] How Anne might have felt about either option is not clear; infidelity, after all, on the part of a man was considered usual at the time, but perhaps some friction can be inferred by the fact that after Anne's death, Richard was far more generous in his treatment of his son than previously.

Back at Middleham, Edward's nursery was presided over by Anne Idley, a widow who was given the title of 'mistress of our ducal nursery'.[10] Prior to his own death, Anne's husband had written a book called *Peter Idley's Instructions to his Son*. This text was no doubt used by his widow in relation to Edward, and maybe she was chosen because of her expertise in this area. The book is interesting in that it instructs the child to honour their mother

Anne, Queen of Richard III.

1. Anne Neville. Image after the Rous Roll.

2. A view of Warwick Castle.

3. The mighty Warwick Castle today. Anne was born here on 11 June 1456.

4. Anne Neville's father, Richard Neville, the 'Kingmaker', 16th Earl of Warwick. This carved relief of him as a mourner on the tomb of his father-in-law, Richard Beauchamp, 13th Earl of Warwick, is the only known depiction of him that was made in his lifetime.

5. Anne's ancestor, John of Gaunt, third surviving son of Edward III. Ralph Neville's marriage to his daughter Joan was possibly the reason why he was made Earl of Westmorland in 1397. Anne was his great-great-grandchild, as was her first husband, Edward of Westminster, meaning they were related in the fourth degree and required a papal dispensation to marry. Anne and her second husband, Richard, were also related in a similar way, both being descended from Ralph Neville and Joan Beaufort. This also meant that a papal dispensation was required for their marriage.

6. One of many plaques, this one at Clare Priory, commemorating the ancestors of Anne Neville and her second husband.

Above left: 7. Anne's future father-in-law and her father's greatest friend and ally, Richard, Duke of York. He led the Yorkist faction and died at the Battle of Wakefield.

Above right: 8. Anne's mother-in-law, Cecily Neville, the mother of her brother-in-laws and second husband: King Edward IV, George, Duke of Clarence, and King Richard III.

Left: 9. Anne's first father-in-law, the Lancastrian King Henry VI.

10. The marriage of Henry VI and Margaret of Anjou. Anne spent a good deal of time with her first, formidable mother-in-law.

11. Anne's older sister, Isobel Neville, wife of George, Duke of Clarence.

12. Anne's brother-in-law twice over, George, Duke of Clarence.

13. Anne's sister-in-law, Elizabeth Woodville. Her marriage to King Edward IV helped to cause a permanent rift between Edward and Anne's father.

14. A coin dating to 1464, depicting Anne's brother-in-law, the Yorkist warrior King Edward IV.

15. Amboise Castle. Anne stayed here, in an earlier building, for a time when she was in France.

16. Men re-enacting the Battle of Barnet in 2023, the battle in which Anne's father was killed.

17. The site of Bisham Priory, burial place of Anne's father and grandfather.

18. Gobes Hall, where, according to tradition, Anne and the other Lancastrian ladies stayed the night before the Battle of Tewkesbury.

19. The Bloody Meadow at Tewkesbury, where the Lancastrian army was finally routed.

Above left: 20. Tewkesbury Abbey interior.

Above right: 21. The plaque that marks the burial place of Edward of Westminster, Anne's first husband and son of Henry VI and Margaret of Anjou.

Left: 22. The grill over the steps in Tewkesbury Abbey, which lead down to the Clarence vault, where Anne's sister Isobel and George, Duke of Clarence, rest.

23. Anne Neville, after the Rous Roll, torn between the crowns of Lancaster and York.

24. The great keep at Middleham Castle, Anne's home for many years.

25. Portrait of Richard III, Anne's second husband, painted by Barthel II after a lost original, for the Paston family. It has been owned by the Society of Antiquaries, London, since 1828.

26. Watercolour of the white boar, symbol of Richard III, and his motto.

27. Artist's impression of Richard, Duke of Gloucester, and the Lady Anne, by Edwin Austin Abbey.

28. An image of the Garter ceremony for Elizabeth Woodville's son by her first marriage, the Marquis of Dorset, in *Writhe's Garter Book*. The women sit to the side of the king. The two at the front are most likely the queen and one of her sisters, but it has been speculated that the two immediately behind them are Anne Neville (on the left) and Isobel.

Above left: 29. The Middleham Jewel.

Above right: 30. Artist's impression of Anne Neville at the time of her coronation.

Left: 31. A statue of Anne's second husband, Richard III, at Middleham Castle.

32. One of the Eton Chapel Wall Paintings, which were painted between 1479 and 1487. This scene depicts an episode from the story of 'The Empress Falsely Accused'. It is suggested that the central empress image is that of Anne Neville, who looks up at the Emperor (Richard III) on his horse. Richard and most likely Anne visited Windsor, close to Eton, many times between 1483 and 1485, so probably saw these paintings.

33. Plaque marking the investiture of Anne's son as Prince of Wales in York.

34. Anne's niece, Elizabeth of York. Anne's feelings towards her remain unclear, as does the question of whether or not Richard III sought to marry her. She married Henry Tudor and together she and her husband founded the Tudor dynasty.

35. The plaque in Westminster Abbey that marks the likeliest location of Anne's final resting place.

and father, to be still and keep a careful tongue as a careless one can cause much pain. It also advises against taking the counsel of covetous men and to not seek worldly goods. It is a manual designed to create a cautious, devout and contemplative mind. It also instructs the young subject to value friendship above all, and to value family.

In 1538, Middleham Castle was surveyed, when the south-west corner tower of the keep was intriguingly referred to as the Nursery Tower, suggesting that it was there that Edward of Middleham was born and his nursery established.[11] The tower had been constructed in the 1300s and was therefore a part of the castle that Anne would have been familiar with from her own childhood. The tower itself is round. On the modern English Heritage plans the nursery is shown as extending out along the west range, over the pantry with its ovens, which would have made it one of the warmest areas of the castle, ideal for family accommodation. Along the south side, this nursery also connected to a series of privy chambers, perhaps where Anne herself slept.[12]

Anne's son Edward was not the only child to have been born in her world during the 1470s. Queen Elizabeth Woodville continued to bear her husband's children and by 1480, they had an impressive brood consisting of Elizabeth of York, Mary, Cecily, Edward (later King Edward V), Richard (later Duke of York), Anne, Catherine and Bridget. Two other children died as infants: Margaret (born April, died December 1472) and George (born March 1477, died March 1479). Anne was also an aunt, as in 1473, her niece Margaret had been born in Farleigh Hungerford Castle to Isobel and George. This was followed in 1475 by the birth of their son and heir, Edward Plantagenet.

As far as we know with any degree of certainty, Anne only ever bore one child, although that does not rule out the possibility that she suffered either miscarriages or stillbirths, which Rous would not necessarily have recorded. Given that her mother also seems to have had gynaecological issues, historian Lisa Hilton suggests that she might have been suffering from tuberculous endometriosis, which affects fertility, but the accuracy of such a diagnosis is hard to assess so retrospectively.[13] There is also the intriguing possibility that Anne bore a second son at some point during this period. The *Chronicle of Tewkesbury*, which took a particular interest in the lives of Anne and her sister due to the family's patronage of the abbey, Anne's mother being its patroness, contains an intriguing entry in a later sixteenth-century copy, which mentions a possible son called George born in 1476 to the Duke and Duchess of Gloucester. This entry is generally considered as having been a clerical mistake, but we cannot completely discount the idea that Anne had borne a second, short-lived, son.[14]

Whilst Anne's days at Middleham would have assumed the regular pattern of a ducal household with which she would have been familiar, her husband was now firmly established as the leading magnate in the north and his brother the king's right-hand man. Unfortunately, once again, Anne now appears only infrequently in the historical records. We do, however, catch fleeting glimpses of her as she carried out her duties as a duchess. In 1477, she actively sought a position for one of her clerks at the vicarage of Bossall, which was in the gift of Durham Cathedral Priory. Her letter had been carried to Durham by a servant of Anne's called Nicholas Hedlam. The position had already been filled so they were unable to honour her wishes, but Prior Richard Bell, who replied to her, begged her to 'take no displeasure' and assured her that he would make it up to her by providing 'another as good'. He clearly wanted to ensure that Anne and Richard continued to support him and he did not want to risk them withdrawing their patronage.[15] Hicks suggests that Bell was later promoted to bishop on their recommendation.[16] As duchess, we also know that Anne deputised for Richard in 1475–6 when he was away in France. During this period, she sent a message to the city of York through Richard's councillors, issuing orders and offering suggestions. On one occasion in particular, members of Richard's council came 'bearing letters from the lady Duchess of Gloucester'. This was a role that Anne would perform many times over the years, and demonstrated that Richard had confidence in his wife's abilities. The right to deputise for one's husband was not automatically conferred and Richard could have nominated someone else. Anne would have been well equipped by her upbringing to perform such a function, and in her immediate family she could have had no shortage of role models; even setting aside her own very capable mother, there are dozens of other examples of the Warwick women deputising for and supporting their husbands.[17] Anne's paternal aunt, Alianor, for example, in a letter she sent sometime in the 1460s, instructed

Wife and Mother

one Piers Werburton to get her concerns sorted, ending with the line that his assistance 'shall cause me to be your gode lady', clearly meaning that he needed to get it sorted quickly if he did not want to incur her displeasure.[18]

Whilst Anne was largely at Middleham, Richard had travelled to France in June 1475 in the company of the king, and he provided 100 archers and at least 100 men-at-arms, fully armoured heavy cavalrymen. The expedition ended without bloodshed as Louis and Edward signed a peace treaty. Richard, it seems, possibly disapproved of Edward's actions; he is conspicuously absent and Commines records that 'the Duke of Gloucester, the King of England's brother and some other persons of quality were not present at the interview [with the French king] being averse to the treaty.'[19] Many of the Englishmen were offered pensions by the French king. John Morton received 600 crowns a year and Lord Howard, 1,200 crowns, amongst others. It seems likely that Richard refused similar financial payouts from the French king. Anne's husband had principles.

It is possible that Anne waited for her husband's return in London and she was certainly there with Richard from 3 to 6 December 1475, and while there, she and Richard purchased cloth, silks and velvet. Richard also bought furs from a man called Thomas Cole, a skinner 'for the use of the most dear consort of the said Duke', Anne. He could go on to become Richard's skinner as king. We also know that one of the men from whom Anne and Richard bought cloth was called Henry Ivy, or Ive, and that he would later become Anne's tailor when she was queen.[20] From this, we can infer that Anne dressed lavishly, as befitted her status. It also seems that Anne personally chose the fabrics she wanted. Although Richard paid, she submitted her order separately to him, suggesting that she had definite ideas as to how she wished to appear and the sorts of fabric she found appropriate and comfortable to wear.[21]

There is also a clue as to the sort of jewellery that Anne would have been wearing at this time. In 1985, near her home of Middleham Castle, a late fifteenth-century pendant was found by a metal detectorist. This pendant is made of gold and set with a large blue sapphire. The inscription around the edges seems to relate to childbirth, so the jewel was likely made for a woman, possibly intended to protect her during childbirth. It also once contained a religious relic, likely a piece of cloth. The word 'Ananizapata', which is engraved, is thought to relate to the pendant's magical powers to protect against epilepsy. The front bears an image of the Trinity; the reverse bears an engraving of the nativity along with the faces of fifteen saints. Given the high-status nature of this find, it has been suggested that this stunning jewel once belonged to Anne Neville. This cannot be proved, of course, but it gives us a dazzling insight into the type of jewellery that she would have worn.

Anne and Richard may have remained at court to celebrate Christmas with the king and his household. At some point around now we know that Richard and Anne leased the London house of Crosby Place, so perhaps it was there that Anne spent time with her husband. Crosby Place was built by Sir John Crosby in the mid-1400s on land that he had leased from the prioress of the Convent of St Helens, Alice Ashfield. Crosby was granted a ninety-nine-year lease, for which he paid 11 pounds, 6 shillings and 8 pence. The house was described by Stowe as being 'built of stone and timber very large and being the highest at the time in London',[22] which might explain why Richard wished to lease it even though he already had accommodation at Coldharbour. While in London, Anne would no doubt have also been a regular visitor at her mother-in-law's London house, Baynard's Castle. Cecily Neville would certainly have approved of the fact that Anne was, in 1476, admitted to the sisterhood of Durham Cathedral Priory, which ensured that the monks would support her in life and pray for her soul after death, and intercede on her behalf in both instances, if necessary.[23] Anne was admitted independently of her husband and it seems to have been something she personally sought, perhaps in light of the fact that several of her family ancestors were buried at the priory. Anne was in fact a great friend to Durham Priory, and as we have seen, she communicated with the prior on several occasions on behalf of members of her household.

Although there is no record, it seems likely that Anne was with her husband and his brothers when they attended the reinterment of their father, the Duke of York, and their brother, Edmund, at the church of St Mary and All Saints, Fotheringhay, on 30 July 1476. Thomas Whiting, who was the Chester Herald, described how the coffins were pulled by seven horses all wearing black and that the mourners also all wore black. On the chariot was placed an effigy of York dressed in a blue gown trimmed with ermine, adding a dramatic splash of colour. Inside the church, we know that Queen Elizabeth, along with two of her daughters, and Cecily Neville and Isobel, were waiting.[24] It seems certain therefore that Anne was there as well, even though the chronicles do not mention her by name amongst the ladies present. York's coffin was buried before the high altar, and Edmund's was placed inside the Lady Chapel. Overnight, servants stood guard over them. The following day, Mass was said and the bodies were interred before a great feast was held at Fotheringhay Castle. Alms were distributed and the feast is said to have fed 20,000 people.

If she did attend, this occasion was likely to have been personally important for Anne, and would have loomed large in her memory, as it was perhaps the last time that she saw her sister Isobel. If Anne's son Edward was born in 1476, perhaps she was pregnant at the time. Isobel certainly was. At the beginning of October 1476, Isobel went into labour and gave birth to a second son, whom they called Richard, in a chamber in the infirmary of Tewkesbury Abbey. The baby was baptised the next day inside the abbey church. The choice of name is interesting in that it suggests that whatever rift may have formed between Anne and Isobel's husbands following the division of the Neville inheritance, it was not serious at this stage. The name Richard could have been chosen for George's father rather than his brother, but given that his first son was called Edward, for the king, it seems probable that it was after Anne's husband that he was named.[25] Perhaps, then, the relationship between the sisters at this point was closer than previously thought. After the birth of her son, Blunt tells us: 'The Lord George and the Lady Isobel removed to Warwick on November 12th … she was then in mortal sickness.'[26] As Isobel began to sicken, did increasingly frantic letters fly between Warwick and Middleham? Between Anne and George? We simply don't know, but it seems likely.

Childbirth during this period was a dangerous business and Isobel's rank of course did nothing to protect her from the dangers inherent to it. She passed away ten weeks after the birth of her son. It is generally considered that she died of either a postpartum infection, which in a pre-antibiotic age would have been a death sentence, or of a consumption, possibly tuberculosis, although the former is considered more likely, given that her death appears to have been unexpected. Ten days later, her baby son was also dead. When the news reached Anne, we cannot know, but her devastation is easy to imagine. Anne would spend a good deal of the next year focusing on realising her and Richard's religious plans; perhaps they were propelled forward by her tide of grief and desire to ensure the safety of her sister's soul.

Isobel's body was embalmed and returned to Tewkesbury Abbey, where it lay for thirty-five days in the choir before she was buried in a vault to the east of the high altar.[27] Anne would have gone into mourning, wearing black for the six months prescribed by the medieval church as appropriate for a sibling. She would also have attended special Masses, and said prayers for her sister's soul.

George, Duke of Clarence, appears to have been personally devastated by his wife's death and his behaviour quickly spiralled towards utter disaster, suggesting that Isobel's influence on him had previously acted as a balance and check for his ambition and resentment. George now became enmeshed with his sister, Margaret, now dowager Duchess of Burgundy, after her husband Charles's death, in plotting to try to secure her stepdaughter's position and protect Burgundy. They seem to have thought of marrying George to Margaret's stepdaughter Mary, but there was simply no chance that Edward would permit his brother to make such a powerful alliance. His Lancastrian blood combined with hers would have placed them in such a powerful position that they might have challenged for the throne of England. It also seems that the clever Margaret did not seriously consider George as a viable option. Though she was fond of her brother, his compliance was all she really needed to strengthen her hand temporarily. Her plan worked and it was enough to spur the Holy Roman Emperor Maximillian into action and he instead proposed an alliance between Mary and his son Frederick. This almost certainly was Margaret's intention all along; the Holy Roman Emperor had a much greater chance of protecting Burgundy from the French than either of her brothers. This was another blow for the grieving George and his political ambitions, and he blamed Edward for it.

On 12 April 1477, four months after Isobel's death, George sent his man Richard Hyde and a local man, Roger Strugge, to take into custody a woman by the name of Ankaret Twynyho, who had been a lady-in-waiting to Isobel and was currently at her manor of Keyford. She was dragged to

Bath, Cirencester and Gloucester before being parcelled off to Warwick. All of this was carried out 'without a writ, warrant or any other lawful authority'.[28] On 15 April, she faced George inside Warwick Guildhall, where he accused her of murdering Isobel, claiming that she had given her ale that she had laced with poison. The jury she faced, which was 'fearful of losing their lives and goods', pronounced her guilty and condemned her to death. Three hours later, she was dead, executed on the gallows at Myton. George's actions caused outrage but by now, he seems to have been losing all grip on reality. In May 1477, a sorcerer called John Stacy was arrested, and he implicated a member of George's household called Thomas Burdet. They were charged with attempting to bring about the death of Richard, Lord Beauchamp. George's defence of them after their execution was a step too far for King Edward, and George appeared at Westminster on 10 June before the king. He was arrested and sent to the Tower.[29]

Where was Anne while all this was happening? She was possibly away from London and undoubtedly grieving. We also know that in 1477 she and Richard were made members of the Corpus Christi Guild in York. In January 1478, a parliament was summoned to try George for high treason. It was now clear that Edward had neither forgiven nor forgotten his past actions, and the attainder began with a list of the 'manifold great conspiracies, malicious and heinous treasons' that he had faced and in which George had been involved.[30] In addition, the attainder referenced a new threat against his life, the queen and his heirs, which 'hath been extended by his brother the Duke of Clarence'. Edward's fury is palpable but he still argued that he might have forgiven George were it not for all his past offences. In combination, though, it was too much; George was found guilty and sentenced to death. On 18 February, George was granted a private execution and according to legend, was drowned in a butt of Malmsey wine, drowning being considered a more gentle way of execution at the time.[31] Anne's brother-in-law died at just 28 years old.

How Anne reacted to these events, we do not know, but in public, the blame for this act seems to have been laid firmly at the queen's door. Fifteenth-century writer Dominic Mancini reported that 'the queen concluded that her offspring would never come to the throne unless the Duke of Clarence were removed and of this she easily persuaded the king … Clarence was thus condemned and put to death.'[32] There is some evidence that Richard may have shared this viewpoint. According to Mancini, he 'was so overcome by grief for his brother ... that he was overheard to say that he could one day avenge [it]'.[33] In 1484, he would compare George's death in a letter to James Fitzgerald, Earl of Desmond, to that of the execution of the earl's father, comparing it as well to the deaths of kinsmen and great friends.[34] As historian Matthew Lewis makes clear, the Fitzgeralds blamed the Woodville faction for George's death, therefore we can possibly infer that Richard shared their views.[35] If so, and Anne agreed and grieved with her husband, attendance at court would no doubt have become increasingly uncomfortable. Perhaps this is in part why they turned their attention to more religious matters. In February 1478, Richard and Anne set in motion plans for the creation of two colleges, one at Barnard Castle and one at Middleham. The one intended for Barnard Castle soon took shape, and the Church of St Mary's was restructured so that it could be developed into a collegiate church, and buildings were provided in the curtilage for the priests' houses by statutes drawn up on 4 July 1478 for it to be elevated to collegiate status, with its own priests and choristers. The church at Middleham was also to be endowed with lands of the value of 133 pounds, 6 shillings and 8 pence, and have a dean, six chaplains, four clerks, six choristers and a priest. Richard stated that the college was intended to 'pray for my lady and mother Duchess of York, me, my wife, my son of Salisbury' alongside the king and queen.[36] Saint Alkelda seems to have had a strong local connection; indeed, she is not honoured with any church outside the Middleham area. Alkelda was a noble, virginal Saxon who had been strangled by the Vikings when they raided the area in around 800 CE. Alkelda's name was possibly derived from the Old English for Holy Well, *haeligkeld*, and it is known that there was a well in Middleham. Alkelda was, according to tradition, buried beneath the nave of the church. All this has led historian Lauren Gilbert to hypothesise that the well at the church therefore may have been known during the medieval period for its healing properties.[37]

In addition to the church's named saints, we know in great detail the saints that Richard, and presumably Anne, wanted to be associated with the new collegiate church. The first stall on the left side was to be dedicated to St George, in an echo of his brother Edward's founding of St George's Chapel at Windsor. The second on the right was named for Saint Catherine, who amongst other things protected against sudden death. Perhaps given George's recent death and the fact that we now know Richard suffered from the chronic condition of scoliosis, this seemed appropriate. The inclusion of the Virgin Mary was perhaps Anne's choice, given that she offered protection to women, and was associated with pregnancy and childbirth. Anne, after all, at this time must have been hopeful that she would bear her husband more children. Saint Ninian was also present – a Scottish saint who first appears in Bede's *The Ecclesiastical History of the English People* in around 731 CE. He was associated during the medieval period with healing and was said to have healed children suffering from physical deformities. He was also strongly associated with the north and given the increasing Scottish threat to English borders at the time, might have seemed appropriate. Saint Cuthbert was also present, the patron saint of the north of England. Saint Cuthbert was buried in Durham Cathedral and his cult was centred on there. Considering Anne and Richard's relationship with Durham, it makes sense that they would honour him. It has been suggested that the choice of Saint Anthony was due to his association with the badge of the boar, Richard's emblem.[38] He was also said to be, as one of the Four Holy Marshals, very effective against plague, which was never a bad thing in medieval England. Saint Winifred was also included; she was associated with the Beauchamp family, and Anne Sutton suggests that her inclusion is indicative of Anne's personal involvement in the choice of saints. She also maintains that Anne had a personal connection to the saint and that William Caxton's book on the life of Saint Winifred was published under her patronage.[39] The cult of Saint Winifred was fostered by the Lancastrians after their victory at Shrewsbury during the reign of Henry IV. For Anne personally, her ancestor Isabella Beauchamp, the Countess of Warwick, had in 1439 bequeathed a rich gown to the statue of St Winifred as a symbol of the family's devotion to her. Likewise, there is a window and chapel dedicated to Saint Winifred in the church of Saint Mary's in Warwick, with which Anne would have been very familiar. It seems likely, therefore, that St Winifred's inclusion at Middleham should be regarded as having been Anne's personal choice.

We do not have any books that Anne may have used during her devotion, although she would certainly have owned a book of hours, a devotional book that was used to pray the canonical hours. Contemporary high-class books of hours, such as that which belonged to Catherine of Cleves, were lavishly illustrated and stunning examples of medieval artistry.[40] As previously mentioned, the only book that we can suggest that Anne owned for certain is Mechtild of Hackeborn's *Boke of Gostely Grace* (*Book of Ghostly Grace*), which bears Richard's signature alongside Anne's, but we do know that Richard owned a vast number of books. His own book of hours was likely made in 1420 on Paternoster Row by someone in the circle of illuminator Herman Scheere.[41]

We also know that Richard owned books such as *Guidance of Princes* by Giles of Rome, which was a book on the correct conduct of princes, and the *De Regimine Principum*, written by Aegidius Colonna (who had studied under Thomas Aquinas) and which had previously belonged to his father. Sutton also suggests that he read and could quote from *The Vision of Piers Plowman* by William Langland, a narrative allegorical poem on such wide-ranging subjects as Robin Hood and the nature of religion, and that even his famous motto, 'Loyalty binds me', was taken from there.[42] Alongside this, we know that Richard owned other books on history, such as the *Chronicle of St Denis*, *The Story of Troy* and *The History of the Kings of Britain*, as well as on law and philosophy. We know that Richard's nephew, Edward, the king's son, was taught law and history as part of his education, and that a good deal of Edward IV's library was devoted to such subjects. No doubt, Richard borrowed and used such books in relation to the education of his own son – books that Anne would have had access to.

If Richard and Anne were upset at Clarence's execution, it did not keep them from court. In January 1479, Richard was with the king at Westminster, and again it seems likely that Anne accompanied him to spend time and exchange New Year's gifts with the king and court.

By 8 April, Edward had granted Richard permission to hold two fayres in Middleham in Whitsun week, and for the three days in between the feasts of Saint Simon and Saint Jude.[43] Anne's relatively quiet life, however, was not to last. In the summer of 1480, Richard was sent north, campaigning against the Scots, having been appointed on 12 of May as 'the king's lieutenant-general to fight against James King of Scotland who has violated the truce lately concluded by the king'. In the autumn, Anne joined him at Sheriff Hutton, and might even have been present when he was told that the Scots were planning to invade.

Chapter 11

Death of the King

> For God's sake, let us sit upon the ground,
> And tell sad stories of the death of kings.
> *Richard II*, William Shakespeare

In October 1474, the Scottish king, James III, had signed a truce with Edward IV, which was to last for forty-five years and would be cemented by a marriage between Edward's daughter Cecily and James's heir, his son, the Duke of Rothesay, when they both were of marriageable age. James, however, broke the truce by raiding into England and in 1480, Edward's envoy to Edinburgh effectively stated that unless James returned the lands seized, including the towns of Berwick, Roxburgh and Coldingham, England would take them back by force. With the Scots threatening, King Edward turned to his brother as Lieutenant in the North to help plan this counter-attack, and in November, Richard was given 10,000 pounds to pay the wages of his men. In mid-July, Richard rode out of York to deal with the ever-treacherous border town of Berwick-upon-Tweed. The town surrendered but the castle held out, and Thomas Stanley was left to deal with blockading the castle whilst Richard marched on towards Edinburgh, burning and looting as he went, to try to force the Scottish king into fighting a pitched battle.

James III was considered weak and ineffective, his court was fatally divided into opposing factions and with Richard approaching, James was taken into custody by one faction of his nobles whilst several of his favourites were hung from Lauder Bridge. James was placed in custody in Edinburgh Castle, where his nobles knew they could withstand a long siege if they had to. Richard demanded that James honour the treaty he had with Edward IV, restore his enemy Albany to his lands and restore order. If he didn't, he threatened he could destroy him with 'slaughter, flame and famine'.[1] Richard, it seems, had hoped to replace James III with the more amenable Albany, but the Scots instead asked that the truce be renewed.[2] While awaiting Edward's verdict, Richard returned to Berwick, where the defenders now realised that help would not be coming from Edinburgh, and despite a small force actually being sent, the castle surrendered on 24–25 August. For his efforts, Edward called Richard his 'most loving brother' when he wrote to Pope Sixtus IV. Anne's husband was riding high and in November, a parliament was called whose purpose was, amongst other things, to reward Richard for his actions. In January 1483, the Rolls of Parliament record that he was made Warden of the West Marches, because:

> by his diligent labours ... has subdued a great part of the west border of Scotland, adjoining England, by the space of thirty miles and more ... and has secured divers parts thereof to be under the obedience of the king to the great surety and ease of the north parts of England.

It was a position that was to pass to his male heirs, firm acknowledgment of the future that awaited Anne's baby son. This position included a number of lordships including that of Carlisle, and lands in, amongst other areas, Liddesdale, Ewesdale, Annandale and Eskdale. He and his heirs were also granted 10,000 marks a year for their service in perpetuity as Warden of the West Marches.[3]

As there is no record of Anne in London at this time it seems most likely that Anne was at Middleham with her mother and son while Richard was dealing with the Scots. There is some question as to whether or not Anne travelled to London with her husband for Christmas 1482, with Amy Licence suggesting she likely did, but Michael Hicks, whilst not discounting the possibility, argues that there is no conclusive proof.[4] Given that Anne and Richard were undoubtedly hoping to conceive another child at this time to expand their family, I suggest that it is probable that she did accompany her husband to court for what would turn out to be Edward IV's last Christmas. We know that Richard was there because not only had a parliament been called for mid-January, but also because he purchased gifts from the goldsmith of the city during December. It is not entirely clear where the court held Christmas, but it was either at Eltham Palace, whose impressive great gall, rebuilt by Edward IV, still stands, or at Westminster, but Eltham seems the more likely given Edward IV's preference for it. Thanks to the *Crowland Chronicle*, we do get an impression of the occasion: the king was 'clad in a variety of the most costly garments, of quite a difference cut to those which had usually been seen hitherto in our kingdom', which included a garment with 'full and hanging robe sleeves greatly resembling a monk's frock and lined with fur'.[5] The royal court 'present[ed] no other appearance than such as fully befits a most mighty kingdom'. Guests included Andrew Palaeologus, who was a member of the fallen house of Constantinople, and it is said that over 2,000 people were fed.[6] There is also a mention in the chronicles of the royal children being present. Perhaps, then, Edward of Middleham also accompanied his parents to London and ran around the great hall with his cousins. It is tempting to hope so, for everything that Anne and her son knew was about to be swept away and their world rewritten by Richard.

The events and motivations surrounding Richard's usurpation of the thrones have been studied and vehemently debated almost since the time of the events themselves. Anne herself seems to have played no part in her husband's actions; whether or not she knew of them, or of what he planned, remains a complete unknown. She has left us no clue as to her feelings or the extent to which her husband may or may not have confided in her. In fact, Anne is never more resolutely silent as she is during the first few months of 1483. We know she returned to Middleham at some point before April, no doubt to pick up the thread of her life as duchess again there. Edward returned to his studies and Anne resumed her duties within the castle and community. She was there on 16 April, when the news arrived that King Edward was dead. There is some dispute over the exact date of the king's passing, though it is usually given as 9 April. However, five days earlier, news of it had reached York. Most people today believe that this was the result of poor information and premature alarm. His death was not expected; he was 40, and although rather less trim than in his youth, there are no reports of his failing health, apart from several contemporaries commenting on his increasing levels of inactivity. Nevertheless, in late March, he had been well enough to go fishing, according to Mancini. He then states that during this trip, Edward caught a cold, was forced to take to his bed and later died. Philippe de Commines, meanwhile, suggests that he had a stroke, and the *Crowland Chronicle* states that his doctors simply did not know what killed their king. French chronicler Jean Molinet, meanwhile, suggests that he ate contaminated salad and then perished in an implausible, unique April heatwave.[7] Today, historians remain at a loss as to what killed Edward IV, suggesting perhaps appendicitis, or a perforated ulcer that turned septic, but neither of these fit the contemporary evidence entirely. Richard was in the north when the official news reached him, probably at Middleham Castle with Anne.[8] Ultimately for us, it does not really matter what killed the king, though no doubt it did matter to both Richard and Anne, who, as far as we can tell, had genuinely loved him as a brother. What matters is that he was suddenly dead, and his son and heir was not yet of an age to rule independently.

This meant that he, and England, were now facing a minority rule. The last king to be a minor had been Henry VI, clearly not something that had worked (or ended) well. There had long been divisions at the English court and the Woodville faction headed by the queen was in conflict with that of Hastings. He accused the Woodvilles of having accrued offices and authority, but whilst this is clearly true, they were positions that had been appointed by Edward IV willingly. This, in the words of Matthew Lewis, that Edward's policy 'would suggest that the queen and her brothers would lead a minority government for his son' should anything happen to him.[9] Hastings would therefore have been ousted. Unfortunately, this is where history becomes increasingly unclear. It was said that Edward on his deathbed changed his mind and named Anne's husband, Richard, as Lord Protector, but there is no absolute documentary proof of this that has ever come to light. Mancini tells us that whilst this possibility was debated, Richard was still in the north, presumably at Middleham with Anne. The council, meanwhile, debated as to whether or not it might be better (whatever Edward's wishes had been) to allow Richard to govern rather than see power more devolved between nobles. Mancini again indicates that it was Hastings who told Richard of these events, and possibly even informed him of his brother's death. He

Death of the King

tells us that Richard was then told that it was his brother's wish that he be protector and that the queen and her allies were seeking to find a way to disregard Edward's wishes. Hastings suggested that Richard 'hasten to the capital with a strong force and avenge the insult done to him by his enemies' and that he should first take his nephew into his protection.[10] London was seething with rumour as both sides sought to establish who should bring the young king to London for his coronation. Elizabeth Woodville was pushing for a quick coronation and to this end, Rivers intended to travel to London with the king 'in all convenient haste'.[11] The Woodvilles had also accessed the treasury but Hastings openly declared that he would flee into exile if the new king were to arrive with a Woodville escort.[12] The piracy of Edward Woodville no doubt also had a bearing on this. We must remember that we cannot prove the intentions of any of the men involved here.

Whilst politics and debate raged on, Edward IV was laid to rest in St George's Chapel in Windsor on 19 April. Two days earlier, King Edward's body had been conveyed to Westminster Abbey and his coffin had been followed by the lords who had been in London at the time. These included Edward and Richard's nephew John de la Pole, who acted as chief mourner, and Lord Hastings, who, at least for now, was reconciled with Dorset, who was also in attendance.[13] After the required religious services, the body was taken in procession to Windsor on a chariot and along with its lifelike effigy,[14] before being laid to rest the next day. Neither Richard nor Anne were in attendance, but it is easy to imagine Anne weeping along with the other ladies in this contemporary lament:

> In May when every heart is light
> And fair flowers doth spread and spring,
> I rose me up before the day bright
> For to hear the birds sing
> I heard woeful lamenting
> Of ladies that were clothed in black
> Wept for King Edwards sake.[15]

Two days later, Richard ordered that a funeral Mass for his brother should be said in York Minster, at which point he seems to have still been in Yorkshire.

Amy Licence suggests that Anne accompanied her husband to the funeral Mass at York Minster, arguing that only ill health could have excluded her from the event.[16] Richard travelled with 300 men, and once in York, he led the nobility in swearing loyalty to the new king, Edward V, and according to the *Crowland Chronicle*, he made a particular point of being 'the first of all to take the oath'. Richard had written letters to the council and the queen, which assured them of his 'duty, fealty and due obedience to his king and lord Edward V'.[17]

It seems the inescapable conclusion therefore that Richard left York with no intention but to see his nephew crowned. Information regarding what happened over the next few days and weeks is shadowy at best. We know that Richard left York and intended to meet up with his nephew before travelling with him to London. The king seems to have travelled as planned, but at one point he went on ahead and Earl Rivers travelled back to meet up with Richard and the Duke of Buckingham. The next morning saw Rivers arrested, and other members of the Woodville escort were arrested when Richard and Buckingham rode to meet with the king the next day. There is not the space nor the scope here to discuss fully Richard's potential motives but by 30 April, Rivers, Grey, Vaughan, and Edward V's comptroller, Sir Richard Haute, were arrested by Richard and sent north. When news of these events reached London, Queen Elizabeth fled into sanctuary with Richard, Duke of York, her son by her first marriage, Thomas Grey, Marquis of Dorset, and her daughters, at Westminster Abbey. What information Elizabeth Woodville might have received is unclear; up until this point there is little evidence for a serious rift existing between Richard and the queen, but now she seems to have immediately feared the worst.

Meanwhile, Richard and the king remained at Northampton until 2 May, and at some point, he, Edward and Buckingham wrote down their mottos on a piece of paper, suggesting perhaps that Richard was seeking to gain the king's trust, Edward, after all, was extremely close to his Woodville uncles and must have been missing them and been apprehensive about the actions that had been taken by his uncle, Gloucester.[18] Richard signs his now famous motto, 'Loyaulte me lie' (Loyalty binds me), with a flourish.[19] By 4 May, the party was approaching London, the date that the Woodville faction had already declared should be the date of Edward V's coronation.[20] The fact that Edward and Richard entered London on that date was no accident; he was making a clear statement that Richard was now very much in charge and sure enough, he was quickly appointed Lord Protector by the council.

During this time, Anne remained in Yorkshire, which is strange because surely as the new king's aunt she would have been expecting to, and expected to, attend the new king's coronation on 4 May. This has been interpreted by Michael Hicks as evidence that Richard had already known before he left York that the coronation would not proceed as planned on that date and that it would be far better for Anne, and their son, to remain safely out of harm's way in the north, where he would not have to worry about protecting them.[21] Whilst again this is by no means certain, it must be considered a possibility, and if Richard knew, by default, Anne must have too. Richard would have had to have told her something.

While Anne waited, she would have heard more shocking family news. The same day that Richard entered London, 4 May, Anne's cousin George Neville died, unmarried and childless. This death was not only a personal family tragedy but also a political disaster for Richard. When the Neville inheritance had been divided, if Gloucester was to retain all the Neville lands, then George had to have children but not form an alliance strong enough to challenge Richard's claim to his lands. To this end, George was placed in Richard's custody, but as he was unmarried and childless when he died, there were no more male Montagu heirs, nor the prospect of any. Under the terms of the 1475 Act of Settlement, it therefore meant that Richard only became a life tenant of the Neville northern lands and they could not pass on to his and Anne's son, Edward. His vast northern kingdom was no more, and he and Anne were no longer the scions of a great northern dynasty. This was a devastating blow to Richard's hopes, and by extension, to those of Anne as well.[22] Already in mourning, Anne now had to grapple with the reality that her husband's northern dominion, based upon her own inheritance, would now exist only as long as he lived: her son would not inherit it.

It was his brother's sons, though, that were Richard's immediate focus and he and the council voted to move Edward V to the Tower of London to await his coronation, which was now to take place on Saturday, 22 June.[23] The

Crowland Chronicle makes a point of stating that this date would go ahead 'without fail', no doubt to try to reassure the queen and those outside the Protector's immediate circle. The nobles were instructed to assemble in London by 18 June for the coronation. Anne now travelled down to London, presumably believing that this was in preparation to attend the new king's coronation. We know that Richard had been staying at his mother's house at Baynard's Castle, after having stayed briefly at Crosby Place, and this is where in all likelihood Anne now stayed.[24] Another possibility is that she went to Crosby Place instead, but it is far more likely that Richard used this time to speak with his wife and bring her up to date with everything that had been happening. Anne would also have brought her own news, on how the death of George Neville had been received in Yorkshire, and what the northern rumours were regarding events in London. Matthew Lewis also suggests that she may have 'brought news that changed Richard's outlook, of a threat or even the possibility of some suspicious circumstances surrounding the sudden death of George Neville'.[25]

Anne remained in London and about a week after her arrival, she would have witnessed the immediate aftermath of the events of 13 June on the nobility and the capital, although she was not personally present at the notorious council meeting where Lord Hastings was killed. As late as 20 May, Hastings had been in Richard's favour, when Richard had made him Master of the Mint and confirmed him in the role of chancellor.[26] On 13 June, the council had gathered in the Tower of London. Anne's husband as Protector was there alongside Buckingham, and the Lords Hastings and Stanley, the Archbishop of York, Thomas Rotherham, and John Morton, now Bishop of Ely, whom Anne knew well. At some point during this meeting, tempers flared and Lord Hastings was dragged outside and summarily executed. Mancini writes that he was 'cut down ... on a false pretext of treason [for his loyalty to Edward IV] ... killed not by those enemies he had always feared but by a friend whom he never doubted'.[27] The fact that Hastings was executed so quickly does not mean that he was executed illegally; as Constable of England, Richard was entitled to try acts of treason and sentence a man to death with no right of appeal. One theory for his actions is that Richard had uncovered a treasonous plot at the meeting and simply legally dealt with the threat to the crown. As regent, Richard was

Death of the King

de facto ruler and treason against him was treason against the king. In fact, it does seem likely that Hastings was actively planning in some way to plot against Richard's regency, but the precise nature of any such plot may never be known as the accounts are contradictory. One theory is that Hastings suspected that Richard was planning to seize power for himself and that he had employed the lawyer William Catesby to report back to him regarding the nature of Richard's numerous meetings held at this time in order that he could plot to prevent him usurping Edward V. On the other hand, it is also possible that there was no plot and that Richard was simply acting to remove someone who could threaten his position and future plans.[28]

Three days after the death of Hastings, a group of lords led by Thomas Bourchier, the Archbishop of Canterbury, went to the queen in sanctuary and compelled her to release her second son, Richard, so that he might join his brother Edward in the Tower in order that he might begin to prepare for the coronation. By now, something had changed and Richard postponed the coronation until 9 November and the parliament until 25 June. Mancini reports that he now 'took off the mourning clothes that he had worn since his brother's death and putting on purple raiment he often rode through the capital accompanied by a thousand attendants'.[29]

At some point during this period, at one of the many meetings that Richard held, he had met with Richard Stillington, the Bishop of Bath and Wells, who told him that in the 1460s, his brother Edward had been precontracted to marry, or had married, a woman called Eleanor Talbot, thus making his marriage to Elizabeth Woodville invalid, and making Richard, not Edward V, the true heir to the throne. A rumour was also by now abroad that Edward IV had not even been the legitimate son of Richard, Duke of York, himself. London was uneasy and seething with such rumours, something that cannot have failed to come to Anne's attention. Did her husband confide in her that he now truly believed his nephews to be illegitimate? Or was his reasoning darker and his ambition had simply spotted a chance to elevate them both to the most illustrious position of all? Did Anne also now cast off her mourning? If she were to appear at the side of her husband, the answer must surely have been yes, to the latter, at least. There is no evidence of enmity having existed between Anne and her sister-in-law Elizabeth Woodville, but likewise, there is no evidence that they were particularly close either. However, as a mother, Anne possibly had a good deal of sympathy for the position in which the queen now found herself, separated as she was from her sons. If Anne did have any qualms, and we can never know, she quickly overcame them sufficiently enough to participate in the events of the next few months and there is no evidence that she did anything but loyally follow her husband's directives.

There were now a number of sermons preached, most notably that by Dr Edmund Shaa at St Paul's Cross on 20 June, which declared that the sons of Edward IV were illegitimate and therefore could not inherit the crown. After which, Mancini records that it was said that:

> the progeny of King Edward should be instantly eradicated, for neither had he been a legitimate king nor could his issue be so. Edward, they said, was conceived in adultery and in every way was so unlike his father, the late Duke of York, whose son he was falsely said to be, but Richard, Duke of Gloucester, who altogether resembled his late father, was to come to the throne as the legitimate successor.[30]

It is possible that Anne accompanied her husband to hear this sermon. There is not room here to address the veracity of these accusations, but what mattered to Anne, whether she personally believed them or not, was that they were the basis upon which her whole future was to rest. After the sermon, Buckingham spoke to the Alderman and Mayor of London at the Guildhall and explained the nature of the precontract. Meanwhile, Richard moved against the Woodvilles. Up in the north, at Pontefract, Earl Rivers, the queen's brother, Thomas Grey, her son and Thomas Vaughan were executed, an act that unusually is condemned by all accounts. Even Rous, usually so firmly in the Neville camp, recorded that they were 'unjustly and cruelly put to death being lamented by everyone and innocent of the deed for which they were charged'.[31] Again, the truth of the charges against them is beyond the scope of this book, but what would ultimately matter to Anne is that there were many who were horrified by the actions of her husband, and whilst many did believe the accusations of illegitimacy, many others were not convinced.

Chapter 12

Queen of England

> God give your graces both
> A happy and joyful time of day
> *Richard III*, William Shakespeare

It is not known whether Anne was present at Baynard's Castle on 15 June, when her husband claimed the crown. Although it has traditionally been maintained that Richard was offered the crown by Parliament, no English parliament sat between February 1483 and the beginning of 1484, so although Parliament would later endorse Richard, as indeed it would later do Henry Tudor, it did not invite him to take the crown at this time. Anne was now to be queen; she was to hold the office that her father had plotted for her to attain when he had married her to Edward. Did she feel that the long struggle had been worth it ... that her father was now to be avenged? Or did she view the future with trepidation? Did she approve of her husband's actions, had she even had prior knowledge of his plans? Or did she long to return to Middleham? We simply have no way of knowing. We have only the facts, and they are thankfully more numerous as Anne begins to step forward into centre stage, whether willingly or unwillingly.

Wanting or needing to move quickly, Richard now set his and Anne's coronation date for 6 July. Nearly everyone who had expected to attend Edward V's coronation was already present in London but there would need to be some alterations made. The robes prepared for Edward V were clearly not suitable and Anne was to be crowned alongside her husband, in what was to be the first double coronation since 1308, when the 23-year-old Edward II had been crowned alongside his 13-year-old wife, Isabella. To this end, Peter Courteys, keeper of the Great Wardrobe, received new orders on 27 June that they would have to provide the robes and necessary items by 3 July.¹ The Great Wardrobe was responsible for the provision of all the clothing and fabrics needed for the coronation for the monarch as well as for their consort and households. There were a number of positions in the Great Wardrobe, one being the position of king's tailor and the king's armourer, who rather than being purely responsible for armour was also responsible for embroidery, probably because long before Richard's time, he had been responsible for embroidering the pennants and banners needed on the battlefield. By Richard's time, there was actually a position of king's embroiderer, whilst the king's armourer largely worked at the Tower. The *Liber Regalis* (Royal Book), a medieval illuminated manuscript that specified the coronation procedure, stated that two sets of clothing were needed for the coronation by the king: crimson for his anointing and purple for his crowning.² Anne, it was decided, would also have two sets of clothing although only one is actually specified for a consort.

One of the seamstresses given the honour of working on Anne's coronation robes was a woman called Alice Claver, who was experienced in working with silks and in making mantles. She had been apprenticed as a child to a silk woman in London and given her later career, we can safely assume she quickly became very skilled at her craft. She married a mercer called Richard Claver and together they made a powerful team. Alice also appears to have traded in her own right, which was a privilege open to the women of London if they declared their position before the mayor and aldermen of the city. As a sole trader, separate from her husband, Alice would have been responsible for her own money and her own debts as well as being bound to the same code of conduct as the city's male traders. It seems that Alice was part of a network of silk women working in London; one Beatrice Fyler would make her executrix of her will and in return, she received a gold ring. Alice practised her trade in the parish of St Lawrence Jewry, and by 1480, she had become a supplier to Edward IV and his Great Wardrobe, and had sewn the mantle lace for the Duke of Ferrara's Garter robe. By the time she was employed to make the lace for Anne and Richard's robes and the white silk and gold lace for Anne's mantle, she was therefore extremely experienced in undertaking such work.³

While the seamstresses were busy sewing, Richard now set about ensuring that the recent change in plan was explained to every corner of his kingdom. The men of England and Calais were informed that they were required to swear oaths of loyalty to Richard III, not Edward V, and the bill declaring that Richard was now king was read aloud throughout the land.

Anne herself finally makes a definite appearance in the historical record on 3 July, when we know that she and Richard exchanged gifts. Richard gave Anne 4 yards of purple cloth of gold and 20 yards of the same fabric but this time decorated with garters, and seven yards of purple velvet. In return, Anne gave Richard 20 yards of purple velvet embroidered with roses and garters.[4] The next day, she and Richard travelled to the Tower, where they lodged in the royal apartments. If her nephews were still there at this point, perhaps Anne went to visit them, or enquired after their welfare. In addition, as Amy Licence speculates, the boys, if they were present, would surely have been curious about the coronation as Anne and her husband arrived.[5] Traditionally, the Tower was where the coronation ceremony began and the next day, Mancini tells us, Richard and Anne left the Tower 'attended by the entire nobility and a display of royal honours with bared head he [Richard] greeted all onlookers who stood along the streets and himself received their acclamations'. When Richard rode out of the Tower, Holinshed and later other historians suggest, Anne's son Edward was present and rode beside his father, but this is not the case; he was in fact still at Middleham, where the next day, the Mayor and Aldermen of York would ride out to present him with specially prepared food and wine.[6]

Richard, instead, was immediately followed by John Howard, Duke of Norfolk, his brother-in-law, the Duke of Suffolk, John de la Pole and the ever-loyal Buckingham. These were followed by the Earls of Northumberland, Arundel, Kent, Surrey, Wiltshire, Huntingdon, Nottingham, Warwick and Lincoln. Viscount Lovell was, of course, also at his master's and friend's side, alongside Viscount Lisle. Lords Stanley, Dudley, Dacres, Ferrers, Powis, Scrope(s), Grey(s), Stourton, Cobham, Morley, Abergavenny, de la Zouche, Wells, Maltravers, Herbert and Beecham were also in attendance. As Matthew Lewis points out, there were also some notable exclusions from Edward IV's old household, including Sir William Brandon and Sir William Norreys, both of whom, despite their attendance, would soon oppose Richard. William Brandon would famously be killed bearing Henry Tudor's standard at the Battle of Bosworth and William Norreys would join Buckingham in his rebellion, and finally return to England as a supporter of Henry Tudor, who would richly reward him for his loyalty. These events, though, were in the future and on the day of the coronation, there was no palpable sign of the troubles to come. The streets of London were filled with cheering citizens, all eager to catch a glimpse of their new king and queen.

Anne and her entourage followed that of her husband. She wore a dress of white cloth of gold, with a cloak and train of ermine, trimmed with the lace prepared by Alice Claver. Despite the fact that Anne and Richard already had a child together, she wore her hair loose in the traditional virginal style, topped with a gold circlet filled with pearls and other precious jewels. Her litter was decorated with white damask and white cloth of gold, and trimmed with ribbon bells and gold. Over her head, bells topped her royal canopy and jangled gently as the litter moved forward, pulled by two palfreys and flanked by twelve knights. There were two guiding ushers, William Joseph and John Vavasour, who represented the duchies of Aquitaine and Normandy. The entourage was led by Richard, Lord Grey of Powis, and her gentleman of the chair was one Thomas Hopton. Four carriages followed, in which travelled seven ladies who would become her ladies of the queen's chamber and twelve great ladies of the realm.[7] This was the culmination of every ambition her father had ever had for his daughter.

Outside St Paul's, Anne was presented with 500 marks as a gift from the city and she and Richard then continued on to the Palace of Westminster, where they took some wine and spices. Most likely, they did so in the King's Chamber, a room that was later described as 'the greatest [of the places] artistic treasures'.[8] The room had been built by Henry III and was used as both a private apartment by the king and as a reception room. At 82 feet long and 28 feet wide, it was best known for its stunning wall paintings, which had been started in 1226. They featured the Virtues and Vices alongside biblical figures, and it would most likely have been beneath these that Anne stood sipping her wine. The King's Chamber was to the south of the East End, by the Queen's Chamber, also known as the White Chamber, which had been originally used by Henry III's queen, Eleanor of Provence. Anne and her ladies might well have retired there during the proceedings, although by this time, the chamber was used by the lords and was where the monarch heard court requests. Later, the royal couple returned to the Tower, where Anne then left her husband, who was to carry out the ceremony known as the dubbing of the Knights of the Bath, which always takes place before a monarch's coronation. Although traditionally, forty-nine knights were dubbed by the king, there are only records showing seventeen who were dubbed by Richard. We know he also took a dinner of fish and a ceremonial bath before beginning his vigil and prayers. Presumably, Anne withdrew to a private chamber to rest, prepare and pray.

The morning of 6 July was warm and the sun was shining. The coronation procession assembled in Westminster Hall at 7 am, suggesting that Anne got little sleep the night before. Anne was dressed by her ladies, including her half-sister Margaret, who surely must have been a welcome presence. Her attire comprised:

> a smock of lawn and a kirtle beneath a royal surcoat. A mantle of crimson velvet with a train ... kept in places by heavy silk and gold mantle laces. All were furred with miniver. The kirtle has seventy annulets for the lacing down the front and probably down the sleeves.[9]

A contemporary description records how:

> our said sovereign Lady the Queen for to have unto her most honourable use ... and for her most honourable coronation: A robe of crimson velvet containing a mantle with a train, a surcoat and a myrtle furred ... and the surcoat garnished with gold of Venice. And the said mantle lace of silk and gold with buttons and tassels of silk and gold.[10]

Her long heavy crimson train was secured with heavier silk and gold laces. Her loose hair flowed down her back and she once again wore a golden circlet. She was proceeded into Westminster Abbey by her chamberlain and she was attended by Margaret Beaufort, the Countess of Richmond, who bore her train.[11] Margaret Beaufort was married to Lord Stanley, who was given the job of proceeding Richard into the abbey, bearing the imperial mace. Margaret was wearing a 'long robe made out of six yards of crimson velvet ... and contained six yards of white cloth of gold'.[12] She did not welcome this coronation but at this stage there is little evidence that, with her son in exile, she was doing anything more than biding her time. Of the women who accompanied Anne, Margaret was given precedence. Others included Margaret Chedworth, Duchess of Norfolk; Anne's sister-in-law Elizabeth, Duchess of Suffolk; Elizabeth Tilney, Countess of Surrey, whose husband was Thomas Howard, who bore Richard's sword of state at the coronation; and Joan Strangeways, Countess of Nottingham, a daughter of Katherine Neville and therefore Anne's second cousin. She probably welcomed having a friendly face because having Elizabeth Tilney next to her must have been somewhat uncomfortable for Anne. Elizabeth had been a long-time lady-in-waiting for Elizabeth Woodville, whose train she had carried at her coronation. Apparently a close friend to Edward IV's queen, she had accompanied Elizabeth into sanctuary and had attended her when she gave birth to Edward V at Westminster when Edward IV was in exile. Whatever the fate of the princes in the Tower, she must have participated in Anne's coronation through somewhat gritted teeth, feeling all the while that the infant she had helped to bring into the world should have been the one being crowned. Elizabeth was no great friend to Anne and when history once again came full circle, she would attend Elizabeth of York's coronation and would later become the grandmother of Anne Boleyn.

Bishops Goldwell and Courtenay flanked Margaret Beaufort and Anne's train as they moved forward. Both bishops were involved in the politics of the age but they were respected primarily as educated and talented men who served their cathedrals well.[13] Trumpets sounded as Anne and Richard entered the abbey and they walked along a carpet of ray cloth. They were preceded by Edmund Audley, the Bishop of Rochester, who carried the cross and who was a distant relation of Anne's; and Henry Percy, the Earl of Northumberland, who carried the sword of mercy. Following him, William Herbert carried the gilt spurs. All of these were men to whom Anne was either related or she knew. The Earl of Bedford had the honour of carrying St Edward's Staff whilst Thomas Stanley followed him. Edmund Grey, Earl of Kent, Francis, Lord Lovell, and Thomas Howard, Earl of Surrey, then processed, each carrying a sword. Richard, in his robes of purple velvet, walked beneath a canopy and his train was carried by Buckingham. Anne, likewise, advanced beneath a canopy and her crown was carried by Edward Stafford. Then came her ladies, followed by her other women, including her aunt, Alice FitzHugh, as well as Elizabeth Parr and Francis Lovell's wife

Anne (although Anne does not seem to have been fond of her – more of that later). Perhaps a much-needed friendlier face was provided by Anne's illegitimate half-sister, Margaret Huddleston, whom she would have known since childhood. 'Divers solemn songs' were sung as they approached the altar. A stage covered in red worsted fabric had been erected under the crossing, where Anne and Richard's thrones had been set. Richard would be crowned on St Edward's Chair, Anne on another, the details of which are unclear, and hers was set to the left and somewhat lower than that of her husband. At the high altar, Richard was anointed with holy oil, invested and crowned, while Anne sat to the side. Anne was then led to the altar, where she prostrated herself on the cushions and then knelt to be crowned and anointed on her temple and breasts with the holy oil. On the fourth finger of her right hand, a ring was placed, a sceptre was put into her right hand, and she was given a rod featuring the dove of peace to hold in her left hand. Then a crown was set upon her head and a High Mass was sung. Anne was now queen consort of England. Following the Mass, Anne and Richard went to the shrine of Edward the Confessor, and then broke their fast and changed into their second coronation outfits. We know from the detailed records of the Great Wardrobe that Anne now wore 'a robe of purple velvet containing a kirtle, a surcoat overt and a mantle with a train'. All her garments were made from 56 yards of purple velvet. 'The said surcoat [was] overfurred with miniver and ermine.'[14]

They returned to their thrones and then to Westminster Hall, after which they withdrew for a short while to their private chambers in Westminster Palace. Anne would have had a chance to speak privately with her husband for the first time that day. She was now Queen of England, and must have felt untouchable. This was the culmination of her father's ambitions for her and the family, and surely, she welcomed her elevation even if she had some reservations.

Her ladies would now have helped her get ready for the next stage of the day. The itinerary sounds exhausting to modern ears but we must remember that Anne had spent her whole life preparing for such a moment; she had been Princess of Wales and sister-in-law to Queen Elizabeth; she knew intimately the role she was now expected to play. It is worth mentioning that there are no contemporary accounts of Anne being either sick or feeble at her coronation, something that later historians would mention as a means of foreshadowing the rebellion and trials that were to come. There is in fact nothing to suggest that Anne was anything other than healthy and strong. When he chose to depict her, Rous opted to draw her in her coronation robes, although heraldic ones rather than the ones she actually wore. A good argument can be made to suggest that it was Anne Neville herself who commissioned the Rous Roll. If so, no doubt it depicted her as she wished to be recorded for prosperity: resplendent, with a determined expression, draped in the arms of her family and of England – the literal physical embodiment of the Warwick family's triumph.

Anne's husband, meanwhile, in the second illustration of him in the Rous Roll, is depicted as every inch the warrior king, wearing armour and holding a sword in his right hand and an orb in his left, with his heraldic boar lying at his feet. The text relating to the image reads:

> The most mighty prynce Rychard by the grace of god kynge of England and of Fraunce and lord of Ireland by verrey matrimony with owt dyscontynewans or any defylynge yn the lawe by eyre male lineally descended from kynge harre the second all avarice set a syde Rewled hys subjettys In hys Realme ful commendabylly poneschynge offenders of hys laws specyally Extorcioners and oppressors of hys comyns and chereschynge tho that were virtues by the whyche dyscrete guydynfe he gat great thank of god and love of all hys subjettys Ryche and pore and great land of the people of all other landys a bowt hym.[15]

This was undoubtedly the image that Anne and her husband wished to portray. The ceremonies continued at four o'clock, when the coronation banquet began and Anne re-entered Westminster Hall, stepping on the cloth of gold that had been laid by the Earl Marshal, the Duke of Norfolk. She sat down at the marble table of the king's bench, to the left of her husband.[16] Archaeology has proved that this table was made of Purbeck marble, from Dorset. Cool to the touch, it would have shone as the sun streamed through the stained-glass windows, reflecting their brilliant colours.[17] Westminster Hall had been remodelled in 1401, when Richard II commissioned the master mason Henry Yevele to raise the walls and add two towers to the north entrance. Numerous high-quality heraldic carvings were also added throughout the hall, so we know that when Anne sat down to her coronation feast, she was surrounded by symbols such as the white hart, a motif related to the name Richard Rich-hart and possibly derived from Joan of Kent, holding the arms of England, as well as number of other heraldic beasts, such as the swan of Henry IV and the arms of Edward the Confessor.[18]

Two countesses attended Anne, tasked with meeting her every need and raising a cloth when she wished to drink. One of these was Jane Berkeley, Countess of Nottingham, who as a daughter of Sir Thomas Strangeways and Katherine Neville was Richard's cousin. The other was Elizabeth Howard, Countess of Surrey, whose first husband had died at Barnet. On the other side of Richard sat the Bishop of Durham. The remainder of the guests were seated at four long tables, Anne's ladies being placed on the second table on the left. Among them was Alice FitzHugh, who was the only one of Anne's aunts to have been invited to the coronation. Alice was joined by her daughter Anne, who had married Francis Lovell, and her daughter-in-law Elizabeth Burgh. Alice's daughter Elizabeth, who had married William Parr, was possibly also present although her husband was not. William Parr claimed he was too unwell to attend but many then and ever since have claimed that this was an excuse and that he did not attend because he did not support Richard's accession as king.[19] Through Elizabeth, Alice would later become great-grandmother to Katherine Parr, the last of the six wives of Henry VIII. Alice, as far as we can tell, seems to have been close to her niece, Anne, and perhaps during the banquet their eyes met across the sea of heads in familial triumph. Anne would later appoint her and her daughter Elizabeth as ladies-in-waiting and it was Anne who most likely had instructed Richard that they were to be gifted the grandest cloth available from which to have their dresses made for the coronation.

It was now time for the food: the two main courses were brought in with great ceremony by Sir Robert Percy, Marshall of the Hall, and their arrival was heralded by trumpets sounding. Anne's food was served on a gilt plate, whilst Richard's was served on gold and the bishop's on silver. Anne ate from dishes including roast capon, quail, egret, chickens, veal, sturgeon with fennel, pike, crab, peacock and custards.[20] Whilst this sounds magnificent, it is in fact nothing remarkable for a medieval royal feast, possibly due to the fact it was put together very quickly, suggesting that the cooks did not have time to prepare new and ever more extravagant dishes. As the second course was being served, a traditional part of the coronation banquet ritual was performed when the king's champion, Sir Robert Dimmock, rode into the hall in armour and with his horse draped in red and white silk. He rode in, throwing his gauntlet down upon the flagstones and challenging anyone who opposed King Richard to combat. No challenges were issued and the hall erupted to a cry of 'King Richard!' He issued the challenge twice more to ensure that everyone had heard it but no one replied. His duty done, Sir Robert was offered a gold cup of wine for his service, from which he took a sip before tipping the rest on the floor. The gold cup he kept as payment for carrying out his duty.

Contemporary records suggest that the banquet lasted for five and a half hours. When Anne and Richard had eaten their fill, it was late into the night. They were served sweet wine by the Mayor of London in a cup that was set with pearls. Richard, presumably accompanied by Anne, now 'returned to his chamber and every man to his lodging'.[21] Sadly, no records exist of the events of the next few days but we do know that Anne and Richard remained at the Palace of Westminster, where they were no doubt entertained by tournaments and jousts, in keeping with tradition. Anne would also have attended more formal meals and Masses of thanksgiving. No doubt she would have met with numerous of her more distant relations, now seeking her favour and patronage. She would also have finally decided upon those who would be her ladies-in-waiting as queen. As we have seen, Alice FitzHugh was amongst them, as was her daughter Elizabeth, who perhaps was keen to show that she was loyal to the new regime whatever her husband might think. One omission, however, was Alice's daughter Anne, who was married to Francis Lovell. Why she was not appointed is something of a mystery; the appointment of ladies-in-waiting was mostly a matter of politics rather than personal pleasure. Although Anne did have some scope to give preference to women she personally liked, politics was usually the overriding consideration. As the wife of Richard's close personal friend and key lord in the government, Anne was entitled to be lady-in-waiting for the queen, but she was not. This raises the question of whether Anne Neville disliked Lady Lovell enough to exclude her. If she did so, it was certainly with the consent of her husband, who perhaps bowed to her personal request. Another possibility is that Anne Lovell herself turned down the honour, possibly because she wished to stay with her husband. The king and queen's royal households were often apart and largely existed separately. If Lady Lovell served her queen, she could expect to see a lot less of her husband than hitherto. If this was the case then perhaps Anne was sympathetic and excluded her kindly on those grounds. Elizabeth Babthorpe was appointed as a 'gentlewoman' to Queen Anne, as was Elizabeth Mauleverer. Grace Poleyn, Katherine Scrope, whose husband was Anne's carver at the coronation, and Anne Tempest also became her gentlewomen.

One other woman in Anne's entourage is worth mentioning and that is her half-sister Margaret – her father's illegitimate daughter who had been born sometime in 1450 (her mother's name is unknown). Anne knew her half-sister well and in 1464, Margaret had been advantageously married to Richard Huddleston, a close associate of Richard's. Anne Sutton suggests that there is enough evidence to suppose that there was 'affection' between Anne and Margaret, and her inclusion in Anne's coronation preparation and ceremony does seem to support this, although due to the scarcity of the evidence we cannot know for certain how often the two women were in each other's company.

We unfortunately know very little about any fifteenth-century queen's household, but even less about Anne Neville's as queen. There are, however, a few suppositions and facts that can be ascertained. We know that it was modelled on that of her predecessor, Elizabeth Woodville. In addition to her ladies like Elizabeth, Anne had two chamberers and five henchmen. Her yeoman of horse was called William Danyell and she had a gentleman of her chair called Thomas Hopton, and two ushers for her chamber called William Joseph and John Vavasour, who would have worked alongside a yeoman of her chamber, who was called John Snowdon, and the yeoman usher, Walter Graunt. These are the men who would have interacted with her on a daily basis. Anne also engaged a troop of musicians, as was customary, to play for her entertainment and to entertain her guests.

The fact that after the coronation Anne received no clothing from the king's Great Wardrobe is evidence that her own Queen's Wardrobe was up and running as it should, even though the records of it do not survive. We do know that it operated out of the Prince's Wardrobe, and had done so since at least 1465. The building had originally been the wardrobe of the Black Prince, hence its name, and stood on the site between Old Jewry, Catte Street, Ironmonger Lane at the Church of St Olaves, north of Cheapside.[22] We also know that as queen, Anne kept a lion, who sometimes accompanied her on her tours of the country. Records for this begin shortly after her coronation, so perhaps the lion was a coronation present.

Following the coronation, Anne remained at Westminster for two weeks, after which she and Richard travelled down the Thames Valley and witnessed elaborate pageantry on their journey. According to Vergil, a 'great confluence of people [turned out] for desire of beholding their new king'. They were at Greenwich by 13 July and then moved on to Windsor, where Anne likely paid her respects at the grave of her brother-in-law, Edward IV. On their journey, people cheered Anne and her husband; she must have felt utterly secure. Yet historian Matthew Lewis makes it clear that he believes that Richard had already made the most serious mistake of his fledgling reign, because whilst it was 'undoubtedly desirable for a new monarch to show himself to his people ... Richard was not well known by the political elite of London and had not given them time to be familiar with him'. As a result, as he travelled north towards his more familiar 'home lands', he left London to its own devices... and to seethe with rumours.[23] It is possible that Anne was also a factor behind their decision to leave London; she no doubt wanted to see her son and likely there was also an element of wanting to show herself as queen in the centre of the northern Neville heartlands.

Initially, Anne did not accompany her husband. She remained at Windsor for about two weeks whilst Richard left on 21 July to travel to Oxford, Woodstock, Tewkesbury, Gloucester, Worcester and Warwick. Again, this has been used by later historians to imply that Anne's health necessitated her remaining at Windsor, but although she was no doubt tired, there is no evidence that she was unwell. It was usual for the king to travel without his queen and Richard's tour took place at a breakneck pace. One other thing to consider is that Richard's tour took in Tewkesbury: whatever her feelings in relation to her first husband, Tewkesbury could hardly have been a happy memory for Anne and perhaps she did not wish to return. It would also not have been political for Anne to go to an area where her presence might remind people just how close she had been to the heart of the Lancastrian regime.

While at Windsor, Anne mostly likely stayed in the room that had been used by Elizabeth Woodville in 1472, which was the largest in the castle. There is some evidence that Richard and Anne initially favoured the chapel. In 1478, a covenant between Richard and the Dean and Canons of Windsor concerned the grant of manors at Bentfield Bury in Essex, Knapton in Norfolk, and Chelsworth in Suffolk to fund Masses for Richard and Anne during their lives and after their deaths. In 1480, the lands were conveyed to them by the then duke, Richard of Gloucester, and in 1482, Richard and Anne granted the advowson of the Church of Olney to the Dean and Canons of Windsor, the final concord of which was issued in 1483.[24] These signs of favour, issued in both Richard and Anne's name, may indicate that Anne spent time there prior to this and felt an affinity to the chapel. If she did, perhaps this is why she chose to remain, presumably attending Mass there for two weeks after her coronation.

Anne and her ladies left Windsor in early August and travelled north to join Richard at Warwick. He arrived there on 8 August and Anne soon afterwards. Also present was Anne's nephew, Edward, the Earl of Warwick, who actually owned the castle.[25] Anne's nephew was now 8 years old and the ward of Thomas Grey, Marquess of Dorset. Thomas Grey was, of course, the son of Elizabeth Woodville, and there was no love lost between him and Richard, who had by now executed his brother and usurped his nephew.[26] Edward does not appear to have been mistreated, although an early twentieth-century account claims that Dorset 'imprisoned' him in the Tower. Today, this is generally accepted as a misreading of the evidence; he probably was often lodged at the Tower simply because Thomas Grey was the Constable of the Tower during this period. Also, we know from the royal household accounts that Edward IV personally bought his nephew several pairs of expensive shoes and boots. Edward of Warwick was to be placed in Anne's care as queen. It seems likely, however, that Anne knew her niece, Margaret, somewhat better. Where Margaret grew up is not recorded, but historian Susan Higginbotham suggests she was most likely raised in the royal household alongside the daughters of Edward IV and Elizabeth Woodville.[27] In January 1482, Edward IV had ordered that forty marks be spent on her clothing and the wages of her servants, followed by another fifty marks later in the year, suggesting that she was treated well and honourably.[28] Given this, it is likely that Anne knew her niece quite well and had watched her grow at the royal court. Although we cannot be certain that Margaret now went to Warwick to be placed in Anne's care like her brother, it seems very likely, as we know that she was later with him in the north.[29]

While Anne was staying at Warwick, she visited Guy's Cliff, a location about a mile from the castle, which, according to legend, was where Guy of Warwick had retired to a hermitage. This led to the founding of a chantry there in 1423 as the Chapel of St Mary Magdalene. It was also the site where Piers Gaveston had allegedly been apprehended during the reign of Edward II before his execution on nearby Blacklow Hill.[30] Rous, now an old man, continued to officiate at Guys Cliffe, and while Anne was there, she was presented with the English version of the Rolls of the Earls of Warwick. This copy focused more than the Salisbury Roll on the direct familial line of descent, which culminated in the image of Anne and Richard in their coronation regalia, literally crowning the achievements of the Beauchamp and Neville families. Given the political circumstances, this must have been a somewhat last-minute addition. We also need to remember that Rous knew Anne far less well than her mother and sister; she had, after all, not been resident at Warwick for many years, nor did she inherit the castle. In contrast, he knew Anne's mother very well, and also her sister Isobel, who had lived there in 1471–6. This discrepancy is highlighted by the fact that Rous gives us the precise dates and places of birth for all of Isobel's children but not for Anne's son, whom he most likely had never met.

Rous also does not uniformly approve of Anne, and he certainly does not approve of Richard. He makes a point of recording the Duchess Anne's tribulations since the Kingmaker's death and he states that it was down to Anne that her mother was 'kept straightly' at Middleham. He later clarifies that when the duchess appealed for her freedom, Duke Richard had locked her up for life. Whether these words were added later or were present in 1483, it is impossible to determine. It is known that Rous later believed that Richard poisoned Anne.[31]

Nevertheless, Anne seems to have been very impressed, for it is almost certain that she now commissioned a biography of her grandfather, Richard

Beauchamp, known as the Beauchamp pageants, which was to be lavishly illustrated.[32] The Beauchamp pageants, a copy of which was made for Anne's mother, survives in the British Library. It contains fifty-five pageants – ink drawings that illustrate Richard Beauchamp's life from his birth to his death and are accompanied by captions. The drawings are stunningly detailed and are renowned 'for their sense of drama, their realism, and their immense detail'.[33] In one of them, the earl jousts at the coronation of Joan of Navarre when she became Queen of England, offering us a tantalising glimpse into the celebrations that Anne had likely just witnessed following her own. In consequence of this visit, Rous would refer to Richard as 'a special good lord to the town and lordship of Warwick' due to the fact that he gave the town unspecified ancient privileges, ones that had not been granted to Clarence.[34]

Anne left Warwick along with the entire royal party on 15 August and travelled via Coventry, Leicester and Nottingham before arriving at Pontefract Castle on the 28th, where she spent the night. This may have been a deliberate choice, being the location so recently of the executions of the Earls Rivers and Grey and Sir Thomas Vaughan. It was also where Richard II had been imprisoned and later died sometime in February 1400. In his play *Richard III*, William Shakespeare calls Pontefract Castle a 'bloody prison. Fatal and ominous to noble peers! Within the guilty closure of thy walls Richard II was here hacked to death and for more slander to thy dismal seat we give thee up our guiltless blood to drink.'[35] For Anne, though, the experience of Pontefract was much happier; she was greeted warmly and while there was reunited with her son, Edward, who had travelled to meet his parents. Anne and Edward would have stayed in the castle's royal chambers, which were relatively new, having been built in the early fifteenth century. There were two towers that flanked a large great hall and the towers were five storeys high, one of which contained the king's accommodation, the other the queen's. The queen's tower had a principle or great chamber, with two bedchambers above it. Below was a room referred to as the nursery during later periods. It was in this tower that Anne stayed, although sadly, we know nothing of the manner in which it was furnished at the time. For Anne, this reunion must have been joyful. Edward was to be at the centre of all the coming celebrations, and feted as heir to the throne of England.

Chapter 13

Queen of the North

> Your gentle souls fly in the air
> And not be fixed in perpetual doom.
> *Richard III*, William Shakespeare

Anne stayed only one night at Pontefract before the royal progress moved on to York, where lavish celebrations had been planned by John Kendal, Richard's secretary. He wrote to the mayor of York and council on 23 August that:

> I verily know the king's mind and entire affection that His Grace Breathe towards you and your Worshipful city, for manifold your kind and loving designs to His Grace showed heretofore, which His Grace will never forget and intendeth therefore so to do unto you that all the kings that ever reigned did never so much.[1]

In response, the council of York had decided to present:

> our sovereign to the king ... at his coming with 100 marks in a pair of basins of silver gilt or in a cup of gold or in a gilt piece and that our sovereign Lady the Queen presented with a hundred pieces of gold in a piece

They also planned numerous pageants. In anticipation of such a warm reception, Richard commissioned 13,000 white boar badges to be made for his loyal supporters.[2]

When Anne left the castle she was accompanied by her husband, son, five bishops (those of Durham, Worcester, St Asaph, Carlisle and St Davids), three earls (Northumberland, Surrey and Lincoln), six lords (Lovell, FitzHugh, Stanley, Strange, Lisle and Greystoke) along with other members of the nobility. Outside the city walls near to the Chapel of St James, they were met by the mayor, accompanied by aldermen and the city councillors. At a meeting on 4 August, it had been decided that the main party would be dressed in scarlet robes and that all the other members of the party would also be dressed in red; anyone who did not wear red would be fined 20 shillings.[3]

As they passed St James's Church and Micklegate, they were greeted by the citizens, who were dressed in 'blue, violet and musterdivilers'.[4] This was a type of mixed grey woollen cloth originally from Montivilliers in Normandy.[5] It seems likely that it was near to Micklegate that the mayor welcomed them with a speech and Queen Anne was presented with 100 pounds of gold.[6] They then 'entered the city honourably' and processed to York Minster. On the way, Anne would have viewed three splendid pageants themed around the Festival of the Beheading of John the Baptist, whose feast day it was. These had been planned by Henry Hudson, the rector of the Church of All Saints. When Henry VII entered the city in 1486, and the city wished to make clear its loyalty to the new king, we know that the pageants put on featured both red and white roses, so perhaps we can assume, as historian Peter Hammond does, that white roses were prevalent during Anne and Richard's procession.[7] Anne then attended a service at the Minster, at which the church officials were all dressed in copes of blue. Richard, it is recorded, was sprinkled with holy water and incense and as Anne was at his side, we can assume the honours were extended to her too.[8] The royal party then retired to the Archbishop's Palace, where they were to stay. Anne's uncle, George Neville, had once lived there as Archbishop of York, so perhaps Anne was already familiar with the palace. She and Richard had, of course, also met as children at his enthronement feast at Cawood Castle, so maybe the memory of that event was discussed between them. Richard often stayed at the Augustinian priory when in York, but Anne and Richard now stayed at the Archbishop's Palace, as befitted their new status. This building lay to the north of the Minster and Anne would have been able to pray in the Bishop's Chapel. Perhaps she also saw the six bays of twelfth-century blind arcading, which survive to this day.

The Archbishop of York at the time was Thomas Rotherham; he was no supporter of Richard and had only been released from the Tower in July, having been charged with involvement in the supposed conspiracy between Lord Hastings and the Woodvilles against Richard.[9] He was the only real fly in the ointment, though, during this period, which perhaps was the happiest of Anne's life. While in York she attended feasts and a Creed play, a type of entertainment that was a regular feature of life in the city and had been since the late 1300s, and which focused on religious subjects and iconography.[10]

The culmination of Anne's visit to York, however, was the knighting of her son and his creation as Prince of Wales, which took place at the Archbishop's Palace on the evening of 8 September 1483, the date of the traditionally celebrated Feast of the Nativity of the Blessed Virgin. Just beforehand, Richard and Anne were 'both crowned ... went in procession to the aforesaid church, the Prince and all other Lords both spiritual and temporal being in attendance', and they presented the church with 'silver and gilt figures of the twelve apostles and many other relics given by the Lord King'.[11] An account of the investiture exists in the Bedern College Statute Book, written in a late fifteenth-century hand:

> On the Feast of the Nativity of the Blessed Virgin, the King and Queen both crowned, went in procession to the aforesaid church, the Prince and all the other Lords, both spiritual and temporal being in attendance. The Bishop of Durham was the officiating prelate and the High Altar was ornamented with the silver and gilt figures of the twelve Apostles and many other relics given by our Lord King. These remained here until the sixth hour. After Mass they all returned to the Palace and there before dinner [Edward] was created Prince by the Lord King in the presence of all.[13]

The Crowland chronicler said that this occasion was almost a second coronation and that after Richard had been crowned it was Anne who personally 'led her son by the hand [to where he was] crowned with so great an honour, joy and congratulation of the inhabitants'. Anne's son was knighted alongside her nephew, Edward of Warwick, and John of Pontefract, Richard's illegitimate son. Following Edward's investiture there was held a great banquet, during which Anne sat crowned alongside her husband and son for around four hours accompanied by 'the Dean Robert Booth, and of the Canons, Treasurer Portington, Archdeacon Poteman of Cleveland, the sub dean, and four other Prebendaries, ten chantry priests, twelve vicars choral together with other ministers of the church'.[14] This was designed, according to *Hall's Chronicle*, so that 'all men should behold and see him and his Queen and prince in their high estates and degrees'.[15] A special order had been placed with the Great Wardrobe for the occasion, which included suits of armour, heralds doublets, five banners depicting the Holy Trinity, Saints George and Cuthbert as well as the king's arms. In addition, an enormous 13,000 cushions, embroidered with the white boar, had been created. Lisa Hilton has suggested that Edward of Middleham was already so unwell at the time of his investiture that he had to be carried into the church, but this seems an impossible suggestion, which is not supported by the contemporary accounts of the events. In addition, it is unlikely that a boy would have been able to walk alongside his mother and then sit wearing a crown for four hours, if he were so unwell.[16] We also know that Edward had not been living the life of an invalid. The castle kept a pack of hounds, which he no doubt enjoyed watching and riding with, he paid local visits and he wore rich clothing, including on one occasion a gown of green velvet. More evidence for his health is suggested by the fact that when Anne had met Richard at Warwick on 8 August, they had received an ambassador from Queen Isabella of Castile and it seems they had discussed the possibility of a future marriage between Prince Edward and Isabella, the queen's daughter – something that seems unlikely if there were serious concerns for the prince's health.

Matthew Lewis suggests that the investiture of Edward as Prince of Wales was carried out spontaneously to thank York for its hospitality and welcome, and this may well be the case.[17] The Great Wardrobe order was not placed until 31 August, when Richard sent a letter to London and then dispatched Sir John Tyrell to collect a 'purple satin doublet, a tawny satin lined one, crimson of gold gowns and a myriad of other articles required for the investiture'.[18] It must briefly be mentioned that many later have considered that this letter, and the messenger who took it to London, was dispatched with a darker purpose – to order the deaths of Edward V and Richard of York – and that upon the messenger's return, confirmed to Richard that they were dead. There is not the scope here to debate the evidence for and against this but it must be mentioned as if it was the case, then no doubt Anne would have also been told upon the messenger's return. Whether it was planned or not, or whether in fact Anne's nephews were dead, it seems clear that Richard chose to invest their son now to powerfully demonstrate that theirs was a stable dynasty, with a male heir to rival any of their nephews. While Richard was in York he was also made aware of trouble brewing in London, where an 'enterprise' had been reported against him. It was not serious enough for him to leave York himself but maybe he thought there would be no better way to assert his dominance firmly than by investing his son. Edward went on to be formally created Prince of Wales by a charter dated to 24 August 1483.

One other event of importance for Anne took place when she was in York and that was the establishment of a formal Household and Council for Prince Edward. He now took over the nominal leadership of Richard's ducal Council and Household in the North, which must have met with Anne's approval.[19] Anne herself was now at the peak of her powers as queen. In September 1483, she was allowed to appoint the mastership of the Hospital of St Mary's in le Horsefair. Her choice was William Cerff, a monk of Molsa. Likewise, she was involved in the appointment of a new chaplain to Holy Cross Church in Cambridge. These were important appointments and they give us a glimpse into the kind of influence Anne was now wielding on a national scale.

At some point in mid-September, likely on the 21st, Anne left York and returned to Middleham with her son, whilst Richard, who left a day earlier, progressed to Pontefract and then down to Lincoln.[20] Anne was accompanied by her household, including Alice FitzHugh, although it seems once again that Elizabeth Parr did not accompany them; her husband was by now dying.[21] The journey from York to Middleham was one of about 50 miles and Anne was feted by the people along the route, who turned out to catch a glimpse of their Queen of the North. This was perhaps enough to alleviate any niggling worries Anne may have had about trouble brewing in the south.

Bad news, however, would have reached Anne soon after her arrival back at Middleham. While in Lincoln, her husband learnt of a rebellion against his rule, known to history as the October Rebellion, led nominally by the Duke of Buckingham. Henry Stafford, 2nd Duke of Buckingham, had been a ward of Edward IV and was made a duke in 1460 after the death of his grandfather at the Battle of Northampton. He had been Richard's closest friend and ally ever since he had pledged loyalty to him on 29 April 1483. Buckingham's betrayal, therefore, cut Richard to the core, and no doubt Anne also felt it deeply. It appears that Richard had trusted Buckingham implicitly and he had been well rewarded for his service. In May, he was appointed Chamberlain and Justiciar of South and North Wales, Constable of all the Welsh royal castles and Receiver General of the Duchy of Cornwall. He was also given the great Bohun lands and the Constableship of England. He was, by this time, undoubtedly the second most powerful man in England. At Lincoln, Richard wrote to the chancellor in London requesting the Great Seal, and the postscript vehemently illustrates his shock and anger at Buckingham's betrayal. He writes:

> Here, loved be God, all is well and truly determined for to resist the malice of him that had best cause to be true, the duke of Buckingham, the most untrue creature living; whom, with God's grace, we shall not be long till that we will be in that parts and subdue his malice. We assure you there never was a falser traitor purveyed for.[22]

By calling for the seal, it is also clear that Richard felt the threat to him was severe, because the seal was the mechanism by which the government operated and through which it could raise troops.

Why Buckingham decided to abandon his king is unclear; it has been suggested that he was unhappy at the delays he was experiencing in receiving the Bohun inheritance, but this seems unlikely as Richard was simply waiting for his parliament to assemble to legally sign the lands over to him. Another possibility is that he now knew that Edward V and Richard of York were dead, and this was a step too far even for Buckingham.[23] Vergil writes that he 'was [now] partly repenting that hitherto of himself he had not resisted King Richard's evil enterprise [and resolved] to separate himself from him'.[24] Another option is that Buckingham was now 'considering pressing his own claim to the throne'.[25] He had in mid-August spoken with John Morton and argued that he had a good claim based upon his own descent from Thomas of Woodstock, the youngest son of King Edward III. At this time, it also seems to have been suggested that he might join forces with Margaret Beaufort, who was plotting for her own son's advancement. Margaret was not with Anne at this time but Anne certainly knew her well. The affairs of the Wars of the Roses, as always, were deeply personal and betrayal was often disguised behind a friendly smile. Historian Dr Nicola Tallis argues that Margaret's plotting by this stage clearly indicated that she believed the princes had now been murdered.[26] Reginald Bray, one of Margaret's most trusted servants, was now sent to Buckingham and enabled communication between the duke and Margaret.[27] Whether Richard or Anne were aware of Margaret's involvement at this time is unclear. Richard, however, was utterly determined to defeat Buckingham.

He achieved his aim relatively easily. Appalling weather hampered him in Wales and although the uprising did occur on 18 October, his men quickly deserted him, forcing him to flee into the Forest of Dean.[28] He was soon betrayed by the locals and was taken to Salisbury, where by now Richard had arrived. Buckingham was beheaded on Sunday, 2 November in the marketplace; not even the fact it was the Sabbath could spare him. He had begged to be allowed to see his former friend and master, but Richard refused to see him.

Anne's thoughts can only be guessed at, but the sense of security she had felt for the past few months must have been totally destroyed. Margaret Beaufort's involvement would come to light over the ensuing weeks, and Anne must have wondered who, if anyone, even in her own household, she could trust. By Christmas 1483, Anne was back in London, though perhaps she did not feel much like celebrating. It seems unlikely that she took on many of Elizabeth Woodville's London household staff. Instead, J.L. Laynesmith suggests that she travelled with many of those women who had been in attendance upon her at Middleham, including Elizabeth Bapthorpe, her half-sister Margaret Huddleston, Elizabeth Mauleverer, Grace Pullman,

Joyce Percy, Katherine Scrope, Alice Skelton and Anne Tempest.[29] Such loyalty to one's attendants and servants was not uncommon. We know that in December 1483, Richard issued a grant for life to a woman called Joan Malpas, who had served both Richard and Cecily, Duchess of York, since Richard's childhood at Fotheringhay. Henry and Isabel Burgh, who had been members of Anne and Richard's household at Middleham, were also now given twenty marks a year for their good service and their care of Prince Edward.[30] It would make sense in this context that Anne continued this pattern in retaining her northern ladies.

We know that Anne spent Christmas 1483 at Westminster, but her primary residence when in London was at Greenwich Palace, which was the traditional seat of the medieval queens of England. In doing so she was walking in the footsteps of her predecessors Elizabeth Woodville and Margaret of Anjou, who had both spent time there.[31] Indeed, it seems likely that Anne would have visited Elizabeth Woodville there on many previous occasions. The medieval palace at Greenwich was known as Bella Court or the Palace of Placentia, and had been built by Humphrey, Duke of Gloucester, in 1443.[32] Margaret of Anjou had enlarged the palace, adding windows, built a pier and laid down terracotta tiles that bore her royal symbol. Edward IV confiscated it from the Lancastrian queen and authorised a programme of alterations that were undertaken by Robert Kettlewell. It was once one of Elizabeth Woodville's favourite residences and makes numerous appearances in Edward IV's royal itinerary.[33] In 1481, a joust had been held there to celebrate their son's marriage to Anne Mowbray, an event at which Anne may have been present, and in 1482 Edward IV's daughter, Anne's niece, Mary, had died there. In 1483, Edward IV had invited the observant friars to establish a house adjacent to the palace, which would have been under construction by the time Anne was in residence as queen and would consist of a chantry with a chapel dedicated to the holy cross. While at Greenwich, Anne was visited by her husband, whose accounts show that he frequently journeyed to and from the palace. Anne and Richard would still have been hoping to have more children, suggesting that they were regularly sleeping together in the fullest sense. The later suggestion by Richard's physician that he absent himself from her bed when she fell ill suggests that prior to that they were known to be often together.[34]

At some point in late 1483, Anne left Greenwich to celebrate Christmas with the court at Westminster. Christmas was kept lavishly, with Richard continuing his brother's tradition of richly rewarding his grooms and pages. He paid 100 pounds to them that Christmas, equal to more than 70,000 pounds in today's money. A groom's bonus was 5,760 pounds – twelve times as much as they received during the rest of the year. It is clear that Richard maintained the majority of household regulations and arrangements for the festivities that were laid down by his late brother.[35] He also made a payment to the goldsmiths of London; in particular, on 22 January 1484, Richard paid 764 pounds 17 shillings and 6 pence to the goldsmith Edmund Shawe in payment for supplying the king's Christmas gifts and other jewels.[36] It seems certain that at least part of this sum was used by Richard to purchase jewels for Anne as her Christmas/New Year gift, although what portion of this was spent on her is unclear.

Edmund Shawe himself is an interesting figure. After finishing his apprenticeship in 1458, he rose quickly and within four years, became an engraver at the Tower of London. He served Edward IV as his goldsmith and lent him money on several occasions, further evidence that Richard was continuing to patronise those who had served his brother. Despite this, Shawe's brother Ralph, a theologian, had preached against the legitimacy of Edward IV's marriage and Shawe, who was serving as mayor of London, according to Shakespeare at least, had been one of those who offered the crown to Richard.

During medieval times, the focus of gift giving was on Epiphany, or twelfth night, when the Magi had visited the baby Jesus with their gifts of gold, frankincense and myrrh. Throughout the Christmas period, Anne would have attended feasts and Masses at Westminster Abbey. On 1 January, there would have been the Feast of Fools, which involved cross-dressing, misrule and general pranks. The clergy on this day were permitted to be silly; a French account dating to the period Anne lived in condemned this occasion where:

> priests and clerks may be seen wearing masks and monstrous visages at the hours of office ... they dance in the choir dressed as women, pander or minstrel. They sing wanton songs. They

eat black puddings ... whilst the celebrants were saying Mass ... they play at dice ... without a blush at their own shame.'[37]

There would also have been a number of feasts, at which peacocks would almost certainly have been served. They were extremely popular, as were swans. One hundred years earlier, one royal Christmas feast had included pasties, sausage, black pudding, fish, fowl roast meat, custards, tarts, nuts, and sweetmeats, all washed down with huge quantities of wine and ale. Henry III had also added lampreys to his Christmas menu, and Henry V had ordered large quotas of crayfish, eels and porpoises. Anne would also have most likely been entertained by mummers (troupes of amateur actors), who were very popular at the time, performing folk plays and pageants.

We know that Richard did not stay long in London after twelfth night. Two days later, he was on his way to Kent, where he travelled to Canterbury and then on to Sandwich.[38] Margaret of Anjou and Elizabeth Woodville had often travelled to Canterbury with their husbands, so it is possible that Anne accompanied Richard there to pay her respects at the shrine of Thomas Becket.[39] Amy Licence suggests that Richard had repaired the roads there, before specifically journeying to Canterbury to coincide with the 400th anniversary of the establishment of the famous hospital, established there in 1084 by Bishop Lanfranc to treat lepers.[40]

Unfortunately, we simply do not know if Anne accompanied her husband; she may just as likely have remained in Westminster, or travelled to Greenwich to relax after the Christmas festivities. What we do know is that her son was not with her; Edward had remained in Middleham for the festive period and did not travel to London to join his parents. With children on her mind, perhaps it was during this period that Anne made arrangements for the accommodation and education of her nephews and nieces. Edward of Warwick was somewhere in the north by late 1483, most likely settled at Sandal Castle, in Wakefield, and it seems likely that Margaret now was sent north to join him. In February 1484, Roger Holdern was granted the manor of Sutton to care for 'Edward son of Isobel and Clarence'. Margaret was certainly with her brother by 8 June, when Richard ordered that cloth of gold, velvets, satins and damask be sent to her. Anne's niece was now around 10 years of age and her future marriage might already have been something that Anne and Richard were giving thought to.[41]

Richard and Anne were back in London and at Westminster by 21 January, when Richard called his first and only parliament, which had originally been due to convene on 11 November but had had to be delayed due to the outbreak of the Buckingham Rebellion.[42] The parliament met on 23 January in the Painted Chamber at Westminster. The number attending included 37 lords, 10 judges and 296 members of the Commons, although there is no way to tell how many were actually present on any given day. The parliament was opened by Chancellor Bishop Russell, who preached on national unity and warned against dissent and individual ambition. The first measure of the parliament was the one of most consequence to Anne: the *Titulus Regius*, the formal recital of Richard's title and claim to the throne. This was important because it confirmed Richard's right to the throne by the invitation of the parliament. This was quite usual but as Mathew Lewis states, it also contained a 'scathing attack on Edward's kingship as delighting in adulation and flattery and led by sensuality and concupiscence ... for Richard to slam his brother so vehemently casting his counsellors as personnes insolent vicious and of inordinate avarice was shocking'.[43] For Richard to attack the very people who had kept government turning during the past turbulent year was, at best, unwise. His assertion that he intended to correct the past wrongs may have pleased the people, but the implied criticism hardly won him the support of the officials and nobles. The parliament also had to elect a speaker, and that post went to William Catesby, who was a member of the parliament from Northamptonshire, and since June 1483 had been the Chancellor of the Exchequer. He was a lawyer and squire of the body from Ashby St Ledgers; he was therefore very much Richard's man, but it is interesting to note that another man, Richard Ratcliffe, 'owed their primary loyalty to the queen through their Neville connections', implying that Richard had won their support at least in part through his marriage to Anne and her illustrious Neville bloodline.[44] The issue of attainders were next on the list and the first set of legislative acts related to Henry Stafford, (late) Duke of Buckingham, Henry Tudor, Jasper Tudor, Thomas Grey (late Marquess of Dorset), Richard Beauchamp and eighty-eight others. The second act named John Morton, Lionel Woodville, Piers

Courtney, Margaret Beaufort and Walter Roberts as having been implicated in the Buckingham plot. These attainders were accompanied by a statute that granted Richard the power to dispose of the lands of those attainted as he wished. Towards the women, however, Richard was lenient. Margaret Beaufort had her lands simply placed into the custody of her husband, Lord Stanley, and the widowed Duchess of Buckingham was granted an annuity upon which to live. There has previously been some suggestion that Anne might have influenced her husband in relation to these matters, urging him to be sympathetic to the light of these women, and indeed, she might have, but there is no firm evidence that she did so. It seems more likely that Richard was trying to bind both families closer to him in the hopes of securing their loyalty going forward. From the little we can ascertain of Anne's character, it also seems unlikely that she would have been overly sympathetic towards a woman who had sought to challenge her son's inheritance and threaten her fledgling dynasty; after all, she did have Margaret of Anjou's example upon which to draw. Likely of most concern to Anne was her son's position and she must have been satisfied when, during the parliament, as the *Crowland Chronicle* relates, the men met 'near the passage which leads to the queens apartments and swore an oath of allegiance and adherence to Edward the king's only son as their supreme lord'.[45]

The parliament also turned its attention to less personal matters – the reforms that Richard had promised. Richard abolished benevolences, perhaps in a bid to shore up political support for his reign. Edward IV had invented the benevolences as a hated form of taxation whereby nobles were required to give a 'gift' to the crown – initiated initially to fund his attempt to invade France in 1475. Matthew Lewis argues that this proves that Richard was determined to take the politically harder route of working with the Commons to gain funding and support rather than effectively going over their heads.[46] He also dealt with matters of English trade and introduced measures that would seek to 'root out corruption in shoddy merchandise'.[47] He clearly was attempting to kick-start the economy, but there was possibly also an ulterior motive. Henry VII would later create a merchant class on which the government could depend – an alternative power base to that of the traditional, and seriously troublesome, nobility.[48]

The administration of justice in England was also a subject that Richard dealt with in his parliament, and he again sought to root out corruption and help the common man – something noble to modern eyes but again, hardly designed to endear himself to the nobility, who were used to running their own lands pretty much as they wished. These reforms, rather ironically, would eventually come to weaken the need for such political alliances as that between Anne and Richard, as the power of the nobility and their ability to influence events through forces of arms would ultimately wane under Henry VII. These reforms in parliament, to begin the rein in the nobility, were something that would actually be used by Henry VII to secure his own dynasty, but Matthew Lewis argues that for Richard they were ultimately a 'mistake ... that probably cost Richard his crown and life'.[49]

What did Anne make of these reforms? We simply do not know, nor do we know how she felt about the fact that Richard now began to parcel up and distribute her Neville inheritance. He was King of England and as such, the Warwick inheritance had ceased to be of such importance. He could also now deal with the issues that had arisen following George Neville's death. As we have seen, under the 1475 act, Richard had held the great northern Neville lands only so long as there was a male heir to the Marquis of Montagu alive. He had sought to cling on to these lands by relegating the threat of George Neville as much as possible, and by gaining the wardship of the next heir, Richard Latimer, but when George died, whilst Richard could keep the Neville inheritance, he could not pass it on to his son. Now that he was king, though, this ceased to matter so much; his son was to inherit the crown so he had no need to hold together his northern dominion in trust for him. Latimer's marriage was sold to Humphrey Stafford, who promptly married him to his own daughter, Anne. It was now he who would succeed to the great Neville estates of Middleham, Sheriff Hutton, Penrith and possibly even the northern West March. Likewise, Lord Abergavenny, who had challenged Richard and George for the lordship of south Glamorgan and the lordship of west Wales, was now granted some of these lands in reward for his loyal service. The meaning is clear: in the words of Michael Hicks, 'Richard no longer cares particularly about keeping the estate intact ... he was giving away his nephew Warwick's lands as well as Anne's own.'[50] Given that there are indications (notably as we have seen the words of Rous in relation to her mother, that Anne was to a degree personally invested in her inheritance), it seems unlikely that she was happy about these actions, although she may have seen them as a political necessity.

One matter that certainly did concern Anne at the beginning of 1483 was the issue of her nieces, who were still in sanctuary with their mother, Elizabeth Woodville. They were the now 17-year-old Elizabeth of York, 14-year-old Cecily, Anne, Catherine and Bridget. The *Titulus Regis* had disinherited them once and for all, so now it was deemed safe and political to encourage them to leave the confines of Westminster. Elizabeth Woodville had strongly resisted all previous attempts; by now it seems certain that she believed that her sons were dead, given that she was in correspondence with Margaret Beaufort, whose son Henry Tudor swore on Christmas Day 1483 at Rennes Cathedral that he would marry Elizabeth of York. She had indeed plotted to get her daughter abroad to safety, but this plan had been discovered, and their escape prevented. Clearly, the ex-princesses could not remain in sanctuary indefinitely and it seemed logical that they should now join Queen Anne's household, where she could keep an eye on them. Richard and Elizabeth Woodville reached terms and on 1 March 1484, Anne's nieces left sanctuary.[51] Vergil records that 'King Richard received all his brother's daughters out of sanctuary into the court', where they were 'conveyed to his palace of Westminster'. Once there, Buck states that they were 'treated with all princely kindness'.[52] Elizabeth Woodville had extracted a promise from Richard that he would 'maintain them in honest places of good name ... [and] marry them to gentleman born'. They did not, however, remain at the court for long, although the reasons why are unclear, and they soon joined their mother, who was also released. Traditionally, they resided at Gipping Hall, but it seems highly unlikely that Richard would have permitted them to stay there with its easy access to the river and therefore to France and Henry Tudor. Instead, Alison Weir argues that she was sent to Heytesbury in Wiltshire, where they would have stayed at East Court, a medieval manor house.[53] Here, John Nesfield, a squire to the king, was trusted with the unenviable task of keeping an eye on them.

Whilst the daughters of Edward IV did not remain in her household, Anne would certainly have been involved in their care, perhaps ensuring that they were suitably attired after their spell in sanctuary. Whether or not she had real affection for them, or warmed to them in light of the fact that Elizabeth of York was, in the eyes of the Tudors at least, betrothed to Henry, is unclear. She certainly knew that they posed a threat to her husband's reign and her son's inheritance.

Anne would have received regular reports about her own son, who was still being cared for by the women of his household in 1483–4. Evidence for his household comes from the Signet Docket Book of those years. We know that the previous year, from May to September, a warrant was issued to the suitors of Middleham to the amount of 196 pounds and 10 shillings from the receiver, Geoffrey Frank. There are fifty-nine items listed, of which 70 per cent relate to Prince Edward's household. His nurse was now called Jane Collins, and she was assisted by Agnes Cooper. Jane spent household goods during the period to the amount of 46 shillings. There are also six male servants listed: Oliver Camer, John Vaughan, Rukes Metcalfe, Anthony Peacock, and Dennis and John Marler. Peacock and Metcalfe were paid to run alongside Edward's carriage when he journeyed out, in addition to their other duties.[54] It seems that the young prince also liked to watch hounds, keeping a group of them at the castle.[55] He had also attended the local May games and was entertained by Martin the fool, as well as keeping up with his studies.[56] Edward also visited Coverham Abbey in North Yorkshire, no doubt to hear Mass and maybe to pay his respects at the grave of Ranulph Neville, 1st Baron Neville (1262–1331), and Jervaulx Abbey, north-west of Ripon. There is again nothing to suggest that the prince was in poor health, or that he was doing anything other than enjoying his privileged childhood in the country air of Middleham – something that must have been of great comfort to Anne as 1484 hurtled towards summer.

Chapter 14

Tragedy

> I would to God that the inclusive verge
> Of golden metal that must round my brow
> Were red-hot steel, to sear me to the brain!
> *Richard III,* William Shakespeare

Anne now accompanied Richard on a progress to the north, likely to visit their son at Middleham. They travelled via Cambridge, where Anne is named in a licence of 25 March 1484, which declares that Queen's College Cambridge existed 'by the patronage of our aforesaid consort'. By assuming the role of patroness there, Anne was following in the footsteps of her predecessors, Margaret of Anjou and Elizabeth Woodville.[1] Given how firmly the grants state that it was Queen's College (there is of course a separate King's College, which Richard patronised), it can be argued that this benefaction was something that Anne personally interceded to ensure.[2] Leaving Cambridge sometime in March, they travelled to Buckden Manor, a fortified brick manor house, which was home to the Bishop of Lincoln.[3] Its two imposing brick towers were added in 1475 and Anne would have seen them and passed beneath the arch of its gatehouse.

Anne and Richard then moved on and were in Nottingham by 17 March.[4] Nottingham was one of Richard's favourite residences and it was sometimes called his 'castle of care'. The castle dominated the medieval skyline and was originally built to guard the point where the king's road crosses the river Trent before wending its way to York, meaning that it was considered to be the gateway to the north. Anne would have entered the castle (which had been largely rebuilt by Edward IV) over a drawbridge with fantastically sculpted beasts and giants looking down upon her from the parapet.[5] Richard had added the great tower, which Leland described as the 'most beautiful part and gallant building for lodging', which was 'carried up for three storeys in stone ... and erected a loft of timber round windows', and it was most likely here that Anne stayed.[6] There was also 'a fair green court fit for princely exercise' around which perhaps she walked to enjoy the early spring sunshine, or perhaps she worshipped in Nottingham's famous rock-cut chapel upon whose walls were painted scenes from the Passion of Christ. In 1447, the chapel had been given to the king in exchange for land in Sherwood Forest, but monks there continued to say prayers for the 'good estate for the King and his family'.[7]

If so, Anne's prayers were not to be answered because it was while staying at Nottingham between 4 and 27 April that Anne and Richard received the devastating news that their son Edward had died at Middleham Castle.[8] Most historians claim that he died on 9 April 1484, exactly one year after the death of Edward IV, but this is by no means certain.[9] The Crowland chronicler says that he died on a 'day not far off King Edward's anniversary'.[10] Rous, who was generally very particular on matters of genealogy, states that he 'died at Eastertide, so some time between the 17/18th April and before the 27th April'.[11] In the medieval church, Eastertide referred specifically to the period between the Easter vigil on the night before Holy Saturday and the Pentecost.[12] This is the only scarce evidence that we have and so it seems likely that neither chronicler knew the date precisely, Edward was, after all, far away in the north and the precise date of 9 April should simply be regarded as historical tradition rather than fact.

Edward's cause of death is likewise unclear but the *Crowland Chronicle* records that his illness was a short and sudden one. Everything from tuberculosis to appendicitis has been suggested ever since, but the simple fact is that there is not sufficient contemporary evidence for us to make even an educated guess.

Anne was utterly devastated by the death of her son and she and Richard were 'in a state almost bordering on madness by reason of their sudden grief'.[13] There is something touching about the image of Anne and Richard being united in their terrible loss. We get no other glimpse into the intimacy of their marriage but their shared devastation paints a picture of an emotional understanding between them, in relation to their son, at least.

Tragedy

Anne and Richard now set out for the north, leaving Nottingham on 27 April, suggesting that the news had not reached them long before that, given the speed with which they now proceeded. By 1 May, Anne and Richard were at York, and they reached Middleham a few days later, either on 5 or 6 May. It has often been assumed that while there they undertook the arrangements for and attended the funeral of their son, but this is not necessarily the case. Royal protocol stated that monarchs should not attend the funeral of their predecessors, spouses, or indeed, children. Notably, despite their devastation, Elizabeth of York and Henry VII did not attend the funeral of Prince Arthur, nor would Henry VII attend the funeral of his mother-in-law Elizabeth Woodville or that of his wife.[14] The question of when Anne's son was buried remains a mystery. Both the Rous Roll and the *Crowland Chronicle* record that he was buried at Middleham, but if so, his tomb has been lost. For many years it was believed that a small alabaster tomb at the church of St Helen and the Holy Cross in Sheriff Hutton was his final resting place but there is no record of Anne or Richard travelling there, and the tomb has now been proven to predate the death of Edward by several years. It contains no bones and the clothing worn by the effigy is stylistically fifty years too early for it to depict Edward. This has led to the suggestion that it was in fact the tomb of either Ralph Neville, a son of Richard, Earl of Salisbury, Anne's grandfather, or that of John Neville, a son of Ralph Neville, the Earl of Westmorland, who would have been an uncle to Richard III. Dr Jane Crease, who has studied the tomb extensively, summarises that:

> the heraldry reliably recorded on the tomb links it with the Nevilles and at the period of its manufacture, Ralph Neville, 1st Earl of Westmorland, held the manor and castle of Sheriff Hutton so it may be one of his children ... the tomb may therefore be that of a kinsman of [Queen Anne] even if it is not her son.[15]

Another suggestion is that Edward was laid to rest temporarily at Sheriff Hutton, something that was common practice in the Middle Ages, while a planned chantry chapel at York was being built, and that Richard intended to bury his son with far greater honours before events overtook him. Another theory discounts any Sheriff Hutton connection altogether and argues that Edward was buried in the church of St Mary and Alkelda in Middleham, where Richard and Anne had founded a college, but not only do no records of such a burial exist, it also seems a very humble burial location for a Prince of Wales. Other suggestions for his burial include Coverham Abbey and Jervaulx Abbey, both of which are very close to Middleham. As we have seen, Edward certainly visited both, but again, if Edward was buried there no records have yet surfaced. If Edward was buried at York, likewise, no definite records have been found, but Hammond argues that there is circumstantial evidence to tentatively suggest that he was buried in York Minster. In August 1484, Richard III planned to found a chantry, 'King's Chapel', intended for 100 priests there. This foundation was set up in a hurry and was very large, clearly intended to be a splendid one befitting a royal chapel, but was never built. Perhaps Richard intended this chapel to be established in honour of his son, and that he would one day rest there himself, alongside him.[16]

For Anne, the death of her son was a personal tragedy, a devastating blow from which she would never truly recover. For her and Richard, as King and Queen of England, it was a dynastic catastrophe for it left Richard with no heir. Without Edward, as Shakespeare has Richard say, his 'kingdom stands [stood] on brittle glass'. They both knew only too well that without a legitimate and unchallenged male heir, support for them would weaken, and their enemies would sense this weakness. Anne was still only in her twenties and the question of whether or not she could bear another child was now of paramount concern. No doubt, she and Richard continued to sleep together in the hopes that she could fall pregnant. In the medieval period, blame for any fertility issues was placed squarely at the woman's door. It was her civic, political and religious duty to bear children. If she did not, or could not, then clearly something was lacking in her. It is possible that Richard shared this view for we now get an account that he spoke to the Archbishop of York, Thomas Rotherham, and complained that 'unto many noble men of his wife's unfruitfulness, for that she brought him forth no children'.[17] However, this account must be treated with caution as it is recorded in Vergil, who was writing after Rotherham's death, meaning

Tragedy

that the account was second-hand at best. Likewise, in September, Thomas Langton, Bishop of St Davids, stated that Richard's sensual and physical needs were not being met by his queen.[18] Taken together, both accounts seem to suggest possible tension in Anne's marriage. What is certain, though, is that Richard's thoughts were dwelling on the succession and that he and Anne were grieving deeply. Richard and Anne were back in York by the end of May and when at Pontefract on 3 June 1484, Richard wrote to his mother informing her that he was replacing in her employ William Colyngbourne (Collingbourne) with Lord Chamberlain Francis Lovell. He also wrote that he was in great need of her comfort – 'your daily blessing to my singular comfort and defence in my need' – and that he wished her to write to him more often.[19] A touching reference to his grief, perhaps.

As for Anne, the Silesian knight Niclas von Popplau, emissary to the Holy Roman Emperor Frederick III, is known to have visited York during this time and he makes no reference to her or her ladies being present, which has led to the suggestion that Anne removed to Middleham with her household to grieve her son in relative privacy. However, it has been argued that as we know Richard was back at Middleham between 6 and 8 May and that he then travelled to Barnard Castle and was there on the 9th to the 10th, Popplau's assertion that he arrived in York on 1 May and 'stayed [at York] for eight days or more and joined him [King Richard] almost every time for the meal at his court' seems therefore to be in error.[20] Likewise, if he had travelled to Middleham, where the town and castle were in deep mourning, the idea that Popplau would not at least mention this fact seems unlikely. Therefore, we cannot use his account as proof that Anne did not accompany her husband at this time. She may have done so; we simply do not know.

The political ramifications of Edward's death were felt immediately. He had been given the title Lord President of the Council of the North, but this was now given to John de la Pole, the Earl of Lincoln and Richard's nephew through his sister, Elizabeth Duchess of Suffolk. In addition, Rous claims that now Edward, Earl of Warwick, Anne's nephew, was named as heir and served first after the king and queen. There are numerous problems with this assertion, not least that there is no legal record of it anywhere. In addition, Edward was barred from inheriting due to his father's attainder. If he was to be heir to the throne of England then this would have to be lifted. Most today believe this record to be more wishful thinking on the part of Rous, who was ever loyal to the direct line of succession of Warwick, than anything rooted in fact. If Rous was merely recording a rumour, though, then he was far from the only one to do so during the next few turbulent months. Looming once again was the threat of invasion from Scotland, as well as from Henry Tudor, currently in Brittany. To address these threats we know that Richard was at Durham, then Scarborough, where he was assembling a fleet to deal with the threat of a naval invasion by Henry Tudor. There is a suggestion that the Queen's Tower was in use at Scarborough when Richard was there, which implies that Anne accompanied her husband and stayed there. Given how desperately they now needed an heir, it would make sense that they were together as much as possible during these months.[21]

In July, the king's 'Household in the North' at Sheriff Hutton, which was now under the governance of John de la Pole, saw the ordering of fabrics for Margaret and Edward. Usually, Anne, as queen, would have had a hand in this, but perhaps her grief was still too raw as there is no mention of her in the records. It must have felt to Anne as if the world was falling down around her as intrigue after intrigue threatened her and Richard's normal life. In August, things were so bad that Richard issued a proclamation that no one could take to sea without first swearing an oath of allegiance to him and offering something as surety for his good behaviour.[22] We know that at some point Anne travelled south to London and that she was in the capital when Richard made arrangements for her ex-father-in-law Henry VI's bones to be moved from Chertsey Abbey to the Chapel of St George in Windsor – something for which he paid the sum of 5 pounds 10 shillings and 2 pence. The body was put into a lead coffin and then into a wooden one before being laid to rest, ironically, opposite to his great enemy, Richard's brother, Edward. The question of why Richard moved Henry VI's body has long been debated. One theory is that, under growing pressure from all sides, he wanted to keep a closer eye on Henry's grave, which had become a place of pilgrimage after reports of miracles having taken place at the tomb.[23] Another is that Richard was considering Windsor as his own burial place, where, in the words of Dr Clare Rider, Archivist and Chapter Librarian, 'interment in proximity to the sacred bones of Henry VI would have been seen as advantageous to their souls.' Yet another possibility is

Tragedy

that Richard was driven by guilt. His own involvement in Henry VI's death remains unclear, but if he had been involved he was acting on his brother's orders and now may have wished to atone for his part in it.

Richard was present at Windsor on 19 August to either witness the reburial or to inspect it and pay his respects. Again, it seems likely that Anne accompanied him there, although this cannot be absolutely proved; she certainly visited Windsor during this period. Anne must have had mixed feelings as she stared at the effigy of her former father-in-law, lying recumbent in armour with a leopard and antelope at his feet, his bearded face serene and at peace. If Anne had accompanied Richard, we know husband and wife soon parted ways again, with Anne most likely travelling back to her palace at Greenwich. Richard, meanwhile, travelled north to Nottingham, where he met with Scottish ambassadors who proposed a truce, sealed by a marriage between James III's son and Richard's niece, Anne de la Pole. With winter looming, the threat posed by Henry Tudor grew. On 7 December, Anne would have known, if not heard, that her husband had been forced to issue another proclamation making clear the damage that Henry Tudor and his followers would bring if they were allowed to invade England. Numerous other traitors were named, including Jasper Tudor, Sir Edward Woodville and, most worryingly, John de Vere, the Earl of Oxford. Oxford was by far the most experienced English military commander left alive, arguably apart from Richard himself, and Richard would have quickly realised that his presence would not only attract more supporters to Henry's cause but also lead to the better organisation of Tudor's forces. The proclamation also reveals that the above were all now in France, not Brittany, with whom Richard had signed a peace treaty. The French king's sister, the infamous Madame la Grande, Anne de Beaujeu, who was regent during his minority, had clearly seen a way in which to further destabilise England and reduce the threat it posed to her own kingdom. It was a brilliant move, but not a surprising one from a woman noted for her intelligence and energy, and who was called 'the least foolish woman in France'.[24]

Chapter 15

Christmastide

> Now is the winter of our discontent
> *Richard III*, William Shakespeare

As winter dawned, things went from bad to worse for Richard and Anne. When Richard came back to the capital around 11 November, Anne most likely returned to the Palace of Westminster to begin her preparations for the Christmas period.[1] If so, she could have had first-hand knowledge of the trial of William Collingbourne, which took place that December. He had been in service of Cecily Neville and it is likely therefore that both Richard and Anne knew him personally. Collingbourne famously wrote the political lampoon 'The Catte, the Ratte and Lovell our dogge ruleth all England under a hogge', referring to Richard (the hogge), Catesby (the Catte), Ratcliffe (the Ratte) and Lovell (the Dogge), which had been posted on the door of St Paul's in the previous July. The longer version, which attacked Richard more directly, may also have been his work:

> The Cat, the Rat and Lovell Our Dog
> Doth rule England under the Hog,
> The Crook-backed Boar the way hath found
> To root out Roses from our ground
> Both flower and bud he will confound
> Till King of Beats and swine be crowned
> And then the Dog, the Cat and Rat
> Shall in his trough feed and be fat.[2]

Collingbourne was not only a writer of insulting rhymes, but when he was arrested in October/November, it quickly became clear that he had been in contact with Henry Tudor and had been working to support his invasion plans, particularly preparing Poole as a possible landing site. Exactly why he opposed Richard is unclear, but he may have been implicated in the Buckingham Rebellion and suffered sanctions as a result, or he may have opposed him on other moral grounds. His previous service in the household of Cecily Neville must have alarmed both Richard and Anne, and if she knew him, perhaps Anne felt his betrayal very keenly. Collingbourne was convicted of high treason and hanged, drawn and quartered on Tower Hill. Tudor historian John Stow later records that his execution was carried out so quickly that Collingbourne was still alive and in shock when his heart was removed.

The reports of such events cannot have raised Anne's spirits and according to the *Crowland Chronicle*, it seems that she was 'sad and preoccupied: neither society that she loved, nor all the pomp and festivity of royalty, could cure the languor or heal the wound in the Queen's breast for the loss of her son'.[3] She was, however, still described by Rous as being 'in presence seemly, amiable and beauteous, and in conditions full commendable and right virtuous, and full gracious'. Despite her low spirits, Anne continued to prepare for the Christmas season and she now invited her nieces to court. There is a record of her sending for them, making clear that they had not been in her household since the spring.[4] Anne welcomed them to court with great kindness and the Crowland chronicler reports that the now adult Elizabeth of York was a particular favourite of hers. It is difficult, though, to get to the truth of their relationship. Anne was ten years Elizabeth's senior though still only in her late twenties herself. Anne may have felt herself something of a protectoress and role model; alternatively, each may have distrusted the other. Elizabeth had spent a good deal of time with her mother in sanctuary, and Elizabeth Woodville clearly mistrusted Richard, evidenced by the fact that she had made Richard swear an oath to safeguard her daughters' future.[5] Perhaps that distrust influenced her daughter and extended to Richard's wife. Later, Holinshed would accuse Elizabeth Woodville of falling under Richard's spell when she released her daughters into his 'care' and of 'blot[ting] out the old committed injury and late executed tyranny', but we must remember that Elizabeth Woodville did not know of Henry Tudor's coming invasion, let alone that it would ultimately be successful.

In one way or another, her sons were out of her reach so she was making the best of a bad situation for her daughters; perhaps she was even relying on Anne to keep them safe. As we have seen, Anne as queen had charge of the care of many children including her nieces and nephews, as well as the six children of John Neville, the wardship of whose five daughters and son had been given to Richard and Anne in 1480. These girls would have been very much part of Anne's household since then and probably served her as queen. The girls all made good marriages, so perhaps with such examples, Elizabeth Woodville had some faith in Anne.

Anne would have been aware that a year earlier, Henry Tudor had sworn to marry Elizabeth and that a dispensation to permit their marriage had been applied for. On 24 March 1484, the Apostolic Penitentiary had released her and Henry 'from the canonical impediment of being related twice in the fourth degrees of consanguinity and legitimised their future issue'.[6] In the absence of her brother, Elizabeth of York was considered by many to be the true royal heir and her marriage was of the utmost importance. Richard had promised, under oath, to make her a suitable match when she emerged from sanctuary but he doesn't seem to have had a particular candidate in mind. A royal unmarried woman who was, by all accounts, 'exceedingly handsome' and of independent age was dangerous: few were more aware of that than Anne Neville. Was there therefore a degree of duplicity behind Anne's offered friendship implied by the Crowland chronicler? Did she hope to bind Elizabeth to her? Certainly, it was a planned advantage to have the daughters of York at court that Christmas, where Richard and Anne could both keep an eye on them.

However, there may have been a darker motive to their presence, one that Anne was initially, at least, unaware of. By Christmas 1484, there were rumours beginning to circulate that Richard intended to put aside Anne and marry Elizabeth of York himself. These were not yet as widespread as they would later become so perhaps Anne was unaware of them as Christmas approached. Anne and Richard prepared for the Christmas festivities by spending 1,200 pounds on new clothes and gifts for the court. Amongst the clothes that Anne ordered was a new dress for herself and one for Elizabeth of York in a similar style. The chronicler Fabyan, who was a draper, alderman and later a sheriff based in London, recorded that the Feast of the Nativity 'was kept at the Palace of Westminster with all solemnity', no doubt with Anne in attendance. This was followed by the Epiphany celebrations, which saw Richard enter the great hall in a state of 'potency and splendour'.[7] Under the leadership of the Lord of Misrule, celebrations followed, including dancing, music and games. There would have been 'good bread and good drink, good fire in the hall ... cheese, apples and nuts ... jolly carols to hear'.[8] As was customary, presents were also exchanged and Richard gave Elizabeth of York a traditional gift of a book, *The Romance of Tristan* or *Prose Tristan*, of which we know Richard himself owned a version or copy. It was one of four romances in his library, the others including 'Palamon and Arcite' by Chaucer and the Anglo-Norman verse *Ipomedon*.[9] Given this, perhaps these are books that Anne also read, and she might have recommended them as a gift for her niece. The fact that Richard's gift was a romantic tale has previously been used as evidence that he was 'wooing' Elizabeth, but this is simply not the case. Such books were not romantic as we would understand the term today and were eminently suitable gifts for one's family. Anne, along with her ladies, would have been present at the Feast of Epiphany on 6 January, and Richard entered Westminster Hall wearing his crown before presiding over a great feast. The mood was not entirely celebratory, however. During the celebrations it was said that Richard received word that 'his enemies would without a doubt invade the kingdom early the following summer or at least attempt to do so'.[10]

Crowland also records that during the Christmas festivities, 'far too much attention was given to dancing and gaiety' and that Anne and Elizabeth were too often dressed the same, which was considered an affront to the natural order of things given the complex sumptuary laws, under which what you could wear was closely governed by rank. Elizabeth was not of Anne's rank and their dressing in the same clothing seems to have attracted almost instant suspicion, from the Crowland chronicler at least. In addition to this, rumours that Richard was planning to set aside Anne and marry Elizabeth of York were now circulating and gaining traction, due in part to the favour he apparently showed her over the Christmas period. It is difficult to untangle the chronology of the rumours surrounding Richard's interest in Elizabeth of York, not least because they were used by his enemies to discredit him, both at the time and ever since.

The best evidence for the existence and power of these rumours dates to three months after Christmas 1485, when Richard III held a meeting in the great hall of St John's Priory in Clerkenwell and he was forced to make it clear that:

> it never came in his thought of mind to marry in such a manner wise nor willing or glad of the death of his queen but as sorry and in heart as heavy as man might be, with much more in the premises unspoken, For the which he admonished and charged every person to clear of such untrue talking on peril of his indignation.[11]

For Richard himself to feel the rumours worthy of public denouncement implies their widespread nature, as does the fact that he summoned the 'mayor, aldermen, councillors and livery companies of London' to hear him speak.

There are also two other contemporary sources for the existence of the rumours prior to March. One, as we have seen, was the *Crowland Chronicle*, which repeatedly hints at 'things as distasteful, so numerous that they hardly be reckoned', and the other, most intriguing, is the report of a letter written by Elizabeth of York herself to her uncle, John Howard, Duke of Norfolk. This letter, known as 'Buck's letter', after the Jacobean historian Sir George Buck, who claims to have found it in 1619, describes 'amounts of precious jewels and rare monuments in the rich and magnificent cabinet of Thomas Howard Earl of Arundel, heir of the recipient to whom it had descended'.[12] In the letter, Buck tells us, Elizabeth asks for her uncle's assistance with regard to her impending marriage to Richard and anticipates Anne's death, which she is impatient for. Indeed, she is enthusiastic about the marriage. Unfortunately, the original of this letter has long since been lost and indeed, Buck's own manuscript was damaged by fire and then heavily edited by his nephew.[13] If the letter is genuine, and most historians today feel that it did exist in one form or another – A.N. Kincaid, for example, argues that Buck must have seen such a letter; he was living under the patronage of the Howards and he simply could never have risked his credibility by entirely making up a letter that his patron would have no doubt asked to see – then does it follow that Richard was actively planning to marry Elizabeth in early 1485? The answer to this simply is not clear. Buck's (and his nephew's) edits are such that whilst it is almost certain that Elizabeth did write to her uncle and that Buck saw the letter, its contents have been distorted; to what extent, though, is uncertain. The closest we can get to the original implies that Elizabeth did call her uncle 'her only joy and her maker in the world and that she was his', but although such words may seem damning to modern ears, we have to remember that Elizabeth was her uncle's subject and such flowery professions of loyalty were usual at the time between a subject and their monarch. Rather than referring to marriage, Elizabeth may simply have been asking Norfolk's help in recovering some of her lands, or indeed, a portion of them, for any future marriage. After all, if she and Richard were so close, why did she need to appeal to her uncle? I, along with most modern scholars, would argue today, on balance, that although this letter did likely exist, its original meaning has been distorted beyond reach. Crowland, meanwhile, clarifies that the way Richard treated Elizabeth 'caused the people to murmur and the nobles and prelates greatly to wonder thereat'.[15]

However, we must not allow the distastefulness of these rumours to prejudice us unduly; Richard was aware by now that Anne was dying and he needed an heir. He also looked abroad to Portugal where he considered Joanna of Portugal as his aide and simultaneously suggested that Elizabeth of York should marry Manuel of Beja to get her safely out of the way. Perhaps Elizabeth welcomed this opportunity and it was to this marriage that she was referring in Howard's letter, something which most historians seem to dismiss but it must not be discounted as a real possibility. Joanna herself seems to have been keen on the plan, despite her having previously expressed a desire for the religious life of a nun, proof that Richard's international reputation at least was positive.

As 1485 dawned, it is clear that rumours that Richard was plotting to set aside Anne and marry Elizabeth of York, whether true or not, were circulating at the court. For Anne to hear such rumours must have been painful, even though she knew realistically that Richard had to remarry, and with Elizabeth of York in her household, they could hardly have hit closer to home. It is now that we get the first definitive evidence that Anne was unwell. The *Crowland Chronicle* reports that a few days after Christmas, she 'began to sicken vehemently'.[16] Up until this point, as we have already seen, it was implied that Richard and Anne were still sleeping together in the hope that they would produce another heir. Now, though, Richard was told by his physicians to 'shun her bed', possibly because they suspected that she had tuberculosis, in which case it was eminently sensible advice, but advice that could hardly have helped Anne's feelings of isolation. Crowland describes how Anne now knew she had become a burden to her husband and that as a barren queen she could be of no further use to him. Hall later tells us that she and Richard were arguing daily at that point, but again, Hall was writing later and could not have known first-hand.

If they were arguing as Anne sickened, perhaps it was because Richard was exploring the possibility of their divorce. Crowland recorded that Richard was seeking to explore whether or not a divorce might be possible and that ultimately, 'he believed had sufficient grounds'. This implies that Anne's death was perhaps not considered to be as inevitable as later writers would have us believe. If Anne was dying there would be no need to spend time considering how or if to divorce her. Richard's exploration of this potential action must have occurred prior to February 1485, after which the seriousness of Anne's illness was apparent and would render it unnecessary. Although the timing may seem callous, in retrospect it must be remembered that Richard's consideration of divorce was not unique when he had no living heir and his wife could not conceive. Henry VIII, after all, would dispose of two wives for ostensibly the same reason, and it was widely agreed that a queen's:

> sexual role was of central importance to the realm ... pregnancy was a powerful image of male versus female ... that forcefully opposes the power to give life and the power to take it away—a conflict as epochal and eternally tragic as that of Cain and Abel. For many queens, the maternal duty was part of the coronation oath, as was intercession, which was explicitly linked to maternity.[17]

Alfonso V would consider, very reluctantly, divorcing his queen of forty-three years, Maria of Castile, when it became apparent that the issue of a legitimate heir could no longer be ignored.

In theological terms, Richard's best hope of divorce was the fact that his and Anne's marriage, as brother and sister-in-law, had never had the proper papal dispensation that should have been necessary. The 1472 dispensation, as we have seen, did not cover all of the key issues affecting their marriage. Indeed, the Warwick inheritance had only been settled with the disclaimer that it would only stand if Anne and Richard did not divorce, implying that the possibility had been considered. To this end, the 1474 parliament had specifically 'ordained that if Richard Duke of Gloucester and Anne be hereafter divorced and after lawfully married... that parliamentary settlement of the Warwick inheritance would be as good as valid'.[18] However, if they divorced and did not choose to remarry and Richard did not marry anyone else while Anne was still living, then he could retain her lands anyway.[19] Richard had chosen to ignore the issues surrounding the dispensation and validity of their marriage when he needed Anne and her inheritance, but now he did not. Indeed, Anne had become a hindrance to the survival of his dynasty. He could now truthfully claim that he and Anne had lived and slept together while, in the words of Michael Hicks, 'being related in the second, fourth, fourth and fourth degrees of consanguinity knowingly without a valid dispensation'.[20] This truth would have horrified the Crowland chronicler, had he known it, so it seems that he did not, which might explain why he gives no reason, or implies that there could be no valid reason for such a divorce aside from Richard's desire for one.

After Christmas 1484, Anne falls even more resolutely silent, so we can only guess her feelings. Was she aware of her husband's tentative exploration of divorce? If so, maybe she was accepting, resigned that for his bloodline to survive, it was becoming clear he would need to have a child with another woman. She had, after all, failed in her primary duty as queen. Alternatively, perhaps Hall was right and she railed at her fate, accusing her husband of falsehood and treachery. He tells us that Richard's desire for Elizabeth was only now stalled by the fact that Anne still lived. Rous tells us that she was 'desperately unhappy', but the truth is, we simply do not know Anne's feelings.

What we do know is that while Anne sickened at Westminster, yet another, more unpleasant, rumour was in circulation. This rumour stated that Anne was in fact already dead – or that Richard was now plotting to kill his wife, perhaps by poison. It seems likely that Anne was now too weak to appear frequently at the court, again evidence that up until this point, she had done so and now her absence was being remarked upon. In keeping with royal precedent, she would have spent a lot of time in her chamber, attended by her ladies, resting and at prayer. If it was tuberculosis that was ailing Anne, historian Anne Sutton suggests that Anne's final few months would fit in with the pattern of her having contracted pulmonary TB during the Christmas festivities of 1484. Once active, without antibiotics the disease usually kills in less than twelve weeks. Another possibility is that Anne had long carried the disease but that it had remained inactive, only to be activated that summer by the trauma of the death of her son.[21] Anne herself would have known people who had died of consumption, as tuberculosis was referred to then. Hundreds of years before the advent of antibiotics, chances of survival were slim. Medieval medical knowledge and treatments derived largely from ancient classical sources. In ancient Greece, tuberculosis was known as 'physis', which Hippocrates defined as a killer disease, especially for the otherwise young and healthy, characterised by lung lesions. By the time of Isocrates, the disease was known to be contagious, something that most medieval doctors would have read about in the works of Aristotle.[22] A doctor instructing a spouse to stay away from an afflicted wife was therefore fairly standard practice. The Romans prescribed a nutritious diet of milk for anyone afflicted. Of less use to Anne would have been other contemporary treatments she might have received: bloodletting, purging, mercury or arsenic. These were all fairly common treatments but we have no way of knowing whether they were now inflicted upon Anne.

Chapter 16

Eclipse of the Sun

> Despiteful tidings! O, unpleasing news!
> *Richard III*, William Shakespeare

As 1485 progressed, Anne and her husband were approaching the new year in very different ways. Anne was dying and Richard was thinking about the future of his dynasty: no longer their dynasty, after the tragic death of Prince Edward. Anne's last days cannot have been happy ones. Outside her sick room the court was alive with gossip. Vergil tells us that the idea that Richard wished his wife dead persisted and she was again forced to speak to him about it.[1] Perhaps, initially at least, Anne believed she would recover and she must have wondered what was to become of her. She was clearly no longer of use to her husband; he had another candidate to hand and she was aware of the grounds that existed for a divorce. The Crowland chronicler writes that Anne understood that she was now a burden to Richard, and that 'she would soon become a burden to herself and [so] wasted away'. It must be remembered, though, that these accusations were levelled by chroniclers who were either hostile or writing at a later date. Richard may well have loved his wife dearly, and if so, though he absented himself from her chamber on the doctor's advice, perhaps he saw her when he could and sent her trinkets or spoke words of comfort.

During the early months of the year, at least, it is likely that Anne would have been well enough to be still aware of what was happening politically in the kingdom, and that the ground was once again shifting beneath her husband's feet. In February 1485, Richard III, who was well aware of the threat posed in particular by Henry Tudor, took out loans intended to fund his military requirements. He was right to be alert. Henry Tudor was already writing to his supporters stating that he would invade soon 'to advance me to the furtherance of my rightful claim, due and lineal inheritance of that crown and for the just depriving of that homicide and unnatural tyrant [Richard III]'.[2]

If Anne was suffering from tuberculosis at about the time her husband was raising these loans, she would likely have begun to cough up blood, and she would also have been struggling to eat. Her ladies no doubt spent their time trying to tempt her and keep her strength up. She may still have been able to move about. Emily Bronte, centuries later, famously held herself upright until almost the hour of her death by sheer willpower alone, but perhaps Anne, broken by her son's death and the political reality, would not have put up so much of a fight. A diagnosis of tuberculosis should not be regarded as certain, though; other possibilities include uterine cancer, which would explain her fertility issues, or even poison. If it was poison, it need not have been deliberately administered on anyone's orders – mercury, after all, was an accepted medical treatment and very easy to kill with. There is also a single, much later, source: Christopher Brooke's *The Ghost of Richard the Third: A Poem*, of 1614, which implies that Anne might have been pregnant at the time of her death. The line 'her issue crawling with worms' perhaps suggests that she was literally with issue.[3] However, given that there isn't a single contemporary source that indicates this or supports this theory, I think it can be discounted. It could alternatively refer to her dead son, who would have been crawling with worms as he lay in his grave.

At some point in February 1485, Anne must have realised that she was dying. Was she afraid? Did she see her fate as punishment, perhaps, for her unlawful marriage? Did her thoughts return to her first husband? Did she welcome death and the chance to be reunited with her son? As ever, we do not know. What we do know is that Anne made no will, which was highly unusual for a woman of means, let alone a queen of England, and the question as to why has puzzled historians ever since. Even if the document itself had been lost, if it had existed there should be references to it in other official documents, but nothing mentions it. As a married woman, of course, legally Anne possessed no property of her own, but it was usual for a husband to allow his wife to dispose of at least a few trinkets or to make religious bequests. A plethora of women's wills exists from the fifteenth century onwards that see women disposing of jewellery, beds, clothing and even small parcels of land. When Elizabeth Woodville died, even though she had been deprived of her lands in 1487 and forced to retire to Bermondsey Abbey, she still made a will in which she stated:

> I bequeath my body to be buried with the body of my Lord at Windsor, according to the will of my said Lord and mine, without pomp entering or costly expense done thereabout ... I have no worldly goods to do the Queen's Grace, my dearest daughter, a pleaser with, neither to reward any of my children, according to my heart and mind, I beseech Almighty God to bless her grace with all her noble issue, and with as good heart and mind as is to me possible, I give her Grace my blessing.[4]

She goes on to ask that her executors pay any debts she has and that:

> such small stuff and goods that I have to be disposed truly in the contentac'on [settling] of my debts and for the health of my soul ... if any of my blood will of my said stuff or goods to me pertaining, I will that they have the preferment before any other.[5]

The document is brief but it is still more than Anne Neville wrote. One theory is that Richard did not allow Anne to make a will; another is that she was too ill to do so, or that she did not wish to. There was no need for Richard to prevent her from doing so. Legally, he had everything he wanted, but we cannot discount the possibility that he simply forgot to make adequate provision for her to do so, given the circumstances in which he was living. As Michael Hicks eloquently puts it:

> If Richard's treatment of Anne was ruthless and cruel, his assessment purely material and utilitarian, we must recognise also that his actions were the desperation of a rat in a trap as Shakespeare indeed so clearly perceived and need not preclude any genuine affection for her.[6]

One last possibility is that we know that Henry Tudor later destroyed a large quantity of Ricardian documents, perhaps Anne's Will was a casualty? We do not know enough about Anne's illness, or her mental state, to comment on either of the other options, but for whatever reason, Anne has remained silent.

On 16 March 1485, Anne Neville died at the Palace of Westminster, on the same day 'when [a] great eclipse of the sun took place'.[7] We do not know if Anne lived long enough to see it; maybe if she did, she saw it as the end of all things as her life ebbed away. Eclipses had long terrified kings and ordinary folk alike, being regarded as an omen of doom. In 1133, Henry I, the son of William the Conqueror, died during an eclipse, and the twelfth-century *Historia Novella* recalls that the 'hideous darkness agitated the heart of men'.[8] The *Anglo-Saxon Chronicle*, meanwhile, states that 'men were greatly wonder stricken and were afrighted'.[9] In 1433, likewise, a 'black hour' occurred in the north of England, which plunged the country into near-total darkness. In each case, the eclipse was said to foretell disaster: the blame for William the Conqueror's death in Normandy was laid at its door, as was later famine in northern England. The eclipse that occurred on the day that Anne Neville died was no different, and many of Henry Tudor's supporters saw this as an omen that predicted the end of the Yorkist king. The bells of London would have tolled to announce the queen's death and as an already seething London heard them, likewise, men began to question whether the eclipse predicted not just her death but also the doom of their king.

Anne's body would have been washed with wine and rosewater by her ladies, to keep away the stench of death, and her hair would have been brushed back, as was Elizabeth of York's. It was quite usual for a king or queen's body to have been embalmed as their mortal remains could not be seen to undergo the process of decomposition. Queen Eleanor of Castile, the wife of Edward I, had had her viscera removed in 1290, and her body had been filled with sweet-smelling herbs, closed and then covered in waxed linen.[10] When Elizabeth of York died, her body was embalmed on the day of her death by the sergeant of the chandlery. We know this because he was given cerecloth (wax-impregnated fabric), gums, balms, spices and wax to use in the process.[11] We know that she was then enclosed in a lead coffin, which bore her name and was then placed inside a wooden coffin, which was draped in black velvet. When it lay in state, it was surrounded by 500 candles and the walls were draped in black. In London itself, Henry VII ordered that 636 Masses be said for her soul, and at Walsingham, 65 pounds of wax candles were burned while the monks prayed for her.[12] We do not know how Anne's body was treated, but we do know that her sister Isobel was embalmed, and even the hostile Crowland chronicler admits that Anne was 'buried with honours no less than befitted the burial of a queen', so it's a reasonable assumption that her body was treated and embalmed, and prayers said in a similar respect.[13]

No details or herald account has survived of Anne's funeral, which took place at Westminster Abbey, but if we again turn to those of Elizabeth of York and Eleanor of Castile, we can perhaps guess at its form. It would have been usual for a lifelike effigy to be placed on top of the coffin for mourners to view. Elizabeth's wore clothes of estate and a crown, her hair flowing about her shoulders, so perhaps Anne's effigy, if she had one, would have appeared similarly. Given that Anne died at Westminster Place, it is unlikely that she had a long procession like both Elizabeth and Eleanor, but her coffin, when it was moved, would have likely been accompanied by her ladies, dressed in black, and some of the city guilds are known to have provided mourning clothes for their members. At Eleanor of Castile's funeral, some stood with lighted candles as the cortège moved by. Richard was probably present at Anne's funeral and if she had laid in state, in the manner of Elizabeth of York, it would have given Anne's friends and relatives a chance to pay their respects as her coffin stood surrounded by torchbearers and light from the candles danced off the Abbey's gilded stones and windows. Prior to burial, Anne's effigy would have been removed and her chamberlain and gentleman ushers broken their staffs of office and thrown them in her grave. Elizabeth of York's funeral cost Henry VII an enormous 300 pounds, but given that Richard was in dire need of money, perhaps we can assume that Anne's was on a smaller scale, although still befitting her status. The writer of the *Great Chronicle* tells us that Anne was buried 'by the south door that leads into St Edward's chapel'.[14] Rous, however, records that she was buried in front of the high altar, but as we have seen, he was at a distance from London, therefore the *Great Chronicle* seems the more likely to be correct.[15]

Why Richard chose to bury Anne at Westminster Abbey is unclear because as we have seen, there is some evidence that he planned for himself, and presumably Anne, to rest in York Minster. Her grave remained unmarked, and if Richard planned to raise a monument over her final resting place, it was never realised and no plans have ever come to light. J.L. Laynesmith speculates that Richard perhaps intended to be buried beside Anne and that a double monument would be raised over them after their deaths.[16] However, this seems questionable given that Richard, whether he was already eyeing Elizabeth of York as his new wife or not, would have needed to remarry in order to secure his dynasty; had he survived the events of 1485, Anne would most likely have always rested alone. Some have asked why she was not buried with her family at Bisham Priory, but primarily this would not have befitted her status as Queen of England. In addition, Richard would not have wanted to draw attention to the fact that essentially, his power had been founded on Anne's inheritance. In the words of Michael Hicks:

> Anne had brought Richard a devoted following united by a family tradition focused on herself that caused them to hazard their lives on her behalf and that endured beyond the grave ... however little control [Richard] allowed her as duchess and queen, they remained hers.[17]

Without Anne, he might have feared that the loyalty of such retainers would weaken. Whether it did or not is unclear; the Neville influence on the Earl of Northumberland and his troops is simply not quantifiable. Anne's burial place remained unmarked until 1960, when the Richard III society erected a memorial plaque to her, close to where Crowland records that her body lies.

ANNE NEVILL[E]
1456–1485
QUEEN OF ENGLAND
YOUNGER DAUGHTER OF RICHARD EARL
OF WARWICK CALLED THE KINGMAKER
WIFE OF THE LAST PLANTAGENET KING
RICHARD III

Eclipse of the Sun

*"In person she was seemly, amiable and
beauteous.....And according to the
interpretation of her name Anne
full gracious"*
REQUESCAT IN PACE.[18]

When she died, Anne had been queen for just twenty-two months and there is no getting away from the fact that her death was extremely convenient for her husband. Her timing was near perfect. Had Richard lived, no doubt he would have remarried within the year and set about securing the future of the Yorkist Plantagenet line. If Anne had lived, would Richard have divorced her? We cannot be certain, but it does seem very likely; Anne's gynaecological issues and her ultimate failure to produce a surviving heir were not something that he could have simply lived with. Anne would have known this and we must not underestimate how much of a humiliation and tragedy this was for her. To be a wife, mother, queen and the founder of a new Neville dynasty was what she had been bred, readied and trained for. She had achieved the ultimate ambition of her father and family. It was a position and status that she was potentially about to lose, and the idea would have been devastating for Anne. Even if Richard didn't want to proceed with divorce, she had failed in her role and in her duty by the standards of the day. As already discussed, the key duty of a medieval queen was to bear her husband's children, and with Prince Edward's death, Anne had failed. Today we know that the fertility issues she and Richard suffered might not have been down to her; with a different husband she might have borne many children, but at the time, any fertility problems were considered the woman's fault.

Anne as a medieval queen was more than a prospective mother, though; she also spearheaded the network of women, she was the go-between of the monarchy and the people, the human face of the monarchy in many respects.[19] She sponsored religious houses, cared for royal wards and interceded with her husband on behalf of petitioners. Anne has traditionally been seen as passive and irrelevant, but as we have seen, she was key to her husband's regime. The lack of evidence means that we can't reliably establish how much power she actually wielded as queen. Her networks of patronage, her accounts and letters have simply not survived, and without them any judgements we make must be treated as circumstantial. We do know that Anne consented to her father's choice of husband and wholeheartedly threw in her lot with Prince Edward. We also know that when Richard came calling she went along with his plan to secure her inheritance and that she married him, lived with him and bore his child, knowing that there was potentially a religious impediment to their marriage that had not been sufficiently dispensed with. This shows ambition, if nothing else. As Richard's duchess, Anne performed her duties flawlessly and won the admiration of the monks at Durham and the council at York, both of which respected and sought to please her – evidence that they regarded her as having influence and power both locally and with her husband. Anne also went along with her husband's usurpation of the throne. Whether she believed the idea of Edward IV's precontract or his illegitimacy is unclear, but she turned a blind eye even if she did not believe it and threw herself behind her husband, performing her queenly duties flawlessly. It is clear, despite later accounts, that Richard did have real support and people who believed in him, and there is no reason why Anne should not be considered a true supporter of her husband. If she did have any qualms, he was offering her the crown of England, surely something that any daughter of the Kingmaker would have jumped at, but there is simply no evidence at all that Anne ever doubted Richard or did anything other than support him completely.

Few women have been better trained or prepared for the role of Queen of England than Anne Neville, and she mattered: she mattered to her husband, her ladies, her son, and to England. Her inheritance was the basis on which Richard's reign was founded and until the death of her son, she had one of the most successful early careers of all the queens of England. In another time, and if circumstances had been different, Anne might have been remembered as a great queen, and the founder of an enduring Yorkist dynasty.

Chapter 17

After Anne

> A horse, a horse, my kingdom for a horse!
> *Richard III*, William Shakespeare

Although this has not been Richard's story, we cannot conclude Anne's properly without taking a look at what happened after her death. Internationally, Anne Neville's death was barely remarked upon, Fabyan wrote that she was 'a woman of gracious fame upon whose soul ... Jesus have mercy'.[1] Agostino Barbarigo in Italy, meanwhile, offered his condolences to Richard on the loss of his beloved consort and told him to 'bear the disaster calmly and resign yourself to the divine will'.[2] Whatever Richard's private feelings might have been, he did not have time to dwell on Anne's passing. On 5 April, less than a month after Anne's death, Richard was forced to write to the city of York, in a letter that was read out publicly and spoke against 'diverse seditious and evil disposed personnes both in our city of London and elsewhere'.[3] Tensions were running high and Crowland reports that 'those who were in arms against the king were hastening to make descent upon England'.[4] Richard did not know exactly where the planned invasion would land but he sent the ever-loyal Lovell to Southampton. Why Richard chose Lovell for this task rather than his Lord Admiral John Howard, Duke of Norfolk, is unclear, but possibly he had more faith in Lovell's loyalty. It appears that he thought the invasion would occur near Southampton, based on a misunderstanding of his intelligence. The *Crowland Chronicle* tells us that Richard was:

> deceived by a quibble on the name of that harbour which had been mentioned by many as the place of their intended descent. For some say that there is a harbour in the neighbourhood of

Southampton called Milford, just as there is in Wales: and there being some persons endowed as it were with a spirit of prophecy, these predicted that those men would land at the harbour of Milford ... besides the kings in this period seemed especially to devote his attention to strengthening the southern part of his kingdom.[5]

Richard, meanwhile, went to Kenilworth and then to Nottingham, somewhere that for him held many memories of Anne and his son.[6] More practically, it was a central location from where he could defend and organise the defence of England. The Great Seal was sent to him there, and placed into his hands during a ceremony witnessed by the Archbishop of York, Bishop of Lincoln, Lord Scrope, George, the son of Lord Thomas Stanley, and John Kendall, Richard's secretary.[7] The same day that Richard received the Great Seal, 1 August 1485, Henry Tudor set sail from Harfleur.

Henry Tudor's invasion force was being financed by Anne of Beaujeu and in May 1485, she finally gave him the support he needed. Henry himself had about 500 men, mostly those on the run from the Yorkist regime. He was now given a few thousand French troops and 'some pieces of artillery'.[8] In command of at least the French troops, and possibly the whole army, was the experienced Philibert de Chandée, whom Henry called his 'dear kinsman, both of spirit and blood'.[9] The fleet itself had sailed under the command of the experienced sailor Guillaume de Casenove in his flagship, the *Poulian De Dieppe*. Henry Tudor landed at Milford Haven in Mill Bay, south-west Wales, on 7 August. It is said that upon coming ashore, he fell to his knees and spoke aloud the words of Psalm 43: 'Judge me, O God, and distinguish my cause'.[10] Tudor then began a slow march into England.

Richard, meanwhile, received news of Henry Tudor's landing, possibly from a man in the service of Sir William Herbert.[11] Richard was staying at the royal hunting lodge at Bestwood, north of Nottingham, when the news reached him.[12] While he had been waiting and mustering his troops, Crowland tells us that Richard was approached by Lord Stanley, who asked to go to his own lands in Leicestershire. Richard agreed but he was closely suspicious of Stanley, who was married to Tudor's mother, Margaret Beaufort, and demanded that his son George remain with him in his place.[13] Nevertheless, allowing Stanley to leave was a fatal miscalculation and there is evidence that he met up with Henry Tudor at Atherstone.[14] Matthew Lewis argues that this action reveals a 'gaping flaw in Richard's character, which prevented him from seeing the motives of others behind their words'.[15]

The Crowland chronicler now accuses Anne's widower of being too slow to act and of being overconfident. Richard, it seems, was relieved that at last the wait for the final confrontation was nearly over.[16] He made it very clear that you were now either with him or against him, and if the latter, then you could expect to lose everything.[17] Richard mustered his forces at Leicester and himself travelled there on 19 August. His army was mustered at Sutton Cheney, whilst according to tradition, Richard III himself stayed at the city's best inn, the White Boar, which was later hastily renamed the Blue Boar Inn after Henry's victory in honour of his commander, John de Vere. The building was pulled down in 1836 but luckily, detailed engravings had been created in the eighteenth and nineteenth centuries, which were rediscovered in 2012 and have enabled a reconstructed model of the building to have been made.[18] This tradition has since been debunked by John Ashdown-Hill but it endured for many years. From Leicester, on 21 August Richard marched west on to Ambion Hill, where he spent the night before the battle.

There are numerous accounts that say the king slept poorly that night, but of course, these were written in hindsight. Of all of them, William Shakespeare's is the most dramatic. He has Richard being confronted by the ghost of those he has wronged, amongst them Lord Hastings, who damns him with the words:

> Bloody and guilty, guiltily awake.
> And in bloody battle end thy days!
> Think of Lord Hastings, despair and die![19]

Anne herself then also appears to her husband, and berates him before addressing Richmond and urging him to victory:

> Richard, thy wife, that wretched Anne thy wife
> That never slept a quiet hour with thee.
> Now fills thy sleep with perturbations

Tomorrow in battle think of me,
And fall thy edgeless sword; despair and die!
[To Richmond]
Thou quiet soul, sleep thou a quiet sleep
Dream of success and happy victory!
Thy adversary's wife doth pray for thee.[20]

Anne would have been horrified to have such words put in her mouth; whatever her feelings towards Richard, she is highly unlikely to have wanted Tudor to prevail. The scene is clearly fiction but perhaps Richard did think of his wife that night, and dwelt on the memory of her. Crowland writes that the next morning, 'there were no chaplains present to perform Divine service on behalf of King Richard nor any breakfast prepared to refresh the flagging spirits of the King.'[21]

We do not know how many men faced each other in battle the next day, but it is generally agreed that Richard had the larger force. Ingram writes that the length of the battlefield 'debris' was over 900 metres, suggesting that both vanguards were about this long, from which a figure of 2,000 men per vanguard had been proposed.[22] Given this, a figure of about 10,000–15,000 men has been proposed for Richard's larger army. John Howard, Duke of Norfolk, was in command of Richard's vanguard, whilst the Earl of Northumberland was placed in command of the rearguard. Stanley was positioned as neutrally as possible, waiting to see how the day would unfold. The *Ballad of Bosworth Field* relates that 'the Stanleys withdrew to a mountain where they looked across the plain and could not see the ground for men and horses.'[23] As for Tudor's much smaller army, it was probably deployed in one main block with the vastly experienced Oxford in a key position. The *Crowland Chronicle* relates that Henry's army advanced first and 'proceeded directly against King Richard'.[24] Norfolk engaged with Oxford and in the melee, Norfolk was killed and his son badly wounded. The question of where Northumberland was and what he was doing remains unclear; it is possible that he had been sent by Richard to encourage him to join him to prevent him from siding with Tudor, or he may have tried to reinforce Norfolk only to be prevented by an area of boggy ground referred to in the sources. There is also the possibility that he, as Molinet writes, 'did nothing except flee, both he and his company abandoned King Richard'. He was certainly later arrested and assassinated on the basis that he had abandoned his 'northern king'.[25]

Things were going very badly and it is now that many sources state that Richard spotted the red dragon banner of Henry Tudor fluttering high in the breeze. Henry was going to meet with Stanley, no doubt to urge him to action.[26] Oxford's tactics when he had formed his troops into wedges had split his lines and there were now gaps. Richard knew that if he could reach Henry and kill him, it would all be over, Henry's men, seeing the danger, likely formed into a protective circle of spears and swords as Richard with his bodyguard and knights charged towards him, hooves thundering on the ground. They smashed into Henry Tudor's bodyguard, and got so close that he killed William Brandon, Henry's standard-bearer, knocking the red dragon to the ground, only for it to be raised again by the Welshman Rhys Fawr. In the blood and the mud, Richard's standard-bearer was then unhorsed and had his legs slashed out from under him. Tudor's forces were threatening to give way under Richards's furious onslaught when Sir William Stanley now led 3,000 men down and into Richard's flank. Exactly when Richard died in the bloodbath that followed is not clear. Vergil tells that he 'was killed fighting manfully in the thickest press of his enemies'.[27] Even Crowland admits that he died 'as a bold and valiant Prince'.[28] King Richard III, Anne's second husband, lay dead on the battlefield at 32 years of age. Following the discovery of his body by archaeologists in 2012, we know that he was stripped naked and that although he was wearing armour, he had not been wearing his helmet when he died. He had suffered eleven injuries at the time of his death; four were dagger stabs to the face, and one, likely to have been fatal, was delivered by a sword to the base of the skull. He also received a blow that penetrated into the brain, likely from a sword or the top of a halberd.[29] His naked body was then draped over a horse and he was symbolically stabbed through the buttocks, an 'insult injury'. This action would also have revealed his scoliosis. There is no way that the curvature of his spine could have been concealed, and it perhaps convinced some onlookers of the just nature of Tudor's victory in an age when any physical deformity was said to reflect a deformity of the soul.

Before his body was given its hasty burial without great honour in the church of the Greyfriars, Leicester, it is recorded that Henry Tudor, now King Henry VII, made the following proclamation:

> Richard Duke of Gloucester, late called King Richard, was slain at a place called Sandeford, within the shire of Leicester, and brought dead off the field unto the town of Leicester, and there was laid openly, that every man might see and look upon him. And also there was slain upon the same field, John late duke of Norfolk, John late Earl of Lincoln, Thomas late earl of Surrey, Frances Viscount Lovell, Sir Walter Devereux, Lord Ferrers, Richard Radcliffe, knight, Robert Brackenbury, knight, with many other knights, squires and gentleman, of whose souls God have mercy.[30]

The proclamation made several errors, including the fact that Francis Lovell was not dead; it is indeed not certain he had made it to Bosworth in time for the battle because if he had, he surely would have died alongside his king in the last Plantagenet charge.[31] Nevertheless, we do know that after Richard's body had been displayed, the Greyfriars asked for permission to bury him and that he was placed in a hastily dug shallow pit inside the church.

Anne's husband was dead, and with him died the last of her dreams and ambitions. Henry Tudor would never again allow families such as the Nevilles to hold so much power and sway. On 25 November 1487, Elizabeth of York, Anne's niece and wife of Henry VII, followed in Anne's footsteps and was crowned Queen of England in a glorious ceremony. Did she think of her aunt, the last crowned Queen of England, that day, as she sat to receive the crown, sceptre and rod of gold?[32] It seems unlikely, for Elizabeth was now an integral cog in the new Tudor regime, just as Anne had once been in Richard's Plantagenet one.

A new day had dawned for England.

Abbreviations

CCR	*Calendar of Close Rolls.*
CFR	*Calendar of Fine Rolls.*
Commines	*Mémoires de Philippe de Commines*, Vol. 1, ed. Troyes, J.D., 1896, Paris.
CPR	*Calendar of Patent Rolls.*
CSPM	*Calendar of the State Papers of Milan.*
Crowland	*The Crowland Abbey Chronicles 1459–86*, ed. Pronay, N. & Cox, J.C., 1986, Gloucester.
Edwards	Edwards, R., 1983, *The Itinerary of King Richard III 1483–1485*, Richard III Society Publication.
Flenley	*Six town Chronicles of England*, ed. Flenley, R., 1911, Oxford: Clarendon Press.
Froissart	*Chronicles*, ed. Brereton, G., 1978, London: Penguin.
Gregory	*The Historical Collections of a citizen of London in the Fifteenth century. Containing John Page's Poem on the Siege of Rouen, Lydgates Verses on England; William Gregory's Chronicle of London*, ed. Gairdner, J., 1876, London.
Head	Head, C., 'Pope Pius and the Wars of the Roses', *Archivum Historiae Pontificiae* 8, 1970: 139–78 (www.jstor.org/stable/23563729).
Hall	*Hall's Chronicle; Containing the History of England, during the reign of Henry the Fourth, and the succeeding monarchs to the end of the reign of Henry the eighth. In which are particularly described the manners and customs of those periods*, ed. Ellis, R., 1809, London: J. Johnson etc.

Hammond	Hammond, P., *The Children of Richard III*, 2018, Stroud: Fonthill Press.
Holinshed	*Holinshed's Chronicles of England, Scotland and Ireland* Vols 3 & 4, 1808, London: J. Johnson etc.
Hicks	Hicks, M., *Anne Neville: Richard III's Tragic Queen*, 2006, Stroud: Amberley Publishing.
Hunter	*Three Catalogues describing the contents of the Red Book of the Exchequer of The Dodsworth Manuscripts in the Bodleian Library*, 1838, London.
Johnson	Johnson, L., *Shadow King. The Life and Death of Henry VI*, 2019, London: Head of Zeus.
Kendall	Kendall, P.M., *Warwick the Kingmaker: A Biography*, 1957, London: George, Allan and Unwin.
Kingsford	*Chronicles of London*, ed. Kingsford, C.L., 1905, London.
Lewis	Lewis, M., *Richard III: Loyalty Binds Me*, 2018, Stroud: Amberley Publishing.
Licence	Licence, A., *Anne Neville: Richard III's Tragic Queen*, 2014, Stroud: Amberley Publishing.
Mancini	Mancini, Dominic, *The Usurpation of Richard III*, ed. Armstrong, C.A.J., 1984, Stroud: Sutton Publishing.
Rous Roll	*The Rous Roll*, ed. Courthope, W.H., 1859.
Schindler	Schindler, M., *Lovell our Dogge*, 2019, Stroud; Amberley Publishing.
Arrivall	*Historie of the arrivall of Edward IV in England and the finall recouerye of his kingdomes from Henry VI A.D. M.CCCC.-LXXI*, 1838, London: Nichols & Sons.
Vergil	*Three books of Polydore Vergil's English History: Comprising The Reigns of Henry VI, Edward IV And Richard III*, ed. Ellis, H., 2010: Kessinger Publishing.
Visser-Fuchs	*Warwick and Wavrin: Two cases studied on the literary background and Propaganda of Anglo-Burgundian relations in the Yorkist period*, doctoral thesis, UCL.
Wavrin	*Recueil des Croniques et Anchiennes Istories de la Grant Bretaigne*, ed. Hardy, W. & Hardy, E.L.C.P, 5 volumes, Rolls Series, 1891.

Abbreviations

Weir Weir, A., *Elizabeth of York: The First Tudor Queen*, 2013, London: Random House.

Worcester *Annales Rerum Anglicarum, Letters and Papers illustrative of the Wars of the English in France*, ed. Stevenson, J., Rolls Series, 1864 ii.

Endnotes

The End

1. Crowland, p. 127.
2. Ibid., pp. 174–5.
3. Weir, p. 122.
4. Buck, *The History of Richard III*, p. 191. The debate surrounding the veracity of this letter is discussed in Weir, pp. 130–4 and in Hicks, pp. 198–201.
5. Crowland, p. 174–5.
6. Vergil, p. 211; Licence, pp. 150–1.
7. Hicks, p. 209.

Chapter 1

1. Rous Roll, British Library MS48976.
2. Benton, John F., 'Trotula, women's problems, and the professionalisation of medicine in the Middle Ages', *Bulletin of the History of Medicine*, 59.1, Spring 1985, p.33.
3. The analysis is presented and discussed in 'Girding the loins? Direct evidence of the use of a medieval English parchment birthing girdle from biomolecular analysis', Sarah Fiddyment, Natalie J. Goodison, Elma Brenner, Stefania Signorello, Kierri Price & Matthew J. Collins, 2021, *Royal Society Open Science. See* an example of a birthing girdle at Wellcome Collection MS.632.
4. Nicolas, S.N.H, 1830, *Privy Purse Expenses of Elizabeth of York: Wardrobe Accounts of Edward the Fourth*, with a memoir of Elizabeth of York, and notes. London: W. Pickering, p. 78.

Endnotes

5. Watt, J., 2004, *The Paston Women: Selected Letters*, London: D.S. Brewer, p. 129
6. Anne also had a half-sister, Margaret, her father's illegitimate daughter. Discussed in Hicks, pp. 231–47.
7. Richardson, R.E., 2018, *Mistress Blanche: Queen Elizabeth I's Confidante*: Langston Press, p. 29.
8. Chisholm, H. (ed.), 1911, Westmorland, Earls of EB, Vol. 28, pp. 552–3.
9. Hicks, p. 37; Kendall, p. 19.
10. Shakespeare, *Henry VI, Part 1*, Act 4, Scene 1.
11. *Bales Chronicle*, in Flenley, p. 140, discussed in Johnson, p. 308.
12. Ibid.
13. Johnson, pp. 311–14.
14. Turner. W.J., 2010, 'Town and country: A competition of the treatment of the mentally disabled in late medieval English common law and charter boroughs', in *Madness in Medieval Law and Custom*, The Netherlands, Leiden, pp. 17–20.
15. Hollman, G., 2020, *Royal Witches: From Joan of Navarre to Elizabeth Woodville*, Cheltenham: The History Press, p. 137.
16. Johnson, p. 310.
17. Ibid., p. 319.
18. Hunter, pp. 277–8; Laynesmith, pp. 62–3; Johnson, p. 320.
19. Rohr's entire text explores the nature of medieval female regency in relation to Yolande of Aragon. Johnson discusses the idea of Margaret of Anjou emulating her on p. 324.
20. Johnson, p. 325.
21. Hanham, A. (ed.) 2015, *Benet's Chronicle: A new English translation*, Palgrave MacMillan: London.
22. Johnson, p. 328.
23. Monro, C. (ed.), 1968, *Letters of Queen Margaret of Anjou and Bishop Beckington and Others: Written in the Reigns of Henry V and Henry VI*: AMS Press, pp. 119–20.
24. Johnston, p. 335.
25. CSPM, Milanese State Archive 'Milan: 1461', in *Calendar of State Papers and Manuscripts in the Archives and Collections of Milan 1385–1618*, Allen B. Hinds (ed.), London, 1912, pp. 37–106, British History Online.

Chapter 2

1. Froissart, pp. 192–5.
2. Sumpton, J., 1990, *Trial by Battle: The Hundred Years War*, Vol. 1, London: Faber & Faber, pp. 532–4.
3. Froissart.
4. Bryant, *The True Chronicles of Jean Le Bel 1290–1360*, pp. 167–8.
5. Ibid., p. 175.
6. Holinshed.
7. *Knighton's Chronicle*, Martin (ed.), pp. 60–4.
8. *Chronicles of London*, Kingsford, C.L. (ed.), Oxford, 1905, p.167. *The Brut: Or the Chronicles of England*, Brie, F.W.D. (ed.), Early English Text Society, cxxxvi, 1908, p. 524.
9. Ibid.
10. MS Lambeth, 853, p. 102.
11. An example of such a letter: British Library MS 43490, p.24. The Paston's literacy is discussed in depth by Richmond, C., 2000–2002, *The Paston Family in the 15th Century*, Vols. 1, 2 and 3, Manchester: MUP.
12. Hewson, M.A, 1975, *Giles of Rome and the Medieval Theory of Conception. A study of the De formatione corporis humani in utero*, London: Athlone Press, p. 100.
13. Image retrieved 13/8/22, from www.habsburger.net.
14. Shakespeare, *Henry VI, Part 2*, Act 4, Scene 10.
15. Johnston, p. 341.
16. PR 1455, item 18.
17. *The Paston Letters*, Vol. 1, p. 378, www.gutenberg.org.
18. Arman, J., 2023, *Margaret of Anjou: She-Wolf of France. Twice Queen of England*, Stroud: Amberley – discusses Margaret's reputation in depth.
19. *Gregory's Chronicle*.
20. PL1, pp. 447–8.
21. Johnston, pp. 365–70, gives an account of the events of Lady Day.
22. Bennett, Josephine Waters, 'The Mediaeval Loveday', *Speculum*, Vol. 33, No. 3, Medieval Academy of America, Cambridge University Press,

Endnotes

University of Chicago Press, 1958, pp. 351–70. The ballad is discussed in depth here: https://thewarsoftheroses.co.uk/loveday-1458/.
23. LP1, p. 369.

Chapter 3

1. These events are discussed by Jeffrey, C., 2021, www.thehistoryofparliament.wordpress.com.
2. Griffiths, R.A., 1981, *The Reign of King Henry VI: The exercise of Royal Authority 1422–1461*, London: Benn, pp. 265–304, discusses York's household in Wales.
3. Brie, F.W.D (ed.), 1906–8, *Brut, The Chronicles of England*, London: Kegan Paul, Trench, Trübner & Co., pp. 526–7.
4. Lander, J.R., 'Henry VI and the Duke of York's second protectorate 1455–1461', *Bulletin of the John Rylands Library*, 43, No. 1, 1960, p. 95.
5. Dr Simon Payling outlines and discusses these events here: https://thehistoryofparliament.wordpress.com/2019/10/10/the-battle-of-ludford-bridge/.
6. CPR 1459, Item 19, and Benet, p. 224.
7. Crowland, pp. 108–11.
8. Johnson, pp. 192–4.
9. Head, pp.139–78.
10. Benet, p. 225.
11. Head, pp. 164–8.
12. Ingram, M., 2015, *The Battle of Northampton 1460*, Northampton: Northampton Battlefield Society, p. 84.
13. Dr Glenn Foard, expert on medieval artillery, discusses the finds and concludes that the cannonball was 'highly likely [to have been] fired during the 1460 battle', www.bajrfed.co.uk.
14. Goodman, p. 38.
15. Johnson, p. 406.
16. Wavrin, pp. 305, 306–8.
17. Wavrin, p. 310.

18. Shakespeare, *Henry VI, Part 3*, Act I, Scene I.
19. Coppini, F., quoted in Weir, A., 2011, *Lancaster and York*, Vintage Digital: Digital Scribe, p. 240.
20. *Great Chronicle*, pp. 194–5, and discussed in Haigh, P., 2014, *From Wakefield to Towton*, Barnsley: Pen & Sword, pp. 31–5.
21. CSPM, Nos 62 and 71, www.british-history.ac.uk/cal-state-papers/milan/1385-1618/, pp.37–106.
22. CSPM, pp. 65–6.
23. *Great Chronicle*, p. 195.

Chapter 4

1. *Hall's Chronicle*.
2. Sadler, J., 2020, *Towton: The Battle of Palm Sunday Field 1461*, Digital Scribe: Pen & Sword Military, p. 76.
3. *Hall's Chronicle*.
4. *See* discussion in: Boylston, A., Holst, M. & Coughlan, J., 2000, 'Physical Anthropology', in Fiorato, V., Boylston, A. & Knusel, C. (eds.), *Blood Red Roses: The Archaeology of a Mass Grave from the Battle of Towton 1461*, Oxford: Oxbow, pp. 36–44.
5. Kendall.
6. Hicks, p. 54.
7. Rous Roll.
8. Hicks, p. 53.
9. Laynesmith, J.L., 2019, *Cecily, Duchess of York*, London: Bloomsbury, discusses Cecily's books and her scholarship in depth throughout.
10. Sutton & Visser-Fuchs, 74 and 87, No. 20.
11. Duffy, E., 2011, *Marking the Hours: English People and Their Prayers 1240–1570*, Yale: Yale University Press, p. 4.
12. Ibid.
13. Discussed in Sutton & Visser-Fuchs, pp. 46–50.
14. Ibid.
15. Marx, W. (ed.), 2004, *An English Chronicle 1377–1461*, Woodbridge, p. 73.
16. Roll of the Exchequer records.

Chapter 5

1. Visser-Fuchs, 2002, pp. 20–142, offers an in-depth discussion and analysis of Richard Neville's reputation in the Burgundian Low Countries, 1450–71.
2. *Gregory's Chronicle*, in: Embree and Tavormina (eds.), p. 115.
3. Ibid.
4. Higginbotham, S., *The Woodvilles*, Digital Scribe, Cheltenham, 2013: The History Press, p. 129.
5. Sutton, A. & Visser-Fuchs, L., *The Entry of Queen Elizabeth Woodville over London Bridge, 24 May 1465*, p. 16.
6. William of Worcester records that the marriage was considered at the time to be 'diabolical' and he felt it was the last straw for Warwick. He was, however, mistaken in his belief that Katherine was 80 rather than in her sixties. John Neville was later executed for rebelling against Edward. The last record of Katherine is at Richard III's coronation, where she was issued with robes.
7. Hicks, p. 70; Weir, pp. 14–17.
8. Stow, J., 1603, 'A Survey of London', reproduced at www.british-history.ac.uk, p. 92.
9. British Library MS 7970.
10. Levitt, E., 'Woodville versus the Bastard', *History Today*, Vol. 66, 2016.
11. Ibid.
12. John Paston letter.
13. Worcester, p. 788.
14. Wilkinson, p.95, based on accounts of the chronicler John Stone.
15. Hicks, p. 69.
16. Wavrin, p. 543.

Chapter 6

1. Hicks, p. 71.
2. Bodleian Library MS, Dugdale 15, p. 75.
3. Base Mérimée: Église Notre-Dame. Ministère Française de la Culture.

4. Chronicle of John Stone, pp. 110–11. Hill, *Cecily Neville*, p. 1959 of 4537, Kindle edition.
5. Crowland, pp. 132–3.
6. Scott, M., 2011, *Medieval Dress and Fashion*, London: British Library, p. 153.
7. Ashdown-Hill, J., *The Third Plantagenet: George Duke of Clarence, Richard III's Brother*, Cheltenham: The History Press, p. 144.
8. Wavrin, p. 579.
9. She was cleared by Edward IV. CPR 1467–77, p. 190.
10. Kendall, pp. 286–7.
11. CSPM.
12. Crowland, Charter Rolls, C.53/105.
13. Parliament Rolls, VI 132, 1470, membranes 3 and 4.
14. Hicks, p. 74; Kendall, p. 256.
15. Wagner, p. 296.
16. Fols 87v–88. Discussed in *Archaeologia Cantiana*, Vol. 127, 2007, p. 399; Searle, p. 110.
17. Commines, Vol. 1, p. 194.
18. Hicks, M., 2002, *Warwick the Kingmaker*, London: Wiley-Blackwell, p. 287.
19. Commines, p. 194.

Chapter 7

1. Broadwell, p. 1.
2. CSPM i 139, referenced in Hicks, p. 77.
3. Sutton, A. & Visser-Fuchs, L., 2023, 'Anne Neville: Heiress and Highest Ornament of her House', in Norrie, A., Harris, C., Laynesmith, J.L., Messer, D.R. & Woodacre, E. (eds.), *Later Plantagenet and the Wars of the Roses Consorts. Power, Influence and Dynasty*: Palgrave Macmillan, p. 242.
4. CSPM 1470.
5. *The Politics of Fifteenth Century England: John Vale's Book*, Kekewich, M.L., Richmond, C., Sutton, A.F., Visser-Fuchs, L. & Watts, J.L. (eds.), p. 217.

6. CSPM i. 140.
7. Hicks, p. 85.
8. Champollion-Figeac, 1848, Vol. 2. pp. 488–91.
9. Hicks, p. 82.
10. *De Laudibus Legum Angliae*, Sir John Fortescue, edited and translated by Chrimes, S.B., 1942, Cambridge: Cambridge University Press.
11. CSPM, referenced in *History of War*, October 2020, www.pressreader.com.
12. McGerr, Rosemarie, 'A Statute Book and Lancastrian Mirror for Princes: The Yale Law School Manuscript of the "Nova Statuta Angliae"', *Textual Cultures*, Vol. 1, No. 2 (2006): 6–59, http://www.jstor.org/stable/30227927.
13. Hicks, M., 2002, *Warwick the Kingmaker*, London: Wiley-Blackwell, p. 289.
14. Ross, C., 1998, Edward IV, Yale: Yale University Press, p. 147.
15. Commines, p.185.
16. Hicks, p. 87.
17. BnF MS. FR. 6758 FOL 67.
18. Clarke, 1021 N.
19. Sutton & Visser-Fuchs, p. 243.
20. Calmette, J. & Perinelle, G., *Louis XI et L'Angleterre*, 1930, Paris, p. 133.
21. James, p. 376.
22. Johnson, p. 516.
23. Sutton & Visser-Fuchs, p. 244.
24. Calmette, J. & Perinelle, G., *Louis XI et L'Angleterre*, 1930, Paris, ref: 134n1 136n4 136n5.
25. Crowland, p. 125.
26. Froissart.
27. Lawne, p. 143.
28. The activities and political machinations of Anne's aunts are explored thoroughly in Baldwin, D., 2009, *The Kingmaker's Sisters*, Digital Scribe, Cheltenham: The History Press.
29. Wavrin.
30. The *Arrivall*, p. 10. *See also* Hicks, p. 89.

Chapter 8

1. Discussed in Kirke, H., 1920, 'Sir Henry Vernon of Haddon, Derbyshire', *Archaeological Journal*, 42, pp. 1–17.
2. Johnson, p. 527.
3. Harrison. H., Harrison, S. & Noronha, M., p. 21.
4. Ibid., p. 24.
5. Warkworth, p.16. John Paston II writes to his mother to inform her that his brother has been injured in the arm by an arrow. The letter can be found online at www.thisispaston.co.uk.
6. Warkworth, p. 16. Hicks, Warwick, p. 310.
7. Thornbury, p. 244.
8. Bisham Priory was the family burial place. It was destroyed in the Reformation and today is a sports centre.
9. Hicks, p. 94.
10. Hicks, Warwick, pp. 315–20, discusses these rumours.
11. The *Arrivall*, p. 23.
12. Hicks, p. 94.
13. *Cerne Historical Society Magazine*, Issue 1, 2020, p. 90.
14. CSPM 1471. The *Arrivall*, p. 23.
15. The *Arrivall*, pp. 23–8, gives an account of these movements.
16. Hicks, p. 96. For a full account of Tewkesbury Abbey's history and the relationship Anne's ancestor had with it, *see The Founders Book: A Medieval History of Tewkesbury Abbey*, a facsimile of Oxford Bodleian Library MA Top. Glouc.d.2. Edited by Julian Luxford, 2021.
17. Lewis, p. 137.
18. The *Arrivall*, pp. 28–31, gives a full account of the Battle of Tewkesbury.
19. Ibid.
20. Shakespeare, *Richard III*, Act 1 Scene 2.
21. Hicks, p. 98.
22. The inscription on Prince Edward's grave marker in Tewkesbury Abbey.

Chapter 9

1. Weir, A., 2011, *Lancaster and York*, Digital Scribe, Cheltenham: History Press, pp. 409–10.

2. Ibid.
3. Margaret's mother had been pregnant at least once more but she likely miscarried soon after her husband's death, which left Margaret as her parents' only surviving child. CPR1441–46, p. 283.
4. Weir, A., 2011, *Lancaster and York*, pp. 409–10.
5. Ibid., p. 410.
6. Hicks, p. 98.
7. Ibid.
8. The *Arrivall*, 31 and Kingsford, C.L., 1913, *English Historical Literature in the 15th Century*, p. 37.
9. Weir, A., 2011, *Lancaster and York*, p. 411.
10. Laynesmith, J.L., 2004, *The Last Medieval Queens*, Oxford: Oxford University Press, pp. 44–7.
11. Eighteen months after entering Beaulieu, Anne's mother was still writing to try to find someone (anyone) to help her assert her rights. British Library MS Julian BXII ff.314-v.
12. Hicks, pp.105–106.
13. Vergil, p. 152.
14. Hicks, p. 103.
15. The *Arrivall*, p. 38; Johnson, p. 537.
16. Crowland, pp. 130–1.
17. Johnson, p. 537.
18. Johnson, p. 538. She goes on to clarify that of course the same logic must apply to them to the potential murder of the princes in the Tower.
19. Kingsford, C.L., 1914, *Historical Notes on Medieval London Houses: London Topographical Records*, Vol. 10, p. 94.
20. If this was the case in medieval London, this might have been why Clarence chose to stay there now.
21. 'A Collection of Ordinances and Regulations for the Governance of the Royal Household made in divers reigns from King Edward III to King William and Queen Mary London', Society of Antiquaries, 1790. Discussed and transcribed in Licence, pp. 147–8.
22. Ibid.
23. Licence, p. 149. Shakespeare, *Richard III*, Act 1, Scene 2.
24. *Richard III: Discovery and identification*, University of Leicester, www.le.ac.uk.

25. Hicks, p. 110.
26. Crowland, pp. 132–3.
27. Paston Letters and Papers, i.447.
28. This was at the expense of Anne's cousin, George Neville, the Duke of Bedford, Monatgu's son and heir.
29. Hicks, p. 19.
30. Crowland, p. 133.
31. Branfield, M., 'Diriment Impediments, Dispensations and Divorce: Richard III and Matrimony', p. 2.
32. Oxford Bodleian Library, MS Digdale, 15 f.75.
33. Hicks, pp. 132–4, discusses the legal intricacies of the situation.
34. Hicks, p. 136.
35. Gairdner, J. (ed.), 2012, *Letters and Papers Illustrative of the reigns of Richard III and Henry VII Volume 1*, Cambridge: Cambridge University Press, p. 22.

Chapter 10

1. Hammond, p. 18.
2. Ibid.
3. CPR 1476–1485, p. 34.
4. Gairdner Paston Letters, Vol. 5, p. 36.
5. CPR 1476–1485, p. 34.
6. Hammond, p. 20.
7. CPR 1476–1495, p. 513.
8. Hicks, p. 158.
9. Licence, p. 163.
10. *Stoner letters and papers of the fifteenth century*, Kingsford, C.L. (ed.), Camden Third Series xxx, 1919, 11 81.
11. Kenyon, K., 2015, *Middleham Castle*, English Heritage, p. 19.
12. www.english-heritage.org.uk/siteassets/home/visit/places-to-visit/middleham-castle/history/middleham-castle-phased-plan.pdf.
13. Licence, p. 163.
14. Hicks, p. 153. Hicks, M., 'One Prince or Two?' *The Ricardian*, Vol. 120, 1993, pp. 467–8.

15. *Historiae Dunelmensis Scriptores Tres*, Raine, J. (ed.), Suratees Society, 1839, ccclviii–ix.
16. Hicks, p. 164.
17. Barnfield, M., richardiii.net/richard-iii-his-world/his-family/anne-neville-wife/.
18. Baldwin, D., *The Kingmaker's Sisters*, p. 153. A letter written to Piers Werburton.
19. Commines, p. 277.
20. Horox & Sutton, p. 269.
21. Ibid., p. 267.
22. Stow, J., 1598, *A Survey of London by John Stowe*, p. 160.
23. *Historiae Dunelmensis Scriptores Tres*, Raine, J. (ed.), Suratees Society, 1839, ccclvii–viii.
24. Lewis, p.199; Licence, p.171.
25. Lewis, p. 201.
26. Blunt, pp. 84–5.
27. Ibid.
28. Lewis, p. 209.
29. Ibid., p. 212.
30. *Roturli parliamentorum*, Vol. VI, London, 1777, p. 193.
31. Ashdown-Hill, J., 2015, *The Third Plantagenet: George Duke of Clarence*, Cheltenham: The History Press, p. 231.
32. Mancini, pp. 62–3.
33. Ibid.
34. Gairdner, p. 68.
35. Lewis, p. 214.
36. Middleham Collegiate church collection, ZRC 17496.
37. Gilbert, L., 2017, 'St Alkelda: Saxon Lady, Martyr and Saint?', https://englishhistoryauthors.blogspot.com/2017/03/st-alkelda-saxon-lady-martyred-saint.html, retrieved 15/1/2023.
38. Lewis, p. 220.
39. Sutton, A.F., 'Caxton and the Cult of St Winifred and Shrewsbury', in Clark, L. (ed.) *Of Mice and Men: Image, Belief and Regulation in Late Medieval England*, 2005: Boydell Press.
40. Morgan Library and Museum, M917 and M945.

41. Lambeth Palace Library, MS 747, and Sutton, A.F. & Visser-Fuchs, L., 1990, *The Hours of Richard III*, Stroud: Ian Sutton for Richard III and Yorkist History Trust.
42. Tiptoft, J., *The Declamation of Noblesse*, quoted in A.F. Sutton, 'A Curious Searcher for our Weal Public': Richard III, Piety, Chivalry and the Concept of the 'Good Prince' in Hammond, P.W. (ed.), *Richard III: Loyalty, Lordship and Law*, pp. 61–2.
43. CPR, Edward IV, 1476–85, PRO, p. 133.

Chapter 11

1. Hall, 1809, pp. 332–3.
2. Lewis, p. 234.
3. CPR, Edward IV, Edward V and Richard III. Edward IV – January 1483.
4. Licence, pp. 175–6; Hicks, p. 162.
5. Crowland quoted in Licence, p. 176.
6. Ramsey, J.H., 1982, *Lancaster and York*, Vol. 2, London: Legare Street Press, p. 448.
7. Ashdown-Hill, J., 2016, *The Private Life of Edward IV*, Gloucester: Amberley Publishing, pp. 205–10, discusses Edward IV's death.
8. Edwards, p. x. *See also* Lewis, p. 244.
9. Mancini, p. 73.
10. Lewis discusses Hastings' role and these events in more detail, pp. 244–50.
11. Edwards, p. xi.
12. Crowland, p. 485.
13. John de la Pole was the son of Edward and Richard's sister, Elizabeth. CPR, Vol.7, pp. 688–90.
14. Sutton, A.F., Visser-Fuchs, L. & Griffiths, R.A., p. 25.
15. British Library MS Harleian, 3952 f.105v.
16. Licence, p. 181.
17. Crowland, p. 486.
18. Lewis, p. 255.

19. Cotton, Vespasian FXIII.
20. Drapers' Company account, f.26.
21. Hicks, p. 167.
22. Hicks, M., *What Might Have Been: George Neville, Duke of Bedford, 1465–83: His Identity and Significance*, p. 325.
23. Harleian 433, Vol. 3, p. 3. Richard often joined his nephew there and numerous documents attest to his presence. For example: PRO PSO 1/56/2884/5 and 1/56/2848.
24. Edwards, p. xi.
25. Lewis, p. 272.
26. Licence, p. 184.
27. Mancini, p. 91.
28. For further discussion *see* Lewis, pp. 272–80.
29. Mancini, p. 85.
30. Ibid., p. 95.
31. British Library MS 48976. John Rous, *Historia Regum Angliae*, Oxford, 1745, pp. 213–14, in Hammond, P.W. & Sutton, A.F., 1985, *Richard III: The Road to Bosworth*, p. 111.

Chapter 12

1. CCR 1467–85 1170. Sutton, A.F. & Hammond, P.W., *The Coronation of Richard III: the Extant Documents*, p. 26.
2. NA: SAL/MS/231.
3. Sutton, A.F., 'Alice Claver: Silk woman of London and maker of the mantel laces for Richard III and Queen Anne', *The Ricardian*, pp. 243–7.
4. Sutton, A.F. & Hammond, P.W., *The Coronation of Richard III: the Extant Documents*, pp. 27–8.
5. Licence, p. 193.
6. Lewis, p. 304. Harleian 433 Vol. 2, p. 25, makes it clear that Edward did not attend. For further discussion *see* Hammond, p. 22.
7. Sutton, A.F. & Hammond, P.W., *The Coronation of Richard III: the Extant documents*, pp. 33–5.

8. *The Fire of 1834 and the Old Palace of Westminster*, PDF booklet at www.parliament.uk/globalassets/documents/WORKS-OF-ART/The-fire-of-1834-booklet.pdf.
9. Sutton, A.F. & Hammond, P.W., *The Coronation of Richard III: the Extant documents*, pp. 35–6.
10. Ibid.
11. Ibid., p. 276.
12. Ibid.
13. Compton-Reeves, A., 'Cathedral Deans of the Yorkist Age', *The Ricardian*, p. 91.
14. Sutton, A.F. & Hammond, P.W., *The Coronation of Richard III: the Extant documents*, pp. 42–3.
15. Digitised translation by the British Library at www.bl.uk/collection-items/the-rous-roll.
16. Baldwin, p. 110.
17. Collins, D.M. *et al.*, 2012, 'The King's High Table at the Palace of Westminster', *The Antiquaries Journal*, Vol. 92, pp. 197–243.
18. Collins, D.M., 2018, 'The Heraldry and Badges of Richard II at Westminster Hall, Palace of Westminster', *The Coat of Arms Annual Journal of the Heraldry Society*, Series 4, Vol. 1, No. 235.
19. Schindler, p. 138.
20. Crowland.
21. Lewis, p. 309.
22. Sutton, A.F. & Hammond, P.W., *The Coronation of Richard III: extant documents*, p. 85.
23. Lewis, p. 310.
24. SGChapel Archives, XI.P.7.9.11/12.
25. Hanham, p. 122.
26. CPR 1476–85, p. 212.
27. Higginbotham, p. 6.
28. Pierce, H., *Margaret Pole: Countess of Salisbury 1473–1541*: University of Wales Press, p. 6.
29. Higginbotham, p. 9.
30. *A History of the County of Warwick*, Vol. 8, 1969, BHO, pp. 434–5.
31. Hanham, A., 1975, *Richard III and His Early Historians, 1483–1535*, Oxford: OUP, p. 121.

32. Hicks, p. 175.
33. British Library, Medieval manuscripts blog: 'The Pageants of Richard Beauchamp, Earl of Warwick', 2/4/2020, at blogs.bl.uk/digitisedmanuscripts/2020/04/the-pageants-of-richard-beauchamp-earl-of-warwick.html.
34. Rous Roll, 59.
35. Shakespeare, *Richard III*.

Chapter 13

1. Hicks, *Richard III*, pp. 146–8.
2. Hicks, p. 178.
3. YHB, Vol. 2, pp. 287–8.
4. Hammond, p. 29.
5. YAS Record Series, Vol. 98, York Civic Records, Vol. 1, 1485–87.
6. YHB, Vol. 1, pp. 288–9, 298.
7. Hammond, p. 30.
8. Ibid., p.31.
9. Davies, R.G., 1995, 'The Church and the Wars of the Roses', in Pollard, S. (ed.), *The Wars of the Roses*, New York: St Martin's Press, p. 142.
10. Wright, S.K., 'The York Creed play in light of the Innsbruck Playbook of 1391', *Medieval and Renaissance Drama in England*, Vol. 5, 1991, pp. 27–53. JSTOR at www.jstor.org/stable/2432089, p. 30.
11. York Minster Library, *Vicars Choral Statute Book*, p. 48. Transcript in Hammond, P.W. & Sutton, A.F., *Richard III: The Road to Bosworth Field*, 1985, London, pp. 140–1.
12. Hammond, p. 31.
13. *Bedern College Statute Book*, p. 48.
14. Ibid.
15. *Hall's Chronicle*, p. 15.
16. Licence, p. 206,
17. Lewis, p. 319.
18. MSS433, Vol. II, pp. 42–3.
19. Hammond, p. 35.
20. PRO PSO 1/56/2865. PRO SC1/46/102. A letter from Lovell to Stonor.

21. Schindler, p. 147.
22. 'The Rebellion of 1483: A study of sources and opinions', Hillier, K., 1982, Parts 1&2, *The Ricardian*.
23. More, T., reprint 2023, *The History of King Richard the Third*, independently published, p. 105.
24. Weir, A., 2014, *Richard III and the Princes in the Tower*, London: Vintage, p. 194.
25. Tallis, N., 2019, *Uncrowned Queen: The fateful life of Margaret Beaufort: Tudor Matriarch*, Kindle Scribe, p. 3036.
26. Ibid., p. 3052.
27. Ellis (ed.), *Three Books*, p. 195.
28. Kingsford (ed.), *Chronicles of London*, p. 191.
29. Laynesmith, pp. 228–9.
30. CPR, *Richard III*, 1483–5.
31. Weir, A., 2001, *Henry VIII: King and Court*, Vintage Digital, p. 10.
32. Richardson, J., 2000, *The Annals of London: A Year by Year Record of a Thousand Years of History*: University of California Press, p. 64.
33. Ashdown-Hill, J., *The Private Life of Edward IV*, pp. 48–9, 62–3, 87–8, 114–15, 117–19, 155–8.
34. Edwards, pp. 11–12.
35. Laynesmith, J.L., 'Richard III's lavish Christmas?' at www.richardiii.blogspot.com, accessed 4/1/2021.
36. E/404/78/2/28.
37. Roos, D., 17/12/2021, 'How Christmas was celebrated in the Middle Ages', at www.history.com.
38. Harleian 433, Vol. 2, p. 75, PRO C81/887/95.
39. Canterbury Cathedral Dean Appeal, *Archaeologia Cantiana*, Vol. 22, 1897, pp. lxiii–lxvi.
40. Licence, p. 214.
41. Higginbotham, p. 9.
42. PRO E404/78/2/27.
43. Lewis, M., 'Richard III Parliament', March 2020, *The Ricardian Bulletin* at https://richardiii.net/richard-iii-his-world/reputation/a-devotion-to-equitable-justice/
44. Hicks, M., 1991, *Richard III and his Rivals*, London: Hambleton, p. 332.

45. Licence, p. 215.
46. Lewis, M., 'Richard III Parliament', March 2020, *The Ricardian Bulletin* at https://richardiii.net/richard-iii-his-world/reputation/a-devotion-to-equitable-justice/.
47. Ibid.
48. Amin, N.
49. Ibid.
50. Hicks, p. 185.
51. Chrimes, S.B., 1972, *Henry VII*, p. 29.
52. Weir, p. 115.
53. Ibid., p. 117.
54. Pollard, A.J., 2001, *One Summer at Middleham: The Worlds of Richard III*, London: Tempus Publishing, p. 143.
55. Ibid., p. 139.
56. Ibid., p. 140.

Chapter 14

1. 'Foundresses and Patronesses', at www.queens.cam.ac.uk.
2. Laynesmith, p. 256.
3. Hammond, p. 36.
4. PRO C81/894/425.
5. Gill, H., 1904, *A Short History of Nottingham Castle*.
6. Ibid.
7. Earp, J., 'The Caves and St. Mary de Roche', at www.ournottinghamshire.org.uk.
8. Edwards, pp. 17–18.
9. Hicks, p. 192; Licence, p. 222.
10. Crowland, p. 171.
11. *Regis Edwardi*, p. 170.
12. Rothenberg, D.J., 2011, *The Flower of Paradise*, Oxford: Oxford University Press, p. 18.
13. Crowland, pp. 170–1.
14. Barnfield, pp. 24–6.

15. Crease, J., 'Is this the tomb of Richard III's son?', Church Monuments Society at https://churchmonumentssociety.org/monument-of-the-month/is-this-the-tomb-of-richard-iiis-son.
16. Hammond, p. 39.
17. Hicks, p. 192; Vergil, p. 121.
18. Weir, p. 121.
19. Edwards, pp. 18–22.
20. Edwards, p. 19; Radzikowski, p. 57.
21. Barnfield, M., 'Lady Anne Neville' at https://richardiii.net/richard-iii-his-world/his-family/anne-neville-wife/.
22. CPR, Edward IV, 1476–85, PRO, p. 493.
23. Griffiths, R., 'The burials of King Henry VI at Chertsey and Windsor', in Nigel, S. & Tatton-Brown, T. (eds.), 2010, *St George's Chapel Windsor*, pp. 104–105.
24. Hackett, F., 1937, *Francis the First*, New York: Doubleday, Doran & Company, p. 25.

Chapter 15

1. PRO E404/78/3/10–11.
2. Hillier, K., Normark, P. & Hammond, P., 'Colyngbourne's Rhyme' in Petre, J. (ed.), *Richard III: Crown and People*, 1985, pp. 107–108.
3. Weir, p. 121.
4. Ibid., p. 118.
5. Licence, p. 237.
6. Clarke, P.D., 'English Royal Marriages in the Papal Penitentiary in the Fifteenth Century', *English Historical Review*, Vol. 120, No. 488, pp. 1024–5.
7. Licence, p. 237.
8. Peachy, S., *Festivals and Feasts of the Common Man 1550–1660*, 1995.
9. Sutton, A.F. & Visser-Fuchs, L., *Richard III's books observed*, 2002, p. 2.
10. Weir, p. 127.
11. Hammond & Sutton, p. 199.
12. Hicks paraphrasing Buck, p. 199.

Endnotes

13. British Library MS, Cotton Tiberius, E.x.f.238v.
14. Crowland, quoted in Licence, p. 238.
15. Crowland, p. 174.
16. Ibid., pp. 174–5.
17. John Carmi Parsons, *The Pregnant Queen as Counsellor and the Construction of Motherhood*, 1998, Yale: Yale University Press.
18. Hicks, p. 203.
19. RP VI, pp. 100–101.
20. Hicks, p. 205.
21. Licence, p. 253.
22. Adams, F. (ed.), 'The genuine works of Hippocrates', London, The Sydenham Society, 1849, *Book 1 of the Endemics. Hippocrates 460–370 BC*.

Chapter 16

1. Vergil, p. 211.
2. Halliwell, J.O., 1848, *Letters of the Kings of England*, p. 161.
3. Licence, p. 245.
4. Abernethy, S., 'The Last Will and Testament of Elizabeth Woodville, Queen of England', 16/12/2016 at www.thefreelancehistorywriter.com.
5. Ibid.
6. Hicks, p. 213.
7. Crowland, pp. 174–5.
8. www.cudl.lib.cam.ac.uk is a digitised copy of the manuscript.
9. Nasa has collated the records and references to and of past eclipses, which can be found at www.eclipse.gsfc.nasa.gov.
10. Stephenson, R., 'Royal Rituals of death – The curious traditions of Royal funerals through the ages', an online talk, viewed 8/10/2022.
11. Weir, p. 405. Abernethy, S., 'The Funeral of Queen Elizabeth of York, the first Tudor Queen of England', at www.medievalists.net.
12. British Library MS45161 ff.41–2.
13. Crowland, pp. 174–5.
14. *The Great Chronicle*, p. 234.

15. Rous Roll, No. 62.
16. Laynesmith, p. 122.
17. Hicks, *Rivals*, pp. 332–3; Hicks, p. 213.
18. The inscription on Anne Neville's memorial plaque, Westminster Abbey.
19. Licence, p. 255.

Chapter 17

1. Licence, p. 254.
2. Venice 1481–1485, CSP Relating to English Affairs in the Archives of Venice, Vol. 1:1202–1509, 1864, pp. 141–59.
3. York Books, pp. 359–60.
4. Crowland, p. 50.
5. *Ingulph's Chronicle*, pp. 500–501.
6. Richard was at Kenilworth by 2 May, Harleian 433, Vol. 1, p. 62, and at Nottingham by 9 June, PRO C81/907/1080. Edwards, p. 37.
7. Lewis, p. 379.
8. Ingram, M., *Richard III and the Battle of Bosworth*, Amherst: Helion & Company, 2019, p. 176.
9. Ingram, M., 'The Battle of Bosworth', at https://richardiii.net/richard-iii-his-world/the-war-of-the-roses/the-battles/the-battle-of-bosworth/.
10. Penn, T., *Winter King: Henry VII and the dawn of Tudor England*, 2011, London: Penguin Books, pp. 1–2.
11. Licence, p. 258.
12. Lewis, p. 380.
13. Crowland, p. 501.
14. Ingram, M., 'The Battle of Bosworth', at.https://richardiii.net/richard-iii-his-world/the-war-of-the-roses/the-battles/the-battle-of-bosworth/.
15. Lewis, p. 380.
16. Crowland, p. 501; Lewis, p. 380.
17. A letter Richard wrote to Henry Vernon makes this very clear. For the text of this letter *see* Lewis, p. 380.
18. A 3D model has been made by Leicester University https://le.ac.uk/richard-iii/richard-iii-and-leicester/blue-boar-inn.

Endnotes

19. Shakespeare, *Richard III*, Act 5, Scene 3.
20. Ibid.
21. Crowland, p. 503.
22. Ingram, M., 'The Battle of Bosworth', at https://richardiii.net/richard-iii-his-world/the-war-of-the-roses/the-battles/the-battle-of-bosworth/.
23. Ibid.
24. Crowland, p. 505.
25. Lewis, p. 383.
26. Ibid.
27. Vergil.
28. Crowland, p. 506.
29. How Richard III died, data and analysis at www.le.ac.uk.
30. Hughes, P.K. & Larkin, J.P., 1964, *Tudor Royal Proclamations*, Vol. 1, New Haven, p. 3.
31. Schindler, p. 194–5.
32. Harris, N. (ed.), 'Memoir of Elizabeth of York', in *Privy purse expenses of Elizabeth of York: Wardrobe accounts of Edward IV with a memoir of Elizabeth of York*, pp. lxxi–lxxiv.

Select Bibliography

Primary Sources – Manuscripts

Bodleian Library
MS Dugdale 15.
MS Top Gloucester D.2.

British Library
MS 43490 f.24.
MS45161f.41-2.
MS 48976.
MS FR 6758 f.67.
MS 7970.
Cotton MSS.
Harleian MSS.
Julian MSS BXII f.314-v.

Lambeth Library
MS Lambeth 853.

Middleham Collegiate Church Collection
ZRC 17496.

The National Archives
C81 Chancery warrants for the Great Seal.
E404 Treasury of receipt Warrants for Issue.
PSO 1 Warrants for the Privy Seal.
SAL/MS/231.

Select Bibliography

Chapel of St George's Archives
XI.P.7.9.11/12.

Primary Sources – Books

Annales Rerum Anglicarum, Letters and papers illustrative of the Wars of the English in France, Stevenson, J. (ed.), 1864, Rolls Series II.

Beauchamp Pageant, The, Sinclair, A. (ed.), 2003, Donnington: Richard III and Yorkist History Trust.

Brie, F.W.D. (ed.), 1906-8, *The Brut: Or the Chronicles of England (1906–8)*, London: Kegan Paul, Trench, Trübner & Co.

Bruce, J. (ed.), *The Arrivall of Edward IV*, 1838, Camden Society, London.

Bryant, N. (ed.), *The True Chronicles of Jean La Bel 1290–1360*, 2011, London: Boydell Press.

Buck, G., *The History of King Richard III*, Kincaid, A.N. (ed.), 1979, Gloucester: A. Sutton.

Calendar of the Close Rolls 1452–94.

Calendar of the Patent Rolls 1452–94.

Calendar of the State Papers Milanese.

Chronicles of London, Kingsford, C.L. (ed.), 1905, London.

Commines, P., *Mémoires*, Calmette, J. & Durville, G. (eds.), 1923–5, 3 Vols,, Paris: Société de l'histoire de France 23–4.

Courthope, W.H. (ed.), *The Rous Rolls*, 1859, privately published.

Crowland Abbey Chronicles 1459–86, The, Pronay, N. & Cox, J.C. (eds.), 1986, Gloucester.

Edwards, R., *The Itinerary of King Richard III 1483–1485*, 1983: Richard III Society Publication.

Froissart's Chronicle, Brereton, G. (ed.), 1978, London: Penguin.

Hall's Chronicle: Containing the History of England during the reign of Henry the Fourth and the succeeding monarchs to the end of the reign of Henry the eighth. In which are particularly described the manners and customs of those periods, Ellis, R. (ed.), 1809, London: J. Johnson.

Mancini, D., *The Usurpation of Richard III*, Armstrong, C.A.J. (ed.), 1969, Oxford.

Marx, W. (ed.), *An English Chronicle 1377–1461*, 2004, Woodbridge.

More, T., *History of King Richard III*, Sylvester, R.S. (ed.), 1963, Yale Edition of the Complete Works, New Haven, Connecticut.

Recueil des Croniques et Anchiennes Istoires de la Grant Bretaigne, Hardy, W. (ed.), E.L.C.P.V 1891, Volumes Rolls Series.

Shakespeare: The Complete Works, Bate, J. & Rasmussen, E. (eds.), 2022, Stratford: RSC Shakespeare.

Six town Chronicles of England, Flenley, R. (ed.), 1911, Oxford: Clarendon Press.

Sutton, A.F. & Hammons, P.W. (eds.), 1983, *The Coronation of Richard II: the extant documents*, Gloucester: St Martin's Press.

Sutton, A.F., Visser-Fuchs, L. & Griffiths, R.A. (eds.), 2005, *The Royal Funerals of the House of York and Windsor*, Richard III Society Publication.

Vergil, P., *Three Books of English History encompassing the reigns of Henry VI, Edward IV and Richard III*, Ellis, H. (ed.), 2010: Kessinger Publishing.

Secondary Sources

Arman, J., *Margaret of Anjou: She-Wolf of France, Twice Queen of England*, 2023, Stroud: Amberley Press.

Ashdown-Hill, J., 2014, *The Third Plantagenet: George, Duke of Clarence, Richard III's brother*, 2014, Stroud: The History Press.

Ashdown-Hill, J., *The Private Life of Edward IV*, 2016, Stroud: Amberley Publishing.

Ashdown-Hill, J., *Cecily Neville: Mother of Richard III*, 2018, Barnsley: Pen & Sword.

Baldwin, D., *The Kingmaker's Sisters*, 2009, Cheltenham: Digital Scribe, The History Press.

Bennett, J.W., 'The Mediaeval Loveday', *Speculum*, Vol. 33, No. 3, Medieval Academy of America, 1958: Cambridge University Press/University of Chicago Press, pp. 351–70.

Benton, John F., 'Trotula, women's problems, and the professionalisation of medicine in the Middle Ages', *Bulletin of the History of Medicine*, 59.1, Spring 1985:33.

Select Bibliography

Chamberlayne, J.L., *A Paper Crown: The Titles and Seals of Cecily Duchess of York*, at www.thericardian.online/the_ricardian.php.

Embree, D. & Tavormina, M.T (eds.), 2019, *The Contemporary English Chronicles of the Wars of the Roses* 2019, Woodbridge: The Boydell Press.

Fiddyment, S., Natalie J. Goodison, Elma Brenner, Stefania Signorello, Kierri Price & Matthew J. Collins, 'Girding the loins? Direct evidence of the use of a medieval English parchment birthing girdle from biomolecular analysis', 2021, *Royal Society Open Science.*

Griffiths, R.A., *The Reign of King Henry VI: The exercise of Royal Authority 1422–1461*, 1981, London: Benn.

Griffiths, R., *King and Country: England and Wales in the 15th Century*, 1991, London: Benn.

Hackett, F., *Francis the First*, 1937, New York: Doubleday, Doran & Company.

Haigh, P., *From Wakefield to Towton*, 2014, Barnsley, Pen & Sword Military.

Hammond, P., *The Children of Richard III*, 2018, Stroud: Fonthill.

Hammond, P., *Edward of Middleham, Prince of Wales* (booklet.), 1973.

Harris, N. (ed.), 'Memoir of Elizabeth of York', in *Privy purse expenses of Elizabeth of York: Wardrobe accounts of Edward IV with a memoir of Elizabeth of York*, pp. lxxi–lxxiv.

Head, C., 'POPE PIUS II AND THE WARS OF THE ROSES', *Archivum Historiae Pontificiae* 8 (1970), pp. 139–78.

Hewson, M.A., *Giles of Rome and the medieval Theory of Conception: a Study of the 'De formatione corporis humani in utero'*, 1975, London: Athlone Press.

Hicks, M., *Richard III and his rivals*, 1991, London: Hambleton.

Hicks, M., 'One Prince or Two? The Family of Richard III', *The Ricardian*, Vol. 122, 1993.

Hicks, M., *Warwick the Kingmaker*, 1998, Oxford.

Hicks, M., *Anne Neville: Queen to Richard III*, 2006, London: Tempus.

Hicks, M., 'What might have been: George Neville, Duke of Bedford 1465–83: His Identity and Significance', at www.thericardian.online.

Higginbotham, S., *The Woodvilles*, 2013, Cheltenham: Digital Scribe, The History Press.

Hilton, L., 2009, Queens Consort: England's Medieval Queens, W&N: UK

Hollman, G., *Royal Witches from Joan of Navarre to Elizabeth Woodville*, 2021, Cheltenham: The History Press.

Hunter, J., *Three Catalogues describing the contents of the Red Book of the Exchequer of the Dodsworth manuscripts in the Bodleian Library*, 1838, London.

Ingram, M., *The Battle of Bosworth*, 2019, Amherst: Helion and Company.

Johnson, L., *The Shadow King: The Life and Death of Henry VI*, 2019, London: Head of Zeus.

Kendall, P.M., *Warwick the Kingmaker: A Biography*, 1957, London: George, Allan & Unwin.

Kenyon, K., *Middleham Castle*, 2015, English Heritage.

Kingsford, C.L., 'Historical Notes on Medieval London Houses', 1914, *London Topographical Records*, Vol. 10.

Lander, J.R., 'Henry VI and the Duke of York's second protectorate 1455–1461', *Bulletin of the John Rylands Library*, 43, No. 1, 1960.

Laynesmith, J.L., *Cecily of York*, 2017, London.

Laynesmith, J.L., *The Last Medieval Queens*, 2004, Oxford.

Laynesmith, J.L., 'Richard III's Lavish Christmas?', 2021, at www.richardiii.blogspot.com.

Lewis, M., *Richard III: Loyalty Binds Me*, 2018, Stroud: Amberley Publishing.

Lewis, M., 'Richard III's Parliament', 2020, at https://richardiii.net/richard-iii-his-world/reputation/a-devotion-to-equitable-justice/.

Licence, A., *Anne Neville, Richard II's Tragic Queen*, 2014, Stroud: Amberley Publishing.

'Milan: 1461', in Calendar of State Papers and Manuscripts in the Archives and Collections of Milan 1385–1618, Allen B. Hinds (ed.), (London, 1912), pp. 37–106. British History Online http://www.british-history.ac.uk/cal-state-papers/milan/1385-1618/pp37-106.

Monroe, C. (ed.), *Letters of Margaret of Anjou and Bishop Beckington and others written in the reigns of Henry V and Henry VI*, 1968: AMS Press.

Nicolas, S.N.H., *Privy purse expenses of Elizabeth of York: wardrobe accounts of Edward the fourth: with a memoir of Elizabeth of York, and notes*, 1830, London: W. Pickering.

Parsons, J.C., *The Pregnant Queen as Counsellor and the Construction of Motherhood*, 1998, Yale: Yale University Press.

Penn, T., *Winter King: Henry VII and the Dawn of Tudor England*, 2011, London: Penguin.

Pierce, H., *Margaret Pole, Countess of Salisbury 1473–1541: Loyalty, Lineage and Leadership*, 2009: University of Wales Press.

Pollard, A.J., *One Summer at Middleham: The Worlds of Richard III*, 2001, London: Tempus Publishing.

Richardson, R.E., *Mistress Blanche: Queen Elizabeth I's confidant*, 2018, Langdale: Langston Press.

Richmond, C., *The Paston Family in the 15th Century Volumes 1 ,2 and 3*, 2000–2002, Manchester: Manchester University Press.

Rohr, Z.E., *Yolande of Aragon 1381–1442 – Family and Power: The reverse of the tapestry*, 2015: Palgrave Macmillian.

Sadler, J., *Towton: The Battle of Pal Sunday 1461*, 2020, Barnsley: Pen & Sword Military.

Schindler, M., *Lovell Our Dogge*, 2019, Stroud: Amberley Publishing.

Sumpton, J., 'Trial by Battle', *The Hundred Years War Volume 1*, 1990, London: Faber & Faber.

Sutton, A.F. & Visser-Fuchs, L., The Entry of Queen Elizabeth Woodville over London Bridge 24th May 1465, www.thericardian.online.

Sutton, A.F. & Visser-Fuchs, L., *Richard III's Books*, 1997, Stroud: Amberley Publishing.

Sutton, A.F., *The King's Work: The defence of the north under the Yorksist kings 1471–1485*, 2021: Richard III and Yorkist History Trust.

Sutton, A.F. & Visser-Fuchs, L., 'Anne Neville: Heiress and Highest ornament of her house', in Norris, A., Harris, C., Laynesmith, J.L., Messer, D.R. & Woodacre, E. (eds.), *Later Plantagenet and the Wars of the Roses consorts: Power, Influence and Dynasty*, 2023: Palgrave Macmillian.

Tallis, N., *Uncrowned Queen: The fateful life of Margaret Beaufort: Tudor Matriarch*, 2019, London: Michael O'Hara.

Turner, W.J., 'Town and Country: A Comparison of the Treatment of the Mentally Disabled in Late Medieval English Common Law and Chartered

Boroughs', in *Madness in Medieval Law and Custom*, 2010, Leiden, The Netherlands: Brill.

Visser-Fuchs, L., *Warwick and Wavrin: Two case studies on the literary background and Propaganda of Anglo Burgundian relations in the Yorkist period*, Doctoral Thesis: University College London.

Watt, J., *The Paston Women: Selected Letters*, 2004, London: D.S. Brewer.

Weir, A., *Lancaster and York: Wars of the Roses*, 2011: Digital Scribe, Vintage Digital.

Weir, A., *Elizabeth of York: The First Tudor Queen*, 2013, London: Random House.

Index

Abergavenny, 7
Abergavenny, Lord, 125, 150
Alkelda, Saint, 110, 156
Amboise, France, 68, 72–5
Angers, France, 70–2
Anglo-Saxon Chronicle, 172
Anjou, Margaret of, 8, 10–13, 21, 32, 61, 68–74, 78, 85, 90, 101, 145–7, 149, 153
Arrivall chronicle of Edward IV, 81–2, 85, 86–7, 89, 90, 184
Ashby, George, 71

Babthorpe, Elizabeth, 133
Barnard Castle, 7, 110, 157
Barnet, Battle of, 80–3, 131
Bayeux, vicar of, 73
Baynard's Castle, 62, 98, 106, 120, 123
Beauchamp, Anne, Countess of Warwick, 4, 5, 7, 8, 20, 51, 83, 98
Beauchamp, Isabella, Countess of Warwick, 111
Beauchamp, Thomas, 17
Beauchamp pageants, 136–7
Beaufort, Edmund, 2nd Duke of Somerset, 11

Beaufort, Edmund, 4th Duke of Somerset, 12–14, 15, 84, 86, 88
Beaufort, Henry, 3rd Duke of Somerset, 26, 33, 36, 38, 84, 86, 88
Beaufort, John, 1st Duke of Somerset, 11, 12, 13, 23, 24, 88.
Beaufort, Margaret, Countess of Richmond and Derby, 88, 91, 127, 128, 144, 149, 151, 178
Beaulieu Abbey, 82, 83, 98, 99, 101
Beauvais, bishop of, 17, 19, 73
Bell, Richard, Prior of Durham, 104
Berwick, 113, 114
Bisham Priory, 45, 82, 174
Bohun, inheritance, 143
Bosworth, Battle of, 3, 125, 180–2
Bourchier, Henry, Earl of Essex, 49, 77
Bourchier, Cardinal Thomas, 23, 32, 56, 68, 121
Brackenbury, Sir Robert, 182
Bristol, 64
Brut chronicle, 26
Buck, Sir George, 151, 164, 165
Buckingham, Duke of and his rebellion, 10, 12, 14, 20, 30, 31,

215

50, 96, 118, 120–5, 128, 143, 144, 148, 149
Burgh, Alice, 102
Burgundy, France, 49, 53, 54, 65–7, 75, 76, 91, 108
Burgundy, Bastard of, 52
Burgundy, Philip of, 52, 53

Calais, France, 15–29, 31, 35, 37, 38, 41, 48, 56–9, 64, 65, 75, 102, 124
Cambridge, Queen's College, 70, 142, 153, 188
Canterbury, 13, 29, 30, 55, 58, 60, 147
Carlisle, 114, 139
Catesby, William, 2, 121, 148, 160
Cawood Castle, 45, 47, 139
  feast at, 45–6, 47, 139
Cerne Abbey, 84, 85
Charles VI, King of France, 10
Chertsey Abbey, 158
Chronicle of London, 75
Clarence, George, Duke of, 27, 52, 54–9, 61, 62, 64, 69, 107–109, 150
Clerkenwell, 164
  Declaration, 2
Coldharbour House, 62, 91–6, 106
Cole, Thomas, 105
Commines, Philippe de, 65, 68, 105, 116
Constance of York, 7
Coventry, 21, 28, 60, 80, 89, 137
Coverham Abbey, 152, 156

Crosby Place, 106, 120
Crowland, anonymous chronicler, 1, 28, 34, 48, 90, 92, 93, 96–77, 115, 116, 118, 120, 140–1, 149, 154, 155, 161–6, 167, 169, 173, 174–5, 177–81, 183

Danyell, William, 133
Dartmouth, 22, 64
de la Pole, Anne, 159
de la Pole, John, Duke of Suffolk, 117, 125, 157, 158
de la Pole, John, Earl of Lincoln, 125, 157, 182
de Vere family, 96
de Vere, John, Earl of Oxford, 45, 81, 159, 179
Despenser family, 85, 98
Devon, Countess of, 85, 89
Devon, Earl of, 38, 60, 84, 86
divorce, 2, 51, 98, 166, 167, 175
Durham, 6, 104, 106, 111, 131, 139, 140, 158, 176

Edward I, 7
Edward II, 123, 136
Edward III, 6, 7, 9, 11, 16, 31, 91, 144
Edward IV, also Earl of March, 2, 14, 25, 27–30, 34–8, 41, 43, 47–50, 52, 53, 55, 58, 60, 61, 63, 69, 72, 74, 75, 78, 80, 82, 87, 89, 96, 112–17, 120–5, 128, 135, 143, 145, 146, 149, 151, 153, 154, 176

Index

Edward V, prince in the Tower, 103, 118, 199, 121, 123, 125, 128, 142, 143
Edward, the Black Prince, 77, 134
Edward of Middleham, Earl of Salisbury and Prince of Wales, 101–103, 107, 115, 137, 141–3, 147, 152, 154–6
Edward of Westminster/Lancaster, Prince of Wales, 12, 13, 32, 35, 68, 69–74, 76, 77, 85–7
Elizabeth of York, 5, 51, 52, 54, 62, 69, 103, 128, 151, 152, 155, 161–5, 172–4, 182

Fabyan, chronicler, 162–3, 177
Farleigh Hungerford Castle, 103
FitzHugh, Alice, 128, 131, 132, 142
Fotheringhay, 106–107, 145
    Castle, 94, 107

George, Saint, 110, 117, 158
Glamorgan, 150
Goldwell, James, Bishop of Norwich, 55, 128
Graunt, Walter, 133
Great Chronicle, 173
Greenwich, 31, 44, 134, 145–7, 159
Gregory's Chronicle, 21, 27, 37, 47
Guy, Earl of Warwick, 7, 20, 136

Hall's Chronicle, 36, 87, 141, 183
Hammond, Peter, 100, 139, 156
Hanley Castle, 7
Harfleur, 76–8, 79, 178

Hastings, Katherine, 49, 128, 131
Hastings, Lord William, 49, 81, 86, 116, 117, 120, 121, 140, 179
Haute, Richard, 118
Henry IV, 6, 9, 91, 111, 131
Henry V, 10, 91, 147
Henry VI, 7–15, 20–2, 27, 31, 32, 34, 35, 68, 69, 75, 77, 80, 89–91, 158
Herbert, Richard, 60
Holinshed's Chronicle, 17, 82, 125, 161
Hopton, Thomas, 126, 133
Howard, Elizabeth, 131
Howard, John, Duke of Norfolk, 2, 55, 105, 125, 164, 165, 177, 180
Howard, Thomas, Earl of Arundel, 128, 164, 133
Huddleston, Margaret, 129, 133, 144

Idley, Anne, 102
Idley, Peter, 102
Isabella of Austria, 19
Isabella of Castile, 141

Jacquetta of Luxembourg, Duchess of Bedford, 47, 48, 51, 61
Jervaulx Abbey, 152, 156
Joanna of Portugal, 165
John of Gaunt, 6, 72
John of Lancaster, Duke of Bedford, 10, 11, 47, 48
John of Pontefract, 141
Joseph, William, 126, 133

Kempe, Cardinal, 10, 12, 13
Kendall, John, 178
Knighton, Henry, chronicler, 16

Langstrother, John, Lord St John, 76
Laynesmith, Dr Joanna, 89, 144, 174
Leicester, 14, 80, 137, 179, 182
Lincoln, 142–3
London, 2, 12, 14, 15, 20–5, 29–35, 49, 51, 53, 55, 60–2, 73–6, 80, 82, 90, 91, 98, 105, 106, 109, 114, 115, 117–24, 126, 132, 134, 141–8, 158, 162, 164, 172, 173, 177
Louis IX, King of France, 47, 48, 54, 66–70, 72–6, 105
Lovell, Lord Francis, 45, 125, 128, 131–3, 139, 157, 160, 177, 182
Ludford Bridge, 27, 28
Ludlow, 25–7

Mancini, Dominic, 109, 110, 116, 120–2, 125
Margaret, Countess of Salisbury, 103, 135, 136, 147
Margaret of York, Duchess of Burgundy, 53, 108
Mary of Guelders, 71
Mary of Scotland, 69
Mary of York, 103, 145
Mauleverer, Elizabeth, 133, 144
Micklegate, York, 33, 139

Middleham, 93, 96, 99, 105, 107, 110, 111, 112, 114, 123, 125, 136, 142–3, 150, 152, 153–7
    Castle, 6, 25, 39–40, 43–4, 49, 60, 93, 100, 102–103, 104, 105, 110, 114–16, 144–5, 147
Montague, John Marquis, 62, 74, 75, 81, 82
Mountford, Osbert, 29

Neville, Alice Countess of Salisbury, 6, 7
Neville, Anne, queen to Richard III:
    ancestry, 4–8
    birth, 4, 5, 7
    upbringing, 18–20, 39–46
    in France (1470–1), 66–80
    first marriage (1470–1), 66–87
    widowed, 88–95
    second marriage (c.1472–85), 96–182
    coronation, 124–35
    death, 1–3, 169–79
Neville, Cecily, Duchess of York, 11, 12, 27, 31, 41, 42, 43, 58, 62, 76, 78, 94, 97, 101, 103, 106, 107, 145, 160, 161
Neville, George, Archbishop of York, 45, 55, 56, 58, 62, 64, 69, 139
Neville, George, Duke of Bedford (d. 1483) 119, 120, 150
Neville, Isobel, Duchess of Clarence, 5, 18, 19, 22, 24, 43,

50, 51, 52, 54–9, 61–5, 67, 68, 72, 74, 70, 90–3, 97, 98, 102, 103, 107, 108, 136, 147, 173
Neville, Ralph, 1st Earl of Westmorland, 6, 43, 97, 155
Neville, Ralph, 2nd Earl of Westmorland, 6, 52, 155
Neville, Richard, Earl of Salisbury, 7, 12, 14, 23–30, 33, 35, 45, 52, 97, 98, 155
Neville, Richard, Earl of Warwick, 6, 12–18, 19–40, 43–55, 57–70, 72–84, 97
Northampton, Battle of, 30, 31, 50, 60, 118, 143, 148

papal dispensation, 55, 57, 72, 73, 97, 167
Paris, 75
Parr, Elizabeth, 128, 142
Parr, Katherine, 131
Parr, William, 131
Parry, Blanche, 5
Paston, John, 54, 96
Paston, Margaret, 101
Paston, Margery, 19
Peacock, Anthony, 152
Penrith, 6, 96, 150
Percy family, 23, 26, 36, 62
Percy, Henry, 128
Percy, Joyce, 145
Percy, Robert, 45, 131
Pius II, Pope, 30, 55, 83
Plantagenet, Richard, Duke of York, 11–15, 20, 21, 23–34, 41

Pontefract, 13, 34, 61, 102, 122, 137, 138, 142, 157
Pseudo-Worcester, chronicle, 54

Raby, 52
Ratcliffe, Sir Richard, 2, 45, 160
Richard II, 131, 137
Richard III, Duke of Gloucester, 2, 3, 39, 42, 44, 45, 62, 78, 91, 92, 94–107, 109–14, 116–25, 128–44, 146–82
Rous, John, 39, 55, 65, 100, 101, 107, 120, 122, 136, 137, 150, 154, 155, 157, 158, 161, 167, 173

St Albans, 14, 20, 24, 28, 33, 34, 47
St Martin-le-Grand, 95, 98
St Paul's, 15, 51, 122, 160
Salisbury Roll, 136
Sandwich, 29, 31, 58
Scarborough, 158
Scotland, 70, 112, 114, 158
Shakespeare, William, 1, 4, 16, 21, 25, 32, 36, 47, 54, 57, 67, 80, 87, 88, 93, 100, 113, 123, 137, 138, 146, 153, 156, 160, 169, 171, 177, 179
Sheriff Hutton, 6, 96, 112, 150, 155, 156, 158
Shrewsbury, 31, 74, 111
Sixtus IV, Pope, 114
Skelton, Alice, 145
Skipton, 40
Southampton, 64, 82, 177, 178

Stanley, Lord Thomas, 113, 120, 125, 127, 128, 139, 149, 178, 179, 180, 181
Stanley, Sir William, 180, 181
Stillington, Richard, 121
Stone, John, chronicler, 58
Swynford, Katherine, 6

Tempest, Anne, 133, 145
Tewkesbury, 7, 85–90, 107, 108, 134
Tewkesbury Chronicle, 100–101, 103–104
Thomas of Woodstock, 144
Towton, 36–8, 71
Tudor, Henry (later Henry VII), 123, 125, 126, 148, 151, 158, 159, 161, 162, 169, 172, 178, 179, 181, 182
Tudor, Jasper, Earl of Pembroke, 14, 33, 74, 85, 148, 159
Tudor, Owen, 34
Tutbury Castle, 55
Tyrell, Sir James, 99, 141

Vaux, Katherine, 88, 89
Vavasour, John, 126, 133

Vergil, Polydore, 32, 55, 100, 134, 144, 151, 156, 169, 181

Wakefield, 33, 34, 37, 39, 45, 147
Warkworth's Chronicle, 81–2, 87, 90
Warwick:
    Castle, 4, 31, 39, 60, 61, 63, 66, 98
    St Mary's Church, 45, 110, 142
Welles, Sir Robert, 38, 63, 64
Wenlock, Lord John, 64, 65
Westminster Abbey, 80, 117, 118, 127, 146, 173, 174
Westminster Palace, 129
Windsor, 13, 110, 117, 134, 135, 158, 159, 171
Woodville, Anthony, Earl Rivers, 48, 49, 52, 53, 64, 111, 117, 118, 122
Woodville, Richard, 1st Earl Rivers, 60

Yolande of Aragon, 13
York Minster, 117, 118, 139, 156, 174